RETURN TO TINNIN

A BIOGRAPHICAL NOVEL

JASPER S. LEE

PUBLISHED BY BAM! PUBLISHING

First Edition

Library of Congress Control Number: 2017943562 Purchase this, and other fantastic BAM! Publish titles using https://diy.bampublish.com/ marketplace.

Printed with BAM! Publishing diy.bampublish.com

Table of Contents

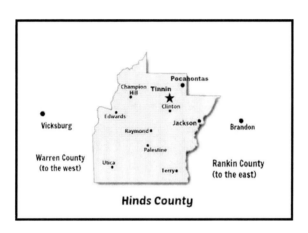

Acknowledgements

Writing this book involved help from a number of people. Some who consciously participated; others did so unconsciously well after their demise.

First, those who consciously helped with the writing will be acknowledged. Ronnie McDaniel, Danville, Illinois, is acknowledged for his copy editing and other suggestions that improved the manuscript. (I was so fortunate to have the assistance of this long-experienced and highly qualified individual.) Three individuals are acknowledged for assistance in reviewing the manuscript: Jacqueline Frost Tisdale, Starkville, Mississippi (she grew up in Clinton); Wally Warren, Clarkesville, Georgia; and Morgan Anglin, Georgia College and State University, Milledgeville. The assistance of genealogist Anne Vanderleest, Brandon, Mississippi, in researching remote family history and being available to clarify situations is acknowledged.

Secondly, those who unconsciously helped by storing and otherwise retaining letters, legal documents, business receipts, and other papers is gratefully acknowledged. Without these documents, the book would have been impossible. The most important individual in this regard was Ellen Loretta Shepard Lee, the main character in the book. Others include George W. Shepard, Ira J. Lee, Doris Sloan Lee, and J. Henry Lee. Amazingly, the old trunk holding the treasure-trove of information was spared from being thrown away a number of times.

Thank you to all family and friends who encouraged me with this undertaking. A special thank you goes to my wife,

Delene, for her patience and help by reading manuscript to assure the story was as it should be.

Special Acknowledgment

A special acknowledgment goes to Ellen Miller Gabardi for her assistance with the image on the cover, entitled Old Home Place (referred to in the book as the Shepard Home). The artist, Ginny Futvoye, is acknowledged for creating a wonderful memory. The painting was prepared in oil on wood. A side note is that Ellen Miller Gabardi is the Great Great Granddaughter of Ellen Loretta Shepard.

DEDICATION

This book is dedicated to the author's granddaughter, Anna Delene. She is the person in the author's life with so many of the wonderful traits of the main character in this book, Ellen Loretta Shepard Lee. Anna Delene is the great, great, great granddaughter of Ellen. No doubt, Ellen would have adored Anna Delene.

I wish you, Anna Delene, much success in life. May you enjoy learning about your ancestors and strive to make them proud in all that you do.

FOREWORD

Return to Tinnin is a biographical novel about the life of a girl who became a young adult in the South during the U.S. Civil War. The main character is Ellen Loretta Shepard Lee. Good times and bad times highlight her life of family, poverty, romance, success, failure, compassion, faith, and love.

Written by her great-grandson, the story is based on considerable research into family history. DNA analysis was a part of determining genetic family relationships. Online searches and visits to historical agencies yielded useful information. Most of all, the attic of the family residence built before the Civil War had a deteriorating trunk that, when opened, yielded a trove of old letters, invoices, and other documents. These provided a great deal of intimate insight into the hardships, joys, and family experiences of Ellen (1847-1918). No doubt to the author, she was a smart, attractive young woman who might possibly have made a better decision about romance, but if she had made a different choice, the author would not be here to brag about her.

SCARY SOLDIERS

"Preacher Hoyle, so good to have you here with us for dinner on this glorious Easter Sunday. You certainly had a powerful message at Mason Chapel this morning about principles of salvation and human love. It was the perfect message for this 1863 Easter. I am sure glad you didn't preach about saving souls from eternal life in the hot fires of hell. Some folks in the congregation sure needed to hear about salvation and love. I was one of them," stated Pa George Shepard.

Ma (George's wife, Sarah) spoke: "Preacher, you are amazing and a real blessing in our community. Here, have another piece of chicken. There are still some 'good' pieces left: a couple of breasts and thighs and a wishbone. The children have plenty on another plate (wings, necks, backs, gizzards, hearts, and feet). I dressed three broilers yesterday. You know, it takes a good bit to feed a family of this size." So goes southern dinner-cooking with the Shepard family, Easter Sunday 1863, on a Tinnin, Mississippi, farm.

Pa spoke up, "You know, Preacher, I am very concerned about this war. I hear that more troops are heading toward Vicksburg for a big battle. They might come through here. Many men have all ready died or been seriously hurt. We have lost so much property to the destructive troops as they moved through. Why can't we get along in harmony?"

With that, Preacher Hoyle responded, "I agree. We need peace and to learn how to get along with each other."

As Ma started passing the plate of remaining fried chicken, the sounds of a horse's hooves could be heard rapidly coming down the long hill moving toward the house. Pa went to the porch on the front of the house. It faced the dirt trail, where dust was in the air from the hooves. The rider, somewhat out of breath, shouted to Pa George that the "Union troops are on the way and will be here tomorrow. The company is about 100 soldiers. And, there may be more." Afterward, the horse and rider sped back up the hill, kicking up even more dust. As many people as possible in the Tinnin community were going to be alerted about the future arrival of the soldiers, and precautions taken to assure safety of families and their property. After all, they had already had Confederate and Union forces to come through, and both were about equally abusive.

George knew some of what had to be done, but he didn't know that his oldest daughter, Ellen, had come to the porch behind him. Ellen, trembling and with tears in her eyes, said, "Pa, what are we going to do? The presence of troops scares me. You know, I am 15 years old. Do you think one of them will take advantage of me? I want to save my 'specialness' until my wedding night; that is important to me and what I have been taught as being right. And, Pa, some men at the Ratliff Store are already looking at me with a gleam in their eyes. You and Ma were married when she was 14, and I was born when she was 15. So..."

Pa replied to Ellen, "Not in my presence will any soldier lay an eye on you. I will shoot straight into the face of anyone who does so in a lustful way." That soothed Ellen a bit, but she knew each soldier had a gun better than Pa's rarely used old double barrel. Pa further said, "Don't let any of those scums at the Ratliff Store touch you either. I will speak to your Grandfather Ratliff about this."

Pa went back to the dining table with Preacher Hoyle, Ma, and Ma's parents, Zachariah and Susan Tinnin Ratliff. Sarah had invited her parents to join them for an Easter meal with the preacher. Ellen went back to the children's table with her seven siblings. (As the oldest child, Ellen was the unofficial leader of the children's table.) Pa announced what the rider had said. "And," he continued, "we just had a Union field artillery company here two weeks ago. They discarded bullets and one cannon ball. Why again?"

Preacher Hoyle immediately said, "I've got to go. It takes at least 15 minutes on horseback to get back to my home in Clinton. I hope I don't run into the soldiers on the way." He grabbed his worn Bible, ran outside, unhitched his horse, and jumped on its back. The horse went up the hill trail faster than the messenger who had brought the word.

Ma was disappointed that Preacher Hoyle left so quickly. "You know," Ma said, "he didn't even say thank you, have a prayer, or anything. He ran."

Pa lamented, "Kind of like preachers around here. You know, a war is going on. If a preacher can't save himself, how can he save the souls of others? He would have been safer if he had stayed here with us until the soldiers passed through. I am sure he was concerned about his family and friends."

And, Ma was also disappointed that she had put so much work into the meal, including the lemon cake that had not been sliced for serving. She had spent Saturday butchering three fine young chickens and hours preparing the meal. Of course, Ellen and others of the older Shepard children had helped some with the collard greens, corn bread, and other fixin's. Unfortunately, they would not see Preacher Hoyle again.

Ma saved the leftover fried chicken in the pie safe over night. Not much there but a neck, back, wing, heart, and half-gizzard. The preacher and the Ratliff and Shepard families had eaten the wishbone, breast pieces, thighs, drumsticks, and the like. Ma had a thought in her mind about hunger among the soldiers, however. She thought they would be hungry and looking for food. That was true with the Confederates who came through a couple of weeks ago. Anyway, since camp cooking wasn't that good, they would especially like to get home cooked food. The lemon cake will make a few really happy.

Preacher Hoyle was an itinerant minister who served at Mason Chapel, a small congregation that pretty well followed beliefs and practices of the Methodist Episcopal Church. The church met in a small frame structure with a couple of privies. It was near the clapboard schoolhouse in the Tinnin community, so the privies were also used by school children and teachers. Just like the Tinnin community, the church congregation was small--not many white folks in the community were brave enough to venture out to church, as a lot of bad stuff was going on due to war and racial tensions. The situation was far more perilous than one preacher could solve. Preacher Hoyle also served a couple of other tiny churches also within a few miles of Clinton. The schoolhouse near Mason Chapel served as a social center in the community.

On his way to Clinton, Preacher Hoyle ran into the company of soldiers (they stormed Clinton before venturing to Tinnin). The soldiers stopped him and looked him over good. They asked if he had money; and, yes, he did from his preaching that morning at Mason Chapel. A Private O'Reilly took his meager earnings and stuffed them into his pocket.

Since the preacher had a fairly good-looking horse, the soldiers decided to keep it and let the preacher go. As the preacher protested that he would have two miles to walk, they pointed guns at him and told him to get going. One soldier was heard to say, "A good horse is far more valuable than an itinerant preacher." One took the preacher's Bible out of the saddlebag and threw it at him; Preacher Hoyle picked it up as it had some sermon notes in it. Because the preacher was not accustomed to such fear and having to walk, his heart pounded so that he fell dead from heart failure. A stranger passing through found his body and alerted a local law official. This did not slow the movement of the soldiers.

At the Shepards, the children were asked to join Pa and Ma and Grandparents Ratliff at the adult table. It was already after 3:00 p.m. because dinner had been delayed until the preacher arrived. His morning sermon had lasted until 1:00 p.m., and then it took a few minutes for him to ride to the Shepard home.

Serious conversation ensued. Pa told the family what the rider had said. The girls cried; the boys were too young to be concerned. Everyone was given a responsibility in preparing for the troops. The Shepards had to protect their limited possessions; the farm hands (slaves) were already about free and not around to help. Overall, life was stressful even without the thought of soldiers coming. Farm work and life had changed so much with the abolition of slavery but it would turn out to be a good change.

Pa continued with the plan that involved hiding things deep in the forest of Shepard Hills, in the attic of the house, and in the ground. The work had to be done before dark that day, with the arrival of the soldiers the next morning. There was some fear that the soldiers would come in the darkness of night, and this was even more scary.

Everyone in the family got involved. Ellen was responsible for the draft animals, which were to be tied in thick brushy hollows in the hills. These included pairs of horses and oxen, along with a mule. She took them to an area filled with small trees, vines, and bushes.

Ellen's sisters Georgia Ann and Sarah were responsible for taking the cured meat (about 150 pounds altogether of hams and bacon sides) from the smokehouse to the attic. Several trips up the ladder were needed. A few small pieces were left in the smokehouse just in case the soldiers demanded some meat. It would be there for their taking. The ladder leading to the attic was cut into pieces and burned in the fireplace, leaving no easy way for the soldiers to get into the attic.

Ellen's sisters Mag and Rachel were responsible for burying the gunpowder in the ground near the stable in a pottery container that would keep it dry. Other small household things were tucked away in places not readily visible. Naomi and James helped with this. Since Ira was only two years old, he wasn't given a responsibility.

Ma Sarah, her mother, and daughters Ellen and Mag quickly cleaned the table and kitchen. Then, Susan and Zachariah departed for their home. It was located in the heart of Tinnin near the Ratliff Store, about a mile away.

Nothing was done to protect the loose chickens, penned pigs, and pastured cows. They would be left vulnerable to the soldiers' whims. But, Naomi, who was six years of age, asked about their dogs, Ritz and Bummer, as well as the barn cats, Oscar and Lucille. Pa said let them stay loose and that "Ritz is the best dog with some training; Bummer turned up as a stray with mange and a bad eye; that makes him kind of mean. It is hard to defend him even though he is a good watchdog, with one eye and all. As for the cats, let them continue their rat patrol of the corn crib. We don't need the rats to get our corn."

Pa had a certain confidence that he could handle the situation with the soldiers. After all, when voting was done to secede from the Union and form the Confederate States of America, Pa had voted the Union ticket. He had moved south from Indiana as a very young man in 1841, searching for opportunity. Many of his values had been shaped by his parents and others in Indiana. Of course, he had several slaves (farm hands) until they were granted their freedom in the early-to-mid 1860s. He lost a small fortune of investment when emancipation occurred. His vote on secession resulted in some people in the community never again trusting him.

He had worked hard to gain his plantation holdings of 1,200 acres (some with government grants from the Choctaw cessation). In 1857, he had built a large home for his family. Various outbuildings supported his family and plantation life. He did not want his property taken or destroyed. He wanted a good future. The future was looking promising until the U.S. Civil War began. The farm was almost in a direct line between Jackson and Vicksburg--a major route for delivery of farm products to the promising foreign markets by way of Vicksburg and its connections to ports in various countries, particularly in Europe.

Easter Sunday night, no one slept well (except baby Ira, who was still breast-fed at age 2). Through the night, there was always a listening ear for the sounds of soldiers. The sun began to rise over Shepard Hills on the Monday after Easter. No sign of soldiers yet. Morning chores were to be done--milk the two cows (Ellen's responsibility) and gather any eggs that were laid early (Mag's responsibility). After chores, everyone was to come into the house. Of course, the sighting of any soldier in the distance was plenty reason to immediately come inside.

Overnight, the remaining farm hands (only a few were still there) and their families disappeared. Where did they go? They didn't tell George or anyone. Some might have been aided by advance men of the Union troops sneaking around before their arrival at the farm. On previous occasions, a few farm hands would return after the troops had moved on. Pa was not harsh on them. He tried to put himself in their places. Everyday life was so chaotic. Whether anyone would be available for producing crops that year was unknown. War had destroyed so much...so little had been gained at this point. Life was hard for everyone.

No one knew if or when the soldiers would arrive. Pa Shepard did not know that they had camped less than two miles away on a hillside just south of a place called Kickapoo. This meant that it wouldn't take long for the soldiers to go down the dirt trail through Shepard Hills to the home. That morning, they broke camp and began movement north toward Tinnin.

About mid-morning, a field artillery company began arriving. Commanded by Captain West, the 100 men made their way into the area surrounding the Shepard home. Men were walking with light weapons and packs. A few with injuries rode horses. Pairs of horses pulled four 12-pounder field howitzer cannons. Captain West ordered the 1st lieutenant to have troops find a site for overnight setup.

Captain West brought a squad (12 men with light arms) with him to the front porch of the house. He fired a shot into the air. He banged on the wooden floor with his gunstock and shouted loudly, "Everyone in the house come out right now!" Pa, Ma, and the eight children came out--all were very afraid. Loaded guns were aimed at them by four soldiers. Smoke from the shot fired into the air was still present. James was so scared that he peed in his pants and cried. The family members were asked to get in a line near the middle of the porch.

Eight armed soldiers got onto the porch. The other soldiers stood in the yard and guarded the goings-on with pointed guns. Then five of the eight went inside to search the house. The three soldiers remaining on the porch looked the Shepards over good. The captain asked questions about food, animals, gunpowder, and the like. Pa provided information but did not reveal where things were hidden. He told the soldiers about the barn, smokehouse, chicken house, and stables. He told them about food in the smokehouse.

A very important question Captain West asked was, "Does a Confederate soldier live here?" None did. Pa said, "No." This appeared to help the soldiers adjust to the family. This truthful answer might have saved both lives and property of the Shepard family. The soldiers with raised, loaded guns lowered them. Stress was only slightly reduced.

While Pa was talking and all family members were distracted, one soldier, Private Cason, approached Ellen. She
was a good-looking young woman and mature for her 15
years of age. He looked her over with lustful eyes and asked
her, "What is your name?"

"Ellen,"she softly replied.

He said, "I will see you later, Ellen," and moved on to other
duties. Ellen was frightened, but there wasn't much she
could do except worry and think about what he might be
up to if he saw her again. She thought about ways to defend
herself from unwanted advances.

Pa told the captain that he had voted the Union ticket.
That seemed to endear the captain and members of the
squad, at least a bit more, toward him. Conversation ensued. Pa, as he later shared with Ma, did learn that this
company of soldiers had come from the Battle of Corinth
to Jackson and then plundered the town of Clinton. They
were now on their way to Vicksburg. There they would join
with other soldiers, including those from Illinois, Indiana,
and Iowa, under Generals Sherman and Grant to engage in
major Union war events at Vicksburg.

Those searching the house found a few things and took
them. Of particular interest were food and beverage items,
such as cornmeal, potatoes, coffee, and whiskey. There was
nearly a half barrel of Dexter Whiskey that Pa had brought
back from Vicksburg--enough for several soldiers that
evening. Pa wasn't much of a drinker but would occasionally take a sip. He supposedly used the bourbon for medicinal
purposes. It was used as an anesthetic in some cases such
as in removing a tooth that had gone bad. Family members, friends, and slaves might get a drink for pain (two if in
considerable pain). Fortunately, the searchers did not take

the small collection of letters and other documents that the family was keeping.

One soldier opened the pie safe and found the plate of leftover chicken and the uncut lemon cake left from dinner with the preacher. He and the other soldiers in the house immediately ate the chicken and spit bones on the floor. Of course, the soldiers who got the heart and half-gizzard had no bones to get rid of. But, considering what they had been having to eat, the soldiers found the cold leftover fried-in-lard chicken to be very tasty. They decided to take the cake with them to their overnight camping site, just a hundred yards or so away in front of the house.

Most of the day was spent pilfering for things of value to plunder. It was then time to set up camp. A relatively level field site near the house was chosen to set up for the night. It was near a dug well with good water and in the fruit and pecan orchard. Being early spring, about the only thing available in the orchard was strawberries and not many of them. The soldiers had packed a few tents and cooking items for camping along their journey.

Four of the soldiers decided to stay the night in one of the vacant shacks that remained after the slaves were gone. Old remnants of beds and a fireplace were available. Because they isolated themselves from the major group, some of the soldiers who stayed in tents thought these four might have been gay. Though this notion was never confirmed, a few soldiers steered clear of them in a discriminating manner. Soldiers weren't always happy being in each other's presence but had to share a common goal of military activity and life.

The soldiers weren't exactly in dress uniform and freshly bathed. Body odors were strong and penetrating. Clothing was frayed and often dirty. A few had stains in their pants because of the diarrhea they had suffered. Their hair was scraggly and their faces were unshaven, for the most part. A few appeared sickly with colds and related ailments, such as ringworm and, perhaps, syphilis. Some had head lice and often scratched their scalps. In spite of all this, it was fortunate that the shots fired on the first day of encampment did not injure anyone. Overall, they were in better condition than the Confederate troops of a couple of weeks ago.

The soldiers searched the outbuildings for anything that would be useful. Small amounts of meat were taken from the smokehouse. Gunshots were heard from near the hog-pen. Two 70-pound pigs were killed, primitively butchered, and, after gutting, roasted over a fire in the encampment. The fire singed the hair off, creating a bad odor; crusted the skin; and, after few hours, somewhat cooked through the carcasses. One soldier took the livers from the two pigs, cut them into slices, and tried to fry the slices in lard. Now, it was time for the troops to eat.

A few of the soldiers who had confiscated Pa's Dexter Whiskey began drinking before the tents were all up. Staggering about and slurring their words were signs they were into it. One, who particularly imbibed, had too much and began throwing up. Sad. Not much was in the vomit except a few particles of chewed chicken gizzard he had taken from the pie safe. He hadn't eaten since breakfast that day except for the leftover chicken. Two soldiers had piccolos and began playing them. Some of the soldiers joined in by singing, clapping, and dancing about. Their euphoria was likely the result of downing the liquor and being in a good camping site.

No one in the Shepard family rested well that night. Soldiers were at hand. Their behavior was unpredictable. Four soldiers stayed up to guard the encampment. One soldier had said he would see Ellen later, and that made her particularly fearful. Ellen made up her mind that she would defend herself as she needed. Also, there were Ellen's slightly younger sisters who might need defending. Of course, Ma was only 33 years of age and still quite attractive. But, everyone made it through the night okay. What would happen when daylight came?

The next morning, the soldiers were out and about at dawn. Fires were started for limited cooking of breakfast. No toilets were available; soldiers relieved themselves wherever convenient but never inside the camping area. Large leaves were used to wipe after 'taking a crap.' The camp was taken down in preparation for the march to the next site a few miles away. But, the soldiers didn't leave immediately.

Shortly after taking down the camp, some continued searching around the outbuildings for things of value. One freshly dug site near the hogpen got their attention. The soldiers checked and found a pottery container of gunpowder. This made some of them furious, particularly their commanding officer.

They returned to the Shepard home, fired three shots into the air, and called out much as they had on the previous day when they arrived. The family fearfully went onto the porch as per orders. Loaded guns were aimed at them. The captain shouted in terse terms about the gunpowder. The family hadn't told the soldiers about it. What else was hidden? None of the Shepards spoke a word.

Several soldiers loudly stepped onto the porch. One was Private Cason, who walked straight to Ellen. He softly asked, "Remember me?" Of course, she did. He struck fear in her on the previous day.

Just when she said, "Yes," Private Cason stood behind her pressing his body against hers. He put his right hand around her waist and pulled her tighter to him. He reached around and put his left hand on her left breast. He stood tightly touching her body. Soldiers who noticed this ignored it; they did not step in to defend Ellen. Such troop behavior was not uncommon among both the Confederate and Union forces.

Just as he pulled her tighter and whispered in her ear, "You are a beautiful woman," she vigorously defended herself, pushing his left hand away from her breast and elbowing firmly into his gut with her right arm. This forced him back about a foot, just enough for Ellen, with all her might, to swing her clinched right fist, hitting him firmly in the belly. He bent over, gasped for air, and stumbled to the edge of the porch. None of her family noticed, as they were distracted by the goings-on and threat of burning by the other soldiers. Ellen never told anyone about this. If Pa knew, he might incite hard feelings and violence.

Just after Ellen had defended herself and Private Cason was on the edge of the porch, a big shout of "Fire!" was heard. Gunpowder had been thrown in a 4-foot long streak on the porch floor. It was to propel a fire that would quickly burn the house. That frightened Private Cason, and he jumped off the porch.

Ellen was free but concerned about her home and what might happen later. Pa pleaded not to set the gunpowder on fire. Ma pleaded the same. The children were sobbing and begging. Ellen and her just younger sister, Rachel, screamed, begging the soldiers not to burn the house.

Anyway, the persuasion by Ma and Pa and the children was sufficient. The captain ordered the soldier not to ignite the gunpowder. The house was spared. Before departing, the captain left a warning: "If this house is ever painted or made fancy, we will come back and burn it to the ground. No Confederate soldiers are to ever live here." That warning was heeded for more than the next 100 years. In fact, no member of the military ever lived in the house, nor did any member of the family serve in the military. It was always Pa's teaching that peace was better than war. He often wondered about the good of the Civil War. He had always felt that slavery wasn't right. He was more progressive than most southern white folks, considering his midwestern orientation. Pa agreed with U.S. President Lincoln's Emancipation Proclamation that had been issued earlier on January 1, 1863. The Confederate states were not in the Union and slavery did not end immediately. Slaves that knew about what was going on would sometimes vanish in the darkness of the night; others would remain a while longer. It was a turbulent time! (Slavery did not officially end until December 1865 when the 13th Amendment to the U.S. Constitution was ratified by three-fourths of the 36 states that were in the Union at that time. Mississippi returned to the Union in 1870 after a time of reconstruction and martial law. Further, Mississippi did not formally submit ratification papers until the year 2013!)

The family rested a little better as the soldiers began their march toward Champion Hill for their next camping site. Some food was gone. All of Pa's Dexter Whiskey was taken (the previous night's imbibing might have helped save the house). Two pigs were prepared and eaten on-site. The horses and other animals hidden in the thick woods of Shepard Hills were still there. Maybe these would be the last troops to come through.

Ritz and Bummer had stayed hidden under the house next to the base of the big chimney. They hardly came out at all during any of the ordeal. But, when the Union soldiers left, they did and wagged their tails at the Shepard children. This helped the family get over their ordeal. As for the cats, they went about their usual work in the corn crib of controlling the rat population.

The Shepard family tried to return to a calm state. They had been spared major tragedy. The house was not burned. Ellen was safe--all family members were safe. Life would go on in the post-slave era, but it was a time of poverty and deprivation. They never knew when another group of soldiers might show up. Actions of Confederate and Union military forces during the Civil War brought great havoc to Tinnin and the Shepard family. Life was chaotic, to say the least.

Pa often shared with his family questions about war. He would begin with, "Why was war needed?" Ellen was always eager to hear his explanations; he sounded so reasoned and eloquent to her. Pa would say that humans are intelligent beings and should be able to settle differences in humane ways without war. He would say that war causes great human loss. It destroys what humans have made through their efforts. Southerners should have agreed with the policies of their Nation. Slavery was not justifiable in a moral society.

Another thing that Pa did not like was the popular notion of guns. He wanted them used discretely and with caution, not flaunted or used as threats. He felt that guns were created primarily for one purpose: to give one human an advantage over another human or over an animal by threatening and/or taking its life. Of course, he and his family had been bullied by men with guns when the Confederate and Union forces came through Tinnin. He was glad that no guns discharged by troops physically injured his family. Soldiers did use guns to harvest some of the animals on the farm. He pretty well thought that anyone who carried a gun was insecure and did so in an attempt to enhance low self-esteem. So, it is just as well that he had only an old shotgun with double barrels.

Pa's ability to lead such discussions was probably a product of his northern upbringing. How he viewed his role as the head of household to embrace fundamentals of education were also midwestern in roots. There were likely times when Pa thought that if he had stayed in Indiana he would have avoided all the turmoil he had found in Tinnin, Mississippi. However, he now thought of Tinnin as his home and the place he should live and seek wealth if any could be found.

Even with war threats and destruction, people in the Tinnin community found pride in where they lived. They felt that there was good quality of life, but that thought was primarily associated with white people who had never traveled any place. Blacks, though they did not enjoy increasing equality in most regards, were adjusting and leaving the area with their newfound emancipation. Members of the Choctaw Tribe had been chased from the area a quarter century earlier by the Federal government and treaties that led to cessation of the land. Hills with wooded areas provided habitat for important meat, such as rabbit, deer, and squirrel. Though Pa was not a hunter, he would let others hunt on his land if they shared their harvest. Creek bottoms provided good lands for row cropping (except following a heavy sustained rain, when runoff water would get the Bogue Chitto Creek out of its banks). Springs in the hills provided good-quality fresh water. The air was clean and free of the pollution found in cities where coal was burned and iron work carried out. Overall, the Tinnin community was a healthful place to live.

But, it was spring, and crops needed to be started. This required work by each individual in the family who was old enough to work in the field. Cotton, corn, sweet potatoes, and pinder (Gullah name for peanut--there were no Gullah people in Mississippi but the name of pinder prevailed) had to be planted as crops. The vegetable garden had to be readied and planted. Fortunately, a few winter vegetable crops had survived, such as collard greens and turnips; these were helpful in getting through times with troops. Before the recent troop experience, potatoes, cabbage, onions, radishes, and lettuce had been planted. Spring and summer vegetable crops should now be planted, which included okra, tomatoes, squash, field peas, and butterbeans. A lot of hard labor was required breaking the land with mule-pulled plows and using hoes to plant by hand.

Orderly life in Tinnin and surrounding area was disrupted by the actions of a few people who held hard feelings toward former slaves and those whites who might have aided them. These small groups would roam around the countryside, create conflict, and be violent. They would burn homes, destroy farm property, endanger human life, and sometimes lynch people who didn't fit right in line with what they wanted. People, particularly children, were sometimes bullied and frightened. One instance near the town of Bolton involved a small group going to a shanty in the night with blazing torches, pulling the man from the house and beating him, and setting the house on fire. Fortunately, the man's life was spared and his wife and children escaped. Their meager possessions were destroyed.

The vigilantes became known as "white-liners;" mention of these words produced fear among people. As a northerner, Pa was somewhat suspect in the South. Some people knew he voted the Union ticket before the U.S. Civil War and that he was always kind toward his slaves. This notion out in the community among the "white-liners" created some additional anxiety among the Shepards; they didn't know what atrocity might be perpetrated upon them next.

Mississippi had seceded from the Union in 1861. The decision was influenced by an elite group of plantation owners. They evidently had confidence that the Confederate states would prevail in the war. Extended battles were fought in the state--several were relatively close to Tinnin such as Champion Hill and, somewhat more distant, Vicksburg. Most battle wins (particularly the major battles) went to the Union. After 1863, astute Confederates could see that there was no future in the war effort. Bringing the War to a close and reconstruction of the South required major leadership and financial investment. Mississippi would return to the Union some nine years after it seceded. Achieving equality for all citizens remained a challenge for many years--even to this day. Many former slaves and their families left the state. Some remained as penniless sharecroppers and tenant farmers.

Youngsters in the Shepard family who were approaching adulthood were unsettled by what they had heard and witnessed. Some were wondering if this war experience would ever end. And, life was hard--lots of work and little income. Things would get better. There would be ups and downs, successes and failures. Pleasures in life had to be gleaned from simple things that didn't require money.

Children in the family began to think about their future. Could they escape such a hard life? Would they have food? Clothing? Safety? Their experiences caused them to grow up fast. School wasn't much of an issue--no one in the family went to school more than a few days each year. The Tinnin schoolhouse was not a very impressive place and usually had one teacher for eight grades. But, all the Shepards could read and write to an extent--at least enough to get by. Some adults in the community could sign their names though others only used an X.

Ellen dreamed of a future romance and life as a wife, mother, and homemaker. She had entered womanhood. She had to sort things out for herself. Sometimes things looked bleak. How could she find a better life? She wasn't sure if a better life even existed. The dream was of a loving, kind, and considerate man who would carry her away to a good, secure life with plenty to live on.

FINDING ROMANCE

Ellen and all the Shepard family adjusted as best they could following their ordeal at the hands of Union soldiers. Now, they hoped the Confederates would stay away and let the family and farm heal. And, they did, as the Union forces had pretty well depleted the will of the Confederate soldiers to fight for a losing cause.

The fall harvest of 1863 had been made. Eleven bales of cotton, worth about $375, had been picked and ginned. Production was down from a couple of years ago when the farm still had slaves. Beyond the money for the cotton, there wasn't much cash income available. Self-sufficiency was so important--grow potatoes, corn, beans, greens, okra, squash, and other foods. Raise a few animals, partic-ularly pigs for butchering and chickens for eggs and meat. Not much was gleaned from hunting game; the Shepard family was never much into hunting. Times were hard.

With the harvest done, Ellen had a little spare time. She did some knitting and general things around the house. Her thoughts began to wonder about a larger world. Ellen and her first cousin Susan Ratliff were about the same age and shared some of the same interests in getting a man. They often talked about what they wanted in a man and assessed local young men in terms of their dreams. Except for an oc-casional outing at a church singing or barbecue, they didn't have contact with many men in the Tinnin community who were eligible or met the standards that they had.

Susan and Ellen would typically find fault with the local young men--they were not bathed, were not considerate, had poor personal skills, lacked education, had little potential for income, were dishonest or not trustworthy, and were immoral by the standards of the day. Some might drink too much whiskey or carry on close relationships with women they deemed inappropriate for the man they wanted.

Thanks to a friend, Susan was about to help change their lack of men. On the second Friday in November, Susan walked over to Ellen's home--about a mile away. Susan told Ellen that she and her friend, Beatrice, were going to Brandon on Saturday. They would spend the night with the family of an aunt and return late Sunday. They invited Ellen to go with them. But, before she went, Ellen wanted to know more about their activities.

Other than the experience being a good outing, the incentive was that there were a few young, single men in Brandon. They had come there to help reconstruct the town and railroad after damage by soldiers in the Civil War. Susan explained to Ellen that these men had jobs and made money. Now, that was appealing. During the war, people had very little money. But, Susan didn't know much about the education, morals, and personal backgrounds of the men--they had come from all around. Maybe they were dodging military service with the Confederate or Union forces, or maybe they had just gotten out of prison, or maybe they had deserted wives and families in other states. Anyway, Susan, Beatrice, and Ellen decided they would go and check out the situation.

Susan explained that the fare on the train from Clinton to Brandon was $1 each way. They would each need $2. They would get Susan's younger brother, Robbie, to drive them to the Clinton depot in the family's wagon and return on Sunday to get them. That sure sounded good to Ellen. She had turned 16 in September and was approaching the age of major interest in men, particularly men who had jobs and made money.

So, Ellen got permission from Ma and Pa to go--not always easy. She told them that her cousin had invited her to go with her and a friend. Ellen didn't tell them that there were possibly some single men of interest. She packed a few things, including a fairly fancy dress and her "prettying-up stuff." She got almost everything ready to go by Friday night.

Saturday morning arrived, and the wagon driven by Susan's brother came but was about five minutes late. Susan and Beatrice were in the wagon. Ellen, always conscientious, was concerned that they might be late arriving at the depot and miss the train. She mentioned it. Robbie popped the lines on the horses' rumps to speed them up. They arrived at the depot in Clinton nearing 9:00 a.m. and caught the 9:23 train to Jackson; it continued on to Brandon.

The train arrived in Brandon at 12:28. Susan's aunt was there to meet them. She took them to her home, where they refreshed and prettied up a tad before going to the barbecue, singing, and dancing at the local Presbyterian Church. (It was a bit more liberal about such activities than the local Mason Chapel in Tinnin and defined *sin*, whatever that is, a little differently.) Ellen was so very pretty and womanly after getting ready. She was enough to tempt any man's eyes.

A small crowd was there when they got to the church on Government Street in Brandon. More people were arriving. Ellen was a tad shy at first. She was experiencing a lot of new things. The aunt introduced her to a few people. She got some barbecued goat, a baked sweet potato, and some corn pone. She, Susan, and Beatrice took their plates over to an empty table outside to sit.

Men in the crowd had been admiring the young women, particularly good-looking Ellen. Three men got their food and sauntered over to sit with the women. The one that sat by Ellen asked her name; she shyly said, "Ellen. What's yours?"

"Jasper," he replied.

"Where do you live?," "Do you like this barbecue?," and such were questions that guided their conversation.

Both Ellen and Jasper instantly felt some sort of attraction to each other. They continued to sit at the table and talk after they finished eating. Susan and Beatrice had left the table with the men they were sitting with. Ellen had overheard Beatrice's man say that there was some fresh, soft hay in the stable on the other side of the church building where folks put their horses during services. Both couples were soon nowhere to be seen. Ellen wasn't sure about what was next with Jasper. She kept remembering what her mother always said, "No young man good enough for marrying wants to marry a used woman." Apparently, Jasper had some of the same feelings, but Ellen didn't know. Ellen carefully structured the conversation and activities in a "safe" direction. She kept remembering what her mother taught her about relationships between men and women.

Ellen wanted an honest man of high morals for a long-term relationship. She wanted a loving husband who would care for her, protect her, father children, and be kind. She wanted a good provider. Ellen and Jasper kept sitting at the table and talking. War had created so much destruction and uncertainty, and it was always on her mind. A time of calmness with an interesting man was good.

Ellen told a little about herself. She began by telling about her family and that she lived with her parents and seven younger siblings. Next, she told about her home and farm. The farm had 1,200 acres of hills and creek bottoms. The Shepards planted cotton (their main source of money), corn, and other southern crops. She told about the little community of Tinnin, where they lived. She told Jasper that he needed to come see it for himself, and he said he might. And, what about him?

Jasper told Ellen that he was in Brandon working to upgrade railroad structures to the east that were damaged by Confederate troops as they left. These structures were toward a little town known as Pelahatchie. The Confederates did not want Union troops to find a usable railroad. On the other hand, they did not want to completely destroy the rails, as they might need them in the future. So Jasper got paid at the rate of $1.75 a day and was provided food and lodging in a nearby boarding house, known as Sister Annie's.

The music was beginning to start under the brush arbor by the church building. The music was provided by an elderly man with a fiddle, a young woman playing a wash tub, a man with a guitar, and former slave named Sam playing a beat-up old piano. There were some chairs around the music group and an open area for dancing.

Jasper took Ellen's hand and asked her to go over near the music. Something new for Ellen--no man had ever taken her hand and asked her to go with him anywhere. She smiled at him. They arose from the bench seat at the table and walked together, holding hands, to the brush arbor. She had a certain feeling of infatuation or something about her that she couldn't readily explain to herself in her mind. She looked at Jasper and tried to size him up. He was kind of tall, relatively thin, but with ample muscles. He was whiskered, and his clothing needed care, though it appeared relatively clean. Something she liked was that he did not have body odor, as did the pungent soldiers she had experienced earlier. His teeth looked okay. Jasper didn't appear sickly. He was well tanned, with calloused hands and blue eyes.

One big question Ellen had was his age: How old was he? He kind of looked almost as old as Pa, but, she thought, he couldn't be. She was reluctant to ask. So, she asked where he was from, and he replied, "Another state back east of here."

Then she asked how long he had been in Brandon, and he answered, "Going on three weeks." Ellen told him she was from the Tinnin community in Hinds County and that she was in Brandon with friends.

Just as Ellen was getting up courage to ask Jasper his age, the old man with the fiddle announced that it was time for a singing. The songs were mostly religious--church hymns such as "Rock of Ages" and "My Faith Looks Up to Thee."

Other songs included "Goober Peas," "I Wish I Was in Dixie," and "Yellow Rose of Texas." This last one would be of particular note in their future, but Ellen and Jasper didn't know it.

Ellen knew some of the words to the songs; Jasper knew a few. They both enjoyed trying to sing. She observed that he knew the words of songs from the South better than those of songs from the North. Of course, Ellen's Pa was from Indiana and had taught his family a few of the songs he knew from the North.

After about 45 minutes, the fiddler announced that the singing was over and that the band would play more music. "Dance if you want to," he said. On the second number, Jasper tugged Ellen's hand, and they were up getting into the dancing. Some numbers were fast; others slow. After a couple of dances, they decided to walk outside. It was getting dark. They would walk into the woods near the church.

Just as they were going out the door, Beatrice and her man were coming inside. No eye contact was made. Beatrice had a couple of pieces of straw in her hair. They went to the dance floor and began doing their do. Susan and her man weren't to be seen.

Ellen and Jasper strolled on their way out holding hands. After they had taken a couple of steps into the woods, Jasper said that Sister Annie's Boarding House was only a short walking distance. He asked Ellen if she would go to the house with him; she said yes. But, "yes" made her quite nervous.

They entered the parlor at Sister Annie's and sat on a sofa. Across the room sitting on another sofa was a couple obviously falling in love or something--maybe the emotion wasn't love but passion. Ellen had all kinds of feelings about this experience. She did not know what Jasper's next suggestion might be, but she kept holding his hand.

Ellen did not have to wait long for Jasper's next suggestion: "Want to see my room?"

She said, "Yes, I would like to briefly see your room." All the while flashing in Ellen's mind was her commitment to herself and family that her "specialness" would wait until her wedding night. She saw in his room and quickly looked around and said, "It is time for me to go back to the church to get with my friends and leave."

Jasper asked, "Are you sure?"

Ellen answered, "Yes, but let's hold hands and talk some more." She did not want this to end. Something about the situation made her want it to last a while longer.

When Ellen and Jasper got back to the Presbyterian Church, both Susan and Beatrice were sitting with their men at one of the barbecue tables. The band had stopped playing for the night. Susan's aunt would soon be there to pick them up.

Jasper told Ellen that he would like to see her tomorrow. Ellen said that she was staying on the edge of town toward Gulde. "We will be leaving early to catch the train to Clinton and home."

Jasper promised he would come early to talk and tell her goodbye. Ellen indicated that she would also like to see him. She told Jasper goodnight and went with Susan and Beatrice to get in the wagon to ride away. Ellen waived at Jasper until they were out of sight--longer than usual because of the bright harvest moon.

Was Ellen excited! She had met a man for whom she had almost immediate feelings. She barely slept that night and was up extra early the next day to see Jasper. Of course, she didn't know if he was a man of his word and would show up. He did; Ellen rushed to greet him. They talked; she told him to write and to visit her in Tinnin. He agreed to do so (even though he wasn't much at writing).

The threesome caught the 11:32 a.m. train in Brandon for Jackson and Clinton. Robbie was there at the depot to meet them at 2:30 p.m. and drive them home in the wagon.

Thoughts kept going through Ellen's mind: Would she ever see Jasper again? Little did she know that Jasper had some of the same feelings for her. He immediately wrote and mailed a letter to her in Tinnin. She got it about the first of December. He wanted to come see her in late December. He said he thought he was falling in love with her. She wrote back and said it would be fine to come for a visit. "I can introduce you to Pa and Ma and my sisters and brothers."

After another exchange of letters, things were set for Jasper to visit the day after Christmas. Ellen talked Pa into letting her use the wagon to go get a young man at the Clinton depot that she had met in Brandon. She talked her sister Rachel into going with her. The horse and wagon with Ellen and Rachel arrived at the depot on December 26 about a half hour before the train.

The train stopped; passengers were getting off and on. No Jasper. Did he stand her up? And, then, he appeared with a small bouquet of camellia blossoms. He was late getting off because he was helping an elderly preacher at the Women's Institute get off. Ellen thought to herself that Jasper was a kind man. She rushed to greet him. And, they hugged. She had never hugged a man other than her father before, but this was a different kind of hug. There was a romantic feel to it. Jasper handed Ellen the camellia bouquet; she looked at the colorful flowers and adored their beauty. She thanked him. Ellen introduced Jasper to Rachel, and they got in the wagon for the five-mile ride to the home in Tinnin.

They arrived at the Shepard home in Tinnin about 4:30. Bummer came from under the house to bark ferociously at the stranger. Rachel jumped from the wagon to calm Bummer by patting his head. She and Ellen knew he could be mean with people he hadn't sniffed before. Ellen and Jasper unloaded, and Ellen tied the horses, still hitched to the wagon, to a post. They all went on the porch. Pa and Ma came out; a couple of sisters peered out through a window.

Ellen introduced Jasper to her father and mother. She said, "I call them Pa and Ma; you can call them Mr. Shepard and Mrs. Shepard."

Pa welcomed Jasper and exchanged a few greetings. He asked him where he was from, how old he was, and what work he did to earn a living. Jasper said he was from back east, 37 years old, and worked for the railroad. Some of those answers didn't satisfy Pa. Other questions went through Pa's mind: What about previous marriages or communal relationships? Had he fathered children he didn't talk about? Had he been involved in crime? What work skills did he have? So many questions; so few answers. Little did Ellen know that she might never learn full details after several years.

Pa, in a stern voice, asked, "What do you mean by back east?"

Jasper related that he had been traveling for quite a while. He had stopped in many places, where he worked a while and moved on. He said he often told people he was born in South Carolina. Pa asked about his mother and father and what they did. Jasper indicated that he had no communication with them and gave no names. Most of these answers did not sit well with Pa.

Ellen said that Jasper was here for a couple of nights and would be leaving three days from now. Ma stated that he could sleep on a pallet in the closet under the steps that go upstairs. "We have some dry fresh-from-the-crib corn shucks in a large cotton-pick sack." Jasper, trying to be gracious, said that would be fine. Ellen was a bit taken back, but she knew that there were Pa, Ma, and eight children in the house and no extra beds. So, she needed to be content; after all she was trying to introduce a new person to her family.

Ellen told Jasper that she wanted to let him look around a bit. She took him into the house and showed him the kitchen, sitting room, bedroom for Pa and Ma, bedroom for girls, and bedroom for boys. The privy was out back and was a two-holer. Water could be drawn from the well. They went outside for Ellen to continue showing Jasper around. Their first activity was to store under the shed the wagon they had ridden in from the depot and release the horses into the lot. Afterward, they walked past the smokehouse, stables, hogpen, chicken house, and other outbuild-ings. Ellen said, "I want to show you the crystal-clear flow-ing water in the spring branch."

They walked across a small area of open pasture; si-multaneously, they reached for each other's hand. Holding hands, they approached the spring branch at the edge of the woods. It was flowing nicely. Ellen told Jasper that the water was very good and that they would sometimes drink it. She showed him where a gourd dipper was kept for get-ting and drinking spring-branch water. Jasper tried the wa-ter and agreed it was good.

At that point, they simultaneously embraced each other. A long kiss followed. Wow! Ellen thought that she was in love; maybe Jasper was in love. After a few moments, they continued their stroll holding hands. Ellen and Jasper were gone on what Ellen called "Jasper's showing-around." It took longer than Pa and Ma thought it should unless the two went to fields some distance away. But, they didn't think that the couple was that interested in the fields. They didn't know that Ellen and Jasper were taking an innocent romantic stroll through the woods past the spring branch. But it was getting late in the December afternoon, and Ellen and Jasper figured they had better soon get back to the house.

Ma was fixing supper with the help of Rachel and Mag. Georgia Ann was looking after Ira, the baby brother who was only a little more than two years of age and the youngest of the Shepard children. Pa was out gathering the last eggs of the day. He would soon be in the house.

As the family gathered for supper, each of Ellen's siblings met Jasper. He tried to talk to them a little. They were very interested in who he was, where he was from, what kind of work he did, and if he had been to school. After all, this was the first man that Ellen had brought home. They sat down at the table; Jasper had a seat next to Ellen. The meal wasn't very scrumptious: fried salt pork meat, dried butter beans, corn bread, and baked sweet potatoes. Jasper ate and expressed appreciation for his meal.

Afterward, Pa said that he wanted to talk with Jasper. Though the weather was kind of cool in the early evening, they went on the front porch. Pa again asked Jasper about his parents, where he was from, and what kind of work he did. The answers weren't very satisfactory. However, Jasper indicated that he had great respect and growing love for Ellen.

Pa assumed, and rightly so, that a courtship was developing between Jasper and Ellen. Answers from Jasper were not very informative. Pa would talk with Ma and Ellen later, particularly Ellen, to see if he could learn more.

It was getting dark. The coal oil lamps were lit. The shutters on the windows had been closed and secured. A fire was built in the fireplace to drive away some coolness in the air. General chatter while watching siblings play lasted about an hour. Then Pa said that it was time to go to bed. He also said to Jasper, "And you know where your bed is, right?" The implication was that Jasper was to stay on the pallet of fresh, dry corn shucks and not approach Ellen. But, Pa didn't know that his daughter might go into the closet.

Everyone was about in bed. Pa went and peed off the porch, as he did each night but in a different place. The coal oil lamps were blown out. A few embers in the fireplace glowed and would keep overnight to start the fire in the morning (with the help of heart pine kindling). After every-one was asleep, Ellen sneaked out and opened the closet door under the steps. Jasper was there but not asleep. She got down on her knees, rubbed the hair on his head, and they kissed. He put his arms around her; she didn't resist. She pulled the closet door shut and lay beside him. They kissed again; he rubbed her shoulder. Passion was high, but Ellen remembered that her "specialness" was for anoth-er time. They lay side by side and talked lowly for about an hour. Ellen then left and went to her own bed without awaking members of the family (the six Shepard girls all shared the same room).

Next morning everyone was up. Jasper got a little sleep on the shuck and cotton-pick-sack pallet in the closet un-der the steps. Ellen wanted to take him around Tinnin and especially to see the Ratliff Store (that her grandparents ran), Mason Chapel, and the schoolhouse (though it was shabby and not exactly a source of community pride). Ellen asked Pa if she could borrow the wagon for this. Pa said no.

Ellen became upset and pleaded. "We will walk." Pa soft-ened his mind and let her borrow the wagon. But, she had to promise to use it carefully and treat the horses kindly. She would also have to do the harnessing and then the un-hitching after the wagon was back. She agreed to this.

However, Ellen didn't have to do the harnessing and the unhitching all by herself; Jasper would help. In fact, he was quite skilled at the tasks. Experience from some past times and places proved useful. He just needed to know the exact ways Pa wanted things done.

While on their outing, they learned of a singing that evening at Mason Chapel. They made plans to go and enjoyed it. The singing was a bit more "churchy" than at the Presbyterian Church in Brandon. As Ellen's Pa had said, sin has a range of meanings: sin in one situation might not be sin in another. This singing might have been a little straight-laced for a couple that was falling in love, or maybe it was more appropriate considering Ellen's moral standards.

If someone wanted a liquid "something" before, during, or after the singing, it was available behind the Ratliff Store. Under the wagon shed, an out-of-towner from Bolton would be there with home brew. Somehow, the Ratliffs always turned to look away from what was going on under the wagon shed. Of course, it wouldn't have been there if some people hadn't wanted it. But, Ellen and Jasper did not go there for a sample. Several others at the singing did, and when they returned, their imbibing was quite evident.

That night, Jasper slept on the same pallet of corn shucks in a cotton-pick sack as the night before. Ellen came into the closet after everyone else in the family was asleep to tell him goodnight, thank him for the day, and remind him of tomorrow's early schedule. Passion was high and ended with a big kiss.

Next morning, Jasper was up and ready to go to the Clinton depot and back to Brandon. It was time to say goodbye. There were hugs and kisses. Jasper asked Ellen to come to Brandon. Ellen asked Jasper to come back to Tinnin. Letters would be exchanged. They would work things out so they could have some time together!

Pa had his say with Ellen. He did not think Jasper would be a good fit in the family. There was too much age difference--he was 37, and she was 16. He was more than twice her age! Ellen would explain the age difference by saying many young women married older men. Most of the time the marriages worked as long as the wives pretty well followed instructions of their husbands. There weren't enough men to go around. The war had caused the deaths of so many men, and others had been permanently maimed. Pa thought that Jasper was little more than a vagrant roaming around the South. He thought that there was a lot he didn't know about Jasper. He wanted Ellen to have a better man! But, Pa didn't change Ellen's mind.

With passion as high as it was, a way would be found for the couple to be together. So, in mid-January, Jasper made another trip to Tinnin. He was there three days. It was hog-killing time, and Jasper knew how to do what needed to be done. He worked side-by-side with Pa for a full day. Their work enhanced meals with fried fresh pork tenderloin and scrambled chicken eggs with hog brains. Delicious! The hog's bladder was removed, drained of liquid, and hung up to dry in the wagon shed. Once dry, baby Ira could play with it like a ball. It would last until it burst, and that could be fairly soon with rough play. And, as during his last visit, Jasper slept on the pallet made of corn shucks in a cotton-pick sack in the closet under the steps. Of course, he and Ellen had time together. Ellen would sneak into the closet to kiss him goodnight and, on the last night, said she loved him. He said the same back to her.

Jasper found his way back to Tinnin at least four more times before the end of February. His and Ellen's romance was moving fast. And Valentine's Day sped the romance along. Jasper came to see Ellen and brought her a small bottle of perfume. She adored it; she had never had perfume before. They embraced--took walks--held hands-- and talked about a possible future together.

They reasoned that Pa and Ma had a big house that could be home to a young couple and that the 1,200 acres of farmland would provide enough for them to get into farming. Life and work would be hard, but that way of life is all they had ever known. They dreamed that they would later get a house of their own and become more independent. Or, as a newly wed couple, they could continue living in Sister Annie's Boarding House in Brandon. He could continue with his job, and she could seek work. But, Jasper didn't like the notion of his bride living at Sister Annie's; there were some tough guys there, and she might not be safe around them.

Jasper and Ellen never knew what soldiers would be doing and when they would pass through the area. The Union troops coming from Vicksburg were under orders to be very destructive. Any Confederates were fairly well demoralized because of the defeats they had experienced. That, however, didn't keep them from being mean. It was best to avoid where soldiers might be, and that wasn't easy, as the line of movement from Vicksburg to the east was along the route of the railroad. Until the war was over and all matters about it settled, uneasiness would always be a part of life in certain areas of the South.

More plans were made before the Valentine's visit was over. Things had to be kept simple; there wasn't much money or time. Those plans would go into early March. And, Ellen was not sure about the feelings of Pa and Ma, particularly Pa. He wanted the best for his oldest daughter. But, with the feelings that Ellen had for Jasper, would she really care? Maybe she should care; Pa was often right about things.

As for Ellen and Jasper, love was all about them. But how could it be? They hadn't known each other that long. There were many uncertainties. They didn't have education, personal possessions, or other things of worth; but they knew how to work and take risks. Ellen was smart, and Jasper was experienced. Together, they could figure things out.

Families Joining and Dividing

The first of March was fast approaching. Ellen and Jasper shared letters. They had made plans for something big in their lives. Jasper was coming to Tinnin on the last day of February, and Ellen was to travel to Brandon on the morning of March 1. (In 1864, February had 29 days--it was leap year and a great time for lovers and marriage!)

Right after Valentine's Day and Jasper's return to Brandon, Ellen spoke to Pa. She waited until he was alone. She told him that she and Jasper were in love and wanted to be married. Pa had a fit! He rarely cussed, but he did on this occasion. He said a lot of bad things about Jasper. He wondered aloud about how they had the money to get married and go about getting life together underway. And ended with, "Hell, no!"

Ellen thought, "How could Pa be so opposed to Jasper?" The next day Ellen again talked to Pa alone. She explained that she didn't think it was right for him to reject Jasper; she said Jasper was a good man who had been so nice to her. She said Jasper was the nicest man she had ever met. He would be coming there on the last day of February to talk about marriage. Pa said that there was no need for him to do so. His mind was set, and he wouldn't change; Jasper was not the right man for her. Neither would Ellen change; her mind was made up regardless of what Pa said.

The last day of February arrived. Jasper rode the train to Clinton and, miraculously, hitched a wagon ride with a stranger to Tinnin. Pa had forbidden Ellen to take a wagon to meet him. Jasper had to walk down the long hill on the dirt road. Bummer started barking as soon as he came into sight. Ellen heard Bummer and went outside to calm him. She looked up the road, and there was Jasper! Pa was out back tending to animals and did not see Jasper coming down the hill--probably just as well.

Ellen was so happy. She ran out to greet Jasper, meeting him about halfway up the hill. She hugged him; he hugged her back. Ellen was nervous when she told Jasper a little of what Pa had said. Anyway, Jasper was at the Shepard home, and he and Ellen would do the best they could. Jasper thought that he loved Ellen so much that her pa's feelings were not about to change his mind. He really didn't like the way Pa was acting toward him. In the back of his mind, he kept thinking that Pa could sense that some things were hidden and weren't being told. Jasper didn't offer any more information.

Ellen invited Jasper into the house. He greeted Ma and the siblings who were present. Pa soon arrived with a few eggs in a basket. He immediately saw Jasper and exclaimed, "What are you doing here!"

Jasper was fairly blunt in answering, "I came to ask for the hand of your daughter Ellen in marriage." Pa was beside himself with anger and dropped the eggs. Rachel cleaned up the mess from the broken eggs.

Pa went on, "Just what else do you have in mind?"

Ellen stepped in, "Pa, Jasper is a good man. I believe he is right for me. I am in love with him. We plan to be married soon." Pa and Ma appeared upset but that didn't "dampen" the romance in the room. Pa stomped out to the porch to cool off. Ellen soon followed him.

Ellen said, "You and Ma always told me that a marriage should be a happy time that brings two families together. You also said that the time of courtship was more important than the wedding day. You know, I think you were likely right. We have been in courtship now for a few months--plenty long enough for us with our level of love and commitment." It was actually a little less than four months since they met at the Presbyterian Church in Brandon.

"Please, Pa. Jasper is my man." Ellen continued, "We will be getting married very soon. Let's work this out so we are all happy." Pa, beginning to cool a bit, said that this didn't sound good to him and he feared for his daughter. Ellen indicated that she wasn't afraid. And, "Pa, Jasper needs to stay here tonight. Okay?"

Pa said, "No." Ellen indicated that if Jasper couldn't stay there that he would leave and she would go with him. Pa stared off the porch into the fruit orchard for a few moments. Then, he relented and said, "Well, okay; he can stay here tonight, but he must leave first thing in the morning. He sleeps on the pallet in the closet under the stairs, and you in your bed." Ellen thanked Pa and said Jasper would leave early the next day.

Ellen went inside and quietly spoke to Ma about what was happening. She explained that she could not understand the attitude of Pa toward Jasper. Ellen said that she and Jasper loved each other and that they wanted to marry and spend their lives together. Ma listened patiently and then said, "You know your Pa. He wants good for his daughters; he wants the best for each of you. I suspect you should heed what he has said."

Ellen continued talking with Ma with thoughts about the future. She said that she and Jasper could live in the house for a short while, work, and then get a place of their own. She also said another way for them to stay was to set aside certain land for them and they would work it. Anyway, the farm was plenty large enough for another worker and to support one additional person. She reminded Ma that the slaves were about gone and that the farm needed more workers to do what they had formerly done. Always promoting Jasper, Ellen indicated that he was a skilled farm worker who knew how to go about getting things done.

After a night of trying to sleep on a pallet of corn shucks in a cotton-pick sack, Jasper was up early. The only family member up was Ellen. Jasper was preparing to leave. But no one knew that Ellen had come into the closet where Jasper slept on a pallet after all were asleep. They agreed that she would be leaving with him. They would catch the train to Brandon and go to the Clerk's office to get a marriage license. Jasper had saved $62 from his work; Ellen had only a couple of dollars.

So, Ellen was also discretely packing. She didn't want to alarm family members and create additional anger. It was soon time to go. Pa did not yet know that Ellen was also leaving. He spoke to Ellen, saying that she could not use the wagon to take Jasper to the depot in Clinton. At that point, Ellen knew she had to provide more details.

"Pa," Ellen said, "I am leaving with Jasper. Our plans are to get married day after tomorrow in Clinton at the home of the Institute for Women (Hillman College) chaplain, Reverend Autry. We will get our license this afternoon at the Clerk's office in Brandon."

Pa shouted, "No!" Ellen indicated that his thoughts didn't much matter at this stage. Pa went further. "You ain't staying at this house--not ever. If you marry him, you leave here." Ellen shed a couple of tears and accepted what her father said.

Ellen was beginning to realize that she might never see her ma, sisters, and brothers again. She hugged each and said goodbye. But, Pa was too bitter for a hug.

Ellen and Jasper left, walking up the hill trail with each carrying a few possessions. They walked to the home of her cousin Susan Ratliff. Ellen knocked firmly on the door. Susan came to the door all sleepy-eyed. Ellen explained that she and Jasper needed a ride to the depot in Clinton and very soon. "We have a train to catch in about an hour." Susan quickly got ready and had her brother join them as they hitched horses to the wagon and headed out.

As they rode to the depot, Ellen told Susan the couple's plans. She asked Susan to go by and tell Ma what they were doing on her way back home. As they approached the depot, they went a hundred yards or so out of the way to Reverend Autry's home. There they met with him and said they were on their way to get a marriage license. He agreed to perform the rites of matrimony the next day at 3:00 p.m. in his home. Ellen said that a few family members and friends might attend but no more than 10 people.

Afterward, Ellen asked Susan to also share the details of the wedding with Ma and Susan's own family; she wanted them to come to the wedding. She asked Susan if she would be her attendant and wear a Sunday school dress. Then Jasper and Ellen bought tickets and caught the train to Brandon.

The train arrived in Brandon just in time for Jasper and Ellen to go to the Clerk's office on Government Street to get the license. The Clerk was Henry Cole. He quickly issued a marriage license dated March 1, 1864. The license granted an authorized individual to "Celebrate the Rites of Matrimony of Jasper H. Lee and Ellen L. Sheppard." (Ellen noticed that her last name had an extra "p," but she didn't say anything.)

Ellen and Jasper then went to Mulholland's Store just across the roadway to get a dress for her and coat and pants for him. Ellen got what she wanted--a simple white dress! It had a tiny waist, had a bow on the back, and properly emphasized her feminine features. Jasper got a navy jacket and pants. Money was short; they would have to wear the shoes they had. They went to the jewelry area of the store and bought $2 wedding bands. Then it was to Sister Annie's Boarding House for the night. They had to share a small bed that night but Ellen remained true to wearing a white wedding dress.

They were up about usual time the next morning preparing to catch the train to Clinton. And, were they excited! Jasper walked about a quarter mile to the job office of the railroad and said that he was quitting. He thanked everyone for allowing him to have the job. Of course, his job supervisor grumbled something about such a short notice. Jasper said he was sorry, but it would have to be that way. He told the desk clerk at the boarding house that he would not be back. He told the people at both places that he was about to marry the woman of his dreams.

Jasper packed what little he had into a small, ragged suitcase. Ellen had what she brought the previous day. They wore their wedding clothes. Jasper folded the marriage license and placed it in the pocket of his coat--he didn't want to lose it.

After a half-mile walk to the depot, they bought tickets and boarded the 11:48 a.m. train to Jackson and Clinton. The train arrived in Clinton at 2:08 p.m.; fortunately it was on time. They walked the short distance to the home of Reverend Autry on the campus of the Institute for Women, or at least what was left of it after Civil War destruction.

They arrived at the house a little early and waited under a tree in the front yard. Just before they were ready to go in, a wagon arrived with Ellen's cousin Susan and Susan's brother and parents. Greetings were exchanged. Close behind was a wagon with Ma, Rachel, Mag, Naomi, and Georgia Ann. The other siblings stayed at home with Pa, who didn't want them to see the wedding. He didn't want Ma or the other children to go either, but Ma was firm and went. Jasper had no family or friends present. Maybe that was appropriate, as no one knew his family, much less anything about him.

Some residents of the Tinnin community thought it was sad that Pa didn't come to the wedding of his oldest daughter. He was very upset. He felt that Ellen was misjudging Jasper. He sent word for the newly married couple not to come to the house and that he never wanted to see Jasper again. This was heartbreaking to Ellen. A family divide had occurred. Ellen might never again see her parents.

Almost everyone wore Sunday school clothes. Ellen freshened a tad in a side room and came out as a radiant bride. The bride and groom quickly reviewed details with the preacher. Jasper gave the preacher the marriage license (which he later signed and returned to the Rankin County Clerk's office).

Reverend Autry performed the ceremony in the front room of the house. Being Baptist, he more or less used Baptist wedding vows. The ceremony was kept simple. Susan held the ring Ellen had for Jasper; Jasper held the ring he had for Ellen. After announcing why they were there, the preacher had a short prayer asking for God's blessing of the union between Jasper and Ellen. He then went into recitation of the wedding vows.

The preacher spoke: "Will you, Ellen, have Jasper to be your husband? Will you love him, comfort him, and keep him, forsaking all others to remain true to him? Will you honor him, submit to him, and strive to follow his direction as his helpmate? If so, say, 'I do.'"

Ellen said, "I do."

The preacher continued. "Repeat after me: "I, Ellen, take thee, Jasper, to be my husband, and before God and these witnesses, I promise to be a faithful, obedient, and true wife.'" Ellen repeated the vow.

Next, Reverend Autry spoke to Jasper: "Will you, Jasper, take Ellen to be your wife? Will you love her, comfort her, and keep her, forsaking all others? If so, say, 'I do.'"

Jasper said, "I do."

The preacher continued. "Repeat after me: 'I, Jasper, take thee, Ellen, to be my wife, and before God and these witnesses, I promise to be a faithful and true husband.'" Jasper looked and smiled at Ellen and repeated the statement.

Reverend Autry called for the exchange of rings. Susan passed Jasper's ring to Ellen. Ellen repeated the words the preacher had asked her to say as she slipped the ring on Jasper's finger: "With this ring I thee wed, and all my worldly goods I thee endow. In sickness and in health, in poverty or in wealth, 'til death do us part."

Jasper took Ellen's ring from his pocket and repeated the same vows as Ellen. He placed it on Ellen's ring finger. The preacher said a short prayer to end the ceremony. The bride and groom kissed and hugged. The preacher now pronounced them Mr. and Mrs. Lee.

Ellen glowed with pride. She walked over and hugged her mother and said goodbye. She also told her mother to tell Pa that she loved him. It appeared that everyone present was happy. Jasper slipped Reverend Autry $2 for doing the ceremony.

As the small group was still gathered, Ellen quietly requested her cousin Susan to ask her parents if the couple could stay at their house that night. Permission was given. Ellen and Jasper had no transportation, so they rode to Susan's home in the Ratliff's wagon with them--made the wagon kind of full. But, it was exciting to the newlyweds.

At Susan's home, the newlyweds brought in their luggage and went to the room that was theirs for the night. It was a small room, isolated away from other family, with a tiny, shuttered window. They got out of their wedding clothes and dressed to take a walk over to the Ratliff Store and otherwise look around the area. They held hands, hugged, kissed, and laughed. Anticipation of their future was exciting but nerve-wracking. They did not know where they would be the next night. A bit later, they joined Cousin Susan's family for supper.

As the morning sun rose, the newlyweds were up and about. They gathered their things together. As they were doing this, Ma arrived in a wagon with a few things that belonged to Ellen. These were going with her as the couple ventured west. Ellen and Jasper were without a destination; they were going wherever the situation merited. Ellen again hugged her mother and said thank you for bringing her things and goodbye.

Susan and her brother drove the newlyweds to the Clinton depot, where they were catching a train to Vicksburg. A lot of things were in disarray, as the Union forces had just moved through the area on their way to the East Coast. The railroad was still operating, however. Some of it had been patched up following damage by military forces. Anyway, it was deemed safe for travel to Vicksburg. Ellen and Jasper hugged Susan and her brother goodbye. They bought tickets and boarded the train.

In Vicksburg, they found a room in a home with a woman widowed by the war, a Mrs. Cornweller. She was a sweet lady of the Old South who could not figure out how the Confederates allowed the Union forces to take Vicksburg-- a major shipping city of the South (her family had operated a dock). She talked about all she had lost in the war, particularly her husband. Their older children were gone from home and living in the Chicago area, and she was alone. She said something about not knowing how she was going to live. She began crying. Ellen hugged her and tried to offer comfort. Ellen encouraged her to have faith in a divine being. She suggested that Mrs. Cornweller might talk with her preacher. Mrs. Cornweller shrugged and muttered, "He is a damn Yankee!" Ellen asked what she meant.

Mrs. Cornweller tried to explain about the preacher at her church. She said he was originally from the North and had protected former slaves and befriended Union troops. He once said that he didn't think slavery was right and that he didn't feel that folks in Vicksburg and the South should go to war to defend it. The preacher even provided special care for an injured Union soldier from Illinois and had him to come to church when she was there. "How could he do that to me!" she exclaimed. She wondered aloud about how any preacher could aid a Union troop. She went on, "Surely, it was a great sin." (Ellen instantly thought about what Pa had taught her about the definition of sin varying. Wow! A perfect example of Pa's wisdom.)

She had curiosity, though, about the Union soldier, as she tried to stand close enough to hear what he said. Mrs. Cornweller said she overheard him talking about his home area in Illinois...the fertile, black soil was so very good for growing corn. He talked about the new equipment that farmers now used to save labor and get more work done. They were able to produce more corn with fewer hours of labor. Mrs. Cornweller probably didn't like it that the Yankees had moved ahead of the South in farming methods. So, Mrs. Cornweller really unloaded on Ellen and appeared to feel better afterward.

Ellen was somewhat shocked by what Mrs. Cornweller went on to say. She said that slavery wasn't that bad. Slaves had food, clothing, and other needs provided by their owners. She further said she could find evidence in the Bible that slavery was a Christian thing. Goodness, Ellen thought, how could anyone feel that way? This caused Ellen to question some of Christianity. But, ever-thoughtful Ellen did not challenge Mrs. Cornweller. The kind of talk just made Ellen more resolute in plans for her and Jasper to leave on their uncertain route for unknown places to the west of Vicksburg.

Jasper got a job at Shawver & Pollock, a commission merchant, located near the dock at the corner of Levee and Crawford Streets. He told a Mr. Shawver that George W. Shepard was his father-in-law and that he needed a job. Mr. Shawver remembered George W. Shepard as a good occasional customer. The firm hired Jasper to do a variety of work, such as unloading shipments, stocking goods, and loading purchases onto wagons. His pay was $1.65 a day.

Ellen helped Mrs. Cornweller straighten and clean her house and the yard around it in exchange for the cost of her and Jasper's room. The location was on the edge of the Vicksburg battlefield. The severe Siege of Vicksburg had occurred there a few months earlier. Destruction was all about, though some effort was underway to clean and reconstruct the area.

One afternoon, Ellen and Mrs. Cornweller took a stroll into some of the area of destruction. It was bad. Building scraps, discarded clothing, shoes, kitchenware, lead slugs from ammunition, and bones from animals or people were about. A couple of obviously human skulls were evident.

Parts of a tiny skeleton that appeared to be that of a young human baby were partially covered with an old cloth. Seeing all this caused Ellen to think back on what Pa said about war. No doubt, war brought out the worst in human behavior. There should be a way to avoid something like this.

After a few days, it was time for Jasper and Ellen to move on. They had to work their way to the West. In spite of their challenges, Jasper always had patience, kindness, and consideration for Ellen; he loved her. She reciprocated.

They crossed the Mississippi River on a ferry from the Vicksburg dock into Louisiana. Ellen and Jasper looked around, and the land was very flat; they liked gently rolling hills. Fortunately, they were able to catch a ride on a wagon with a man who had brought people from Tallulah, Louisiana, to catch a ferry to Mississippi. He drove them to the train depot in Tallulah for 25 cents. They found that Union gunboats had set fire to and burned the depot of the Vicksburg, Shreveport, and Texas Railroad Company. A shack-like temporary depot was being used--not much of a place, but it worked.

Ellen and Jasper caught a train for Monroe and Shreveport, Louisiana. The stop in Monroe let passengers who had reached their destination off and new passengers on. The land still looked too flat for Ellen and Jasper's liking, though there were a few hills off in the distance. It appeared that a lot of crop farming went on the area. Lots of mules and horses and not many goats or cattle were evident. Just maybe Ellen and Jasper would like a mix of hills and flat land.

They thought Shreveport would be their destination, but it was not to be. The Red River in Shreveport offered more flat land but not a very wide expanse compared with the Mississippi River Delta of Louisiana. More of the West was on their minds. They decided that they would sleep that night on benches in the Shreveport depot before boarding an early morning train to Athens, Texas. Ellen was fearful of sleeping in a depot. There might be some "bad" people who would beat them up and rob them; also, the good-looking, newly married woman might be assaulted. Jasper assured Ellen that he would protect her. They were not alone in the depot, as three other people also stayed in it that night. All of them seemed to be honest, law-abiding folks who did not pose threats of robbery or assault.

They had heard that the Athens area was nice hill country and a good place to put down roots. They boarded the train in the early morning for Athens, Texas. Along the way, Jasper and Ellen peered out the window of the train car. They liked the lay of the land and what they saw. It wasn't flat like the Mississippi River Delta in Louisiana or steep like the loess hills around Vicksburg. They saw a few homes and farms with animals and fields being readied for another crop year. It appeared to be an okay area to them.

About noon, the train arrived in Athens, Texas. Ellen and Jasper got off. They saw a poster that said Texas became a state in 1845 and Henderson County was established in 1846. The largest town around was Athens, with about 300 people but growing fairly rapidly. The lay of the land was appealing, and the Trinity River was nearby. They learned that the climate was hot and humid in the summer and mild to cool in the winter. They were excited about this being a place where they might settle down.

They walked the short streets, carrying their suitcases. They looked around for a boarding house or other place to stay or to work. The didn't see much that appealed to them or that they could afford. They were getting anxious. Particularly Ellen was nervous in this new place with strange ways of doings things. Jasper could sense that Ellen was uneasy; he gave her a hug, said "I love you," and assured her that everything would work out.

As they walked, they came upon a couple of mercantile stores, a saloon, and a couple of churches. One of the churches was a Methodist Episcopal, and the other was a Presbyterian. The thought quickly came to their minds about the importance of the Presbyterian Church in Brandon, Mississippi, in helping them get to know each other. Ellen reminded Jasper of where they first met and began to fall in love. Jasper was quick to respond, "Yes, that was a great place to me." The steps of the Presbyterian Church were a spot to sit briefly, rest from their walking, and contemplate.

Ellen remembered one of the sing-along songs from the evening they first met: "The Yellow Rose of Texas." She started trying to sing it, and Jasper sort of joined in. Yes, that song helped bring them closer together now that they were in Texas! But, they had not seen a yellow rose!

For the first time since marriage, Ellen began to think back to her family. She had never been away more than a night at a time. She remembered Ma and Pa. She remembered her sisters and brothers. And, she couldn't forget Bummer, who once notified her that Jasper had arrived in Tinnin. But she didn't have long to let her mind wander. The couple had things to do.

The conversation turned to the role of church in their lives. Ellen said she and her family had sometimes gone to

Mason Chapel in Tinnin. It was small and had an itinerant Methodist Episcopal preacher. Mostly, not much went on since Preacher Hoyle had died of a heart attack after fright from Union troops on Easter Sunday of last year. She stated that her family had a large Bible in which important dates and events were recorded. But, they seldom read from it and seldom had prayer other than a blessing before Sunday dinner. Ellen did say that she was christened as a small girl by the preacher at Mason Chapel. She continued, "I think that involved sprinkling a few drops of water on my head. How about you, Jasper?"

Jasper didn't have much to say about church. He said he had seen a few preachers. He said he once went to a brush arbor revival and was scared by the preacher's message of "burning in hell." He said it "sounded hot and bad" to him. He said that when the folks were singing and the preacher was begging people to come forward and "accept Jesus Christ as savior," he went down to the front. He said the preacher shook his hand and said a brief prayer. The preacher said Jasper would be baptized at the local creek by immersion. Jasper said, "I asked him what that meant. He said dunking me under the water." That scared him. Jasper continued that he "left that town before baptism." Maybe some day he would be baptized. He never learned who Jesus Christ was, either. It would take some explaining to make a "believer" out of him. But, that didn't matter to Ellen. She was with the man of her dreams. She knew that their love was more than being about going to church and the like.

It was time to walk some more. They had a good conversation on the steps of the church. It would probably serve as a foundation for future church endeavors of Ellen and Jasper and any children they might have. In general, they were in agreement on the role of church in their lives. They tried to accept Pa's explanation that the definition of sin varies with the situation and who is involved but that one should always attempt to do what is right and moral. Treat others as you would like to be treated. They would affiliate in some way with a church once they had found a place for settling down. They had little idea about the church and preacher that lay ahead in their lives.

Finally, as night was approaching, they came upon the Witherspoon Hotel and its saloon. The saloon had its own name, Spoon Saloon, and was often known locally as "The Spoon." The hotel wasn't new nor fancy at all, but a room was available at a rate they could afford. Jasper paid $1.50 for three nights. Since Ellen and Jasper didn't drink (with their limited money, they couldn't afford to), the presence of a saloon didn't seem important.

There was one more thing Ellen wanted to do: write a letter to Mrs. Cornweller in Vicksburg. She wanted to thank her for befriending them by allowing the couple to stay in her home, but mostly she wanted to cheer her up. Mrs. Cornweller had seemed so down on life and her ability to survive. That night in their room at the Witherspoon, with the light of a flickering lamp, Ellen wrote a letter for mailing the next day. She wanted to help Mrs. Cornweller feel better and adjust to life after the Civil War. Though she didn't say so in the letter, she really wanted to set Mrs. Cornweller straight on slavery; that could be something for another time as it would probably aggravate her at this time of grieving in the death of her husband. Maybe, in the back of her mind, Ellen really wanted to write her parents and tell them where she was, but she did not do so, because the joining of her and Jasper had created a family divide.

Ellen and Jasper could now relax a bit after their trip from Vicksburg. But, serious relaxation would be a tad difficult and elusive. They had a future to plan and realize. And, they had to face the challenges of getting through tomorrow, the next day, and the days afterward.

LIFE WITH JASPER

On their first day in Athens, Ellen and Jasper found a place to stay at the Witherspoon Hotel and Saloon. It wasn't all that comfortable, but it had to do. Of course, they had never had anything but the bare essentials. There was no luxury in their lives!

After all, Athens was to be the place where they would settle down in life. They were going to see what might be good for them. They knew it would be hard. They might have to work for or sharecrop with a farmer or do other work. Then, with a little luck, they might get a few dollars and buy a horse and other things for their needs. They could get a small farm using credit from a local merchant or bank. They were willing to work for what they got. They were willing to be honest and fair in all that they did. Maybe some of their goals would take a few years. But, there were more pressing needs, such as making it through the night at the Witherspoon.

The small room they got was on the second floor and had a tiny wood-burning fireplace. The toilet was downstairs and out back of the building. A wash pan on the floor of their room took the place of a tub or lavatory. The bed was small for two people. It had a mattress of cotton cloth apparently stuffed with unginned cotton. Though they couldn't see inside, it was similar to the dry corn shucks in the cotton-pick sack that Jasper had slept on in the closet under the steps of the Shepard home back in Tinnin. At 50 cents a night, this would have to do.

When they went to bed that night, all seemed well. Shortly, however, both Ellen and Jasper had bites that were itchy and reddish. Small bugs came out of hiding and bit them. They were not flying, like mosquitoes; they were about three-eights of an inch long and crawling under the bed sheets and in crevices. The bugs preferred darkness and tended to hide in light.

Jasper told Ellen that he had seen those bugs before at a place he stayed sometime ago. He said they were called bed bugs. The couple was able to mash and kill a few of the bugs. When mashed, the bugs gave off a bad odor. Ellen and Jasper couldn't be choosy, as they had little money. They would have to tough it out for the three nights that were paid at the Witherspoon. Despite the bugs and other inconveniences, there was time for the tender and loving touches of newlyweds!

The next day, Jasper searched for work. He heard that there was a farmer out of town a ways looking for someone to help with crops, and maybe on a sharecropper basis. He had no way to travel to the farm other than walk. It wasn't that far; he could walk a couple or so miles. So, on the morning of the third day, he set about to walk to the farm. He left Ellen at the Witherspoon.

Ellen, being industrious, asked the barkeeper and manager in "The Spoon" if any jobs were available. Yes, there were. Ellen was a tad nervous; she had never been in a bar before and wanted to hear more. One was as a barmaid in "The Spoon." With some slightly tight clothing and her flirtatious good looks, she could likely make some good tips. The barkeeper said that he made the drinks and that a person named Bonito could give her some tips on being a barmaid. The other job was cleaning the out-back toilets and the stable area, where guests who rode would keep their animals. Ellen said that she would talk with her husband and come back later.

Ellen waited for Jasper to return from the farm. It seemed to be taking him a long time. When he was back, she told him what she did and about a couple of jobs at "The Spoon." He told her about his day and that sharecropping would be available on Smith Farm on April 1, which was still nearly two weeks away. So, Ellen and Jasper decided to continue staying at the hotel for another few days. They would pay 50 cents a night and battle the bed bugs.

With Ellen's insistence and some reluctance, Jasper agreed that she could be a barmaid at "The Spoon." One condition was that the barkeeper permit him to sit over to one side where he could protect her from any patrons who became unruly. But, of course, Ellen was capable of defending herself, as she did against Private Cason on the porch of the Shepard home when the Union troops came through.

Ellen didn't know much about being a barmaid, so she went to "The Spoon' the next mid-morning before it opened for details on the job. Bonito was there and told her a few things about greeting customers, taking orders, and serving liquor. She would be paid $1 each day, and she could keep any tips she made. The saloon would provide an outfit for her to wear. She looked at it, tried it on, and thought it was a tad on the tight side. However, the skirt did go to her ankles.

Bonito also told Ellen that some customers who had too much to drink might try to take advantage of her. Occasionally, she said, one might ask Ellen if she would come to his room after closing. Bonito told her not to go, though larger tips would result. Ellen knew better than to go.

Of course, Ellen was not that kind of person, anyway. She had been brought up to follow high moral standards. She was also newly married and would never betray her husband. Ellen was comforted knowing that her man, Jasper, would be there in "The Spoon" to protect her if a situation was more than she could handle.

Ellen agreed to do the work. She also asked if the job for someone to clean the toilets and stable area was still available. The answer was yes. She said her husband might like to take it. But, she was reluctant, as she thought Jasper was qualified for a better job. The couple needed money, and this was the best job available. Maybe something better would come along in a day or so.

Jasper took the job as toilet and stable cleaner and did the cleaning early in the day before "The Spoon" opened. He then sat in "The Spoon" while Ellen greeted customers, mostly men, at the place. Ellen was really quite glamorous-looking in her outfit. She appealed to the men, particularly those who didn't know her husband was sitting over on one side.

Ellen provided service to the seven small tables; most of the time, only four or so were occupied. The barkeeper took care of customers sitting at the counter. Some customers would first sit at the counter and then move to a table once they saw good-looking Ellen. She greeted everyone and offered light conversation. Though being a barmaid was new to her, she carefully took orders and relayed them to the barkeeper. After the drinks were ready, she brought them to the customers. She collected money for the drinks and took it to a cashbox at the bar. She tried to keep everything straight; she didn't want to make errors.

Being a barmaid went well for Ellen the first three nights. She got tips of a dollar or more each night. On the fourth night, one of the customers who had drunk three whiskeys became loud. He called Ellen over and ordered another whiskey. As he did, he slapped her on the butt, and she walked away. She brought his whiskey to him, and he asked her to sit with him. She said, "No."

He grabbed her arm and pulled her onto his lap and whispered something into her ear like "You are a hot woman."

Ellen thought she knew how to fend off a man. She had done it before. This time she flung the back of her right elbow as hard as she could into his upper gut. He turned her loose. She got up and began walking back to the bar. He coughed and quickly took a sip of whiskey and then another and another. Things could get worse the way he was behaving.

Jasper saw this indiscretion by a customer; he couldn't accept it. He rushed to the man and told him not to ever grab or touch Ellen and that she was his wife. He asked him to apologize, give a nice tip, and leave "The Spoon." Jasper said, "If you don't, I will drag you outside and beat the living hell out of you." The customer complied; he could tell Jasper was upset and meant what he said. A full dollar tip was left. All else was routine for Ellen that evening and for the next few nights.

The first of April was approaching. Jasper's farm sharecropping would start. Both Ellen and Jasper told the barkeeper at "The Spoon" that their last day would be March
30 (they needed one day to get settled on the farm before
Jasper's job began). And, Jasper never really liked the idea
of his wife being a saloon barmaid. Too many men had eyes
for her. She was a mature, good-looking 16-year-old bride!

So, on the morning of March 30, Jasper and Ellen placed
their belongings in a couple of old suitcases and a sack,
checked out of the Witherspoon, and started walking to the
Smith Farm. They arrived mid-morning and knocked on the
house door. A somewhat aging, relatively heavy-set woman
came to the door. Jasper told who he was and introduced
Ellen. He said that Mr. Smith had agreed for him to sharecrop beginning April 1. He was a day early because he wanted to get settled in and be ready when the time came.

The woman said her name was Candy. She was nice to
them and identified herself as the wife of Mr. Smith. She also said that she served as a midwife in the local community (something that Ellen and Jasper might want to know
about). Candy said that Mr. Smith was out on the farm and
would be back by noon to work out the details with them.
Faithfully, Candy always called her husband Mr. Smith.

She showed Ellen and Jasper the place where they would
stay. It was a shed room attached to the main house. It had
an outside door and one window with hinged shutters (no
glass) that could be opened and closed. One corner of the
room had a wood-burning, flat-top, cast-iron heater-stove
for use in both heating and cooking. There were a couple of
straight rough-wood chairs and a small table. A bed for two
was next to one wall. The mattress was stuffed with moss
or leaves; one couldn't tell with it sewn together. A couple

of blankets and a deerskin were in the room. It was not a particularly appealing place but would have to do.

Candy spoke briefly about the community. She said that according to the U.S. Census, Willow Springs was a small place in Henderson County. It had a store that was open only a few hours a week, the Flowing Waters Church, no doctor, no lawyer, and really not a lot of anything. One needed to go into Athens for many things.

Mr. Smith returned and greeted Jasper and met Ellen. They discussed their sharecropping. It was to be on thirds; Jasper and Ellen would get two-thirds of what was produced, and Mr. Smith would get one-third. Mr. Smith would provide the land, mules for plowing, needed tools, and the seed. He would also provide a wagon with team to transport the harvested crops.

The main crop would be cotton. Some corn and vegetables would be grown. The young couple's piece of land would stretch from the big oak tree to the cedar tree and then over the hill to the property line. The field had about 27 acres divided by a small creek. Jasper and Ellen should be able to make 8 to 10 bales of cotton, a couple hundred bushels of corn, and garden vegetables without planting all 27 acres. Mr. Smith would keep an account of things they needed, sometimes called "furnishings." This included occasional cash advances. The account would be settled-up after the crops were harvested.

Jasper and Ellen would be responsible for all the work growing the crops. The cotton would be ginned in Athens, weighed, and sold. The seed removed in ginning would be exchanged for the cost of ginning.

It was time to begin getting the crops in. Ellen would work quite a bit in the field helping. Jasper hook up Jonas the mule to the turning plow and went through several acres of field. This broke up the land but did not get it into planting condition, as there were too many big clods. He then used a mule-pulled single-row harrow to break and smooth the clods. Sometimes he would stop and throw old roots or limbs out of the field. After a few days, he had five acres done. This was slow, hard, and important work to a crop farmer.

More acres needed to be prepared for planting. Ellen agreed she would run the harrow behind Jasper if Mr. Smith would let them use another mule. He did. The field preparation now went about twice as fast. They soon had 14 acres ready for cotton and turned their attention to five acres for corn, which they hand planted right off. They also prepared a couple of acres for a garden, with a half acre being planted to sweet potatoes and another half acre to peanuts. Potatoes, beans, peas, greens, cabbage, okra, and a few other things were to be planted. Producing food was very important in their lives.

It was now time to plant the cotton (it likes warm weather). No mechanical planters were available, so Jasper and Ellen set about planting the cotton by hand. They would make a small trench with a corner of the hoe blade and drop four seeds about every 15 inches. The seeds would then be covered with about an inch of soil. It took a few days for the 14 acres to be planted. All was finished by May 14. Fortunately, a nice shower came, and enough of the seeds germinated to produce sufficient plants in a few days. It was certainly good to see the plants emerge from the soil!

Commercial fertilizer was available on a limited basis. Jasper and Ellen decided to put a little out by hand on only about five acres, as they would be charged on their account for whatever they used. The soil was fertile and had been cropped only a few years after being taken out of grass. It should produce a decent crop. After all this hand work, they were glad to hear that mechanical drills, planters, and fertilizer distributors were slowly becoming available. They hoped Mr. Smith would buy a drill, planter, and distributor before next year.

Almost every crop came up to an okay stand. Jasper and Ellen had enough growing plants by the first of June to feel a little early success. But, now it was time to keep the weeds down. This was by hand pulling or cutting with a hoe. A lot of time and work went into this, particularly in a process called "chopping cotton." A hand hoe would be used to cut or dig up weeds and grass in the cotton. Care was used not to damage or destroy any cotton plants. A mule-pulled cultivator tool would be used to remove weeds from the middles between the rows.

Farming, as Jasper well knew, is not without problems and setbacks. After the corn was about 18 inches tall, deer got into the field one night and bit off some of the stalks. They also attacked the garden a little. Fortunately, Mr. Smith had a big dog named Pluto. He did not like deer, and they did not like him. He chased the deer off. In doing so, some of the plants were damaged, but they survived. From then on, Pluto was allowed to run loose at night until the crops were nearly ready for harvest. There weren't any more problems with deer getting into the field.

As the summer passed, the crops grew as well as could be expected. Keeping weeds down was a never-ending job.

Some cotton began to bloom about the first of July. Jasper and Ellen always enjoyed seeing cotton blooms. The blooms are formed in a bud structure called a square. Blooms are white the first day they are open in the early morning and turn to pink when aging on the second day. Cotton bolls (fruit structures) begin to grow after the blooms fade and shrivel. In a few weeks, the bolls are rounded and a little more than an inch in diameter. Mature bolls turn brownish and begin to open in a few weeks, exposing the white cotton fibers containing seed. Once about half the bolls have opened, hand picking begins. A second picking will be done to get the remaining cotton. Keeping fibers white (discoloring typically results from rain sustained over more than a few hours) and free of trash is important in getting a higher grade product and a better price for the harvested and ginned cotton. A farmer is always excited to see the different stages of development of a cotton crop.

The corn began to tassel and silk. Everyone knew having two or three silks on a stalk was good. Silks develop into ears of corn. The tassels produce pollen that will be released into the air and come into contact with silks. This results in the development of corn kernels in rows on the developing cob, which is enclosed in green shucks. A few showers are needed to help the ears grow to full size.

Work began to slow a little after mid-July. This allowed time to experience a few things in the local area, like getting to know people and getting involved in church. The tiny Flowing Waters Church held a revival. Jasper and Ellen went. There was singing, clapping, shouting, and amens as Brother Yonah gave one of his fire-and-brimstone sermons. Some of the dozen or so people there would get into a frenzy, waving hands, shouting, and swaying their bodies.

After the service each evening, people would socialize a bit. This helped Ellen and Jasper meet a few local citizens. Bertha and Samuel Hendrick were similar to Ellen and Jasper in age and, like them, were just getting started in farming. They had moved from the Delta area of Louisiana near Tallulah. They were accustomed to flat land. Maybe Ellen and Jasper could help them adjust to the hills of Henderson County.

One evening after the service, Brother Yonah said he would like to come by and visit. Ellen and Jasper agreed that a visit would be fine. They would like to get better acquainted with their preacher. "How about Saturday morning?" he asked.

"Yes," they replied almost in unison.

Brother Yonah was there mid-morning on Saturday. They didn't have much but did serve him some coffee. He sat in one chair, Jasper sat in the other chair, and Ellen sat on the bed.

Brother Yonah opened with a prayer and began some guilt-making discussion about church, sin, hell, and Jesus. He wanted to know who had been saved and baptized. Ellen said she had been christened into the Methodist Episcopal Church at Mason Chapel in Tinnin, Mississippi. Jasper said he made a commitment at a brush arbor revival one time but never went to be baptized. Brother Yonah said he could take care of that with Jasper next Sunday morning at the special baptizing service.

Brother Yonah told Jasper to read his Bible and make a profession of faith in the Lord Jesus Christ. Jasper said he would but continued, "I don't have a Bible. Once I looked at one and could probably read most of the words. It has some long words that I can't read, say, or understand."

The preacher said not to worry about those long words and that he would take care of his not having a Bible; he had a new testament in his saddlebag and would give it to him. "Remember," the preacher said, "our slogan is 'Quenching the Fires of Hell - QFH.'"

Jasper wanted to know the denomination of the church, so he asked, "What is Flowing Waters Church?"

Brother Yonah said, "It is an independent Christian church that teaches old-time Bible beliefs, such as people should love and look after each other and fear of the fires of hell. Men are superior to their wives. Everything that happens is God's will. Men are to father children, and women are to give birth to them. Sometimes snakes and other animals are used to show the power of God." Brother Yonah said, "I run the place."

Now, Ellen didn't necessarily agree with all he said, but she kept quiet. After all, she had been taught to respect preachers and trust what they say and do. But, should she with Brother Yonah? Something in her mind raised a red flag.

Ellen said, "Brother Yonah, tell us about yourself."

He said that he was going to tell them some very private things and asked that they not tell other people. He told that he began his pastoring in the Blue Ridge Mountains of Northeast Georgia in the late 1840s. He stated that this was not long after the Cherokee Indians were chased westward out of Georgia and across the Mississippi River to the Cherokee Nation area of the Louisiana Purchase. This was for the benefit of the white folks in a big land grab. He talked about burying slaves in the Nacoochee Valley in graves that were not marked so they wouldn't create a problem. He further talked about slaves buried separately from whites and outside of cemetery fences. He said a lot of people of Scottish ancestry lived in this area of Georgia and they liked to make whiskey. He said that whiskey was the downfall of people who drank too much. He went on to say that before he came to Texas, he would sample some of it and sometimes drank way too many samples and would pass out. Those folks knew how to make great moonshine! He said that when he became a preacher, he quit most of his drinking. He continued, "A preacher needs to know how drinking affects church members. It takes money that could be given to a church and be used to pay the preacher."

Brother Yonah also indicated that money from whiskey-makers was often used in doing church work. Money from bad sources sometimes results in good work. Gold mining and timber harvest were also ways folks worked and got wealth. He described how the town of Helen, Georgia, was stripped of nearly all harvestable wood by greedy loggers. He told about a few farms and houses in the area that were particularly identified with the wealth of influential southerners connected to the aristocrats of the Old South in Milledgeville. Things sometimes went on there that weren't of the decent Old South. The owner of one fine home sometimes tethered his wife on hooks in their bedroom, deemed her insane, and went to another room in the house to carry on in various ways with her attractive nurse. Of course, his wife was called "crazy" rather than insane. Brother Yonah went on to say that one of the high officials of the Confederate States lived in the tiny town of

Clarkesville in nearby Habersham County. Things went on there that resulted in the front direction of the Presbyterian church being changed. The building was turned so that it no longer faced his house!

Brother Yonah told them that he needed something new after time in the mountains. He needed to get away from slave brutality in the Piedmont area and crushing of the Cherokee Indians by the U.S. government. He blamed U.S. President Andrew Jackson for the brutality the Cherokees received in what is known as the Trail of Tears. President Jackson established an Indian removal policy to force them to go to lands a distance west of the Mississippi River. They would also be forced to walk in the winter so that sickness and death resulted. Most of all (though he didn't say so), Brother Yonah wanted to get away from his wife of 19 years and five children. She had worked some in the little mountain town of Helen in a café and boarding house. She had met and entertained men and had opportunities to meet many others. In a frank statement, Brother Yonah said he wasn't sure if he was the father of all the children that he was responsible for feeding and clothing. He would never know.

He described Helen as a quaint mountain town with a small crystal-clear river that flowed through the middle of it. He said that Helen was an early goldmine and timber town. Many men came to the town for work. Some of the men had become very close friends with Brother Yonah's wife. He did not like what was going on. Divorces were about impossible. So, he deserted her and moved to Texas in 1862 and formed Flowing Waters Church. He made no attempt to keep in contact with any of his children. It seemed that he had made a move to escape responsibility, but neither Ellen nor Jasper would ask about that. Brother Yonah indicated that he had prayed to God for forgiveness of his past sins and that he felt forgiven.

By then, it was time for Brother Yonah to go. He said a goodbye prayer and told Jasper that he would baptize him next Sunday at Watson Creek. No more than a hundred yards from the church, a small pool in the creek was often used for baptizing. He again asked Jasper and Ellen to keep the private matters he discussed to themselves. It would be embarrassing if the information got out in the community. Brother Yonah rode off on a fine horse.

After the preacher left, Jasper and Ellen talked a bit. Jasper decided he would go to be baptized. He didn't want a big deal made out of it. He told of a person who was baptized, got into some home brew afterward, and went home drunk and beat his wife. "You know," he said, "churches are not always what they are supposed to be. They may be more about taking up collection than anything else." Jasper also did not think that the preacher should have deserted his wife and five children. Had Jasper ever heard of such before? It sometimes happened, but no decent man would desert his family or, at least, no man would be decent if he deserted his wife and children. Families needed the support (food, a place to stay, and clothing to wear) that a man might be able to offer. He spoke in a very straightforward manner to Ellen about how wives and children need a man to care for them.

The summer moved on. Ellen and Jasper continued with Sunday services at Flowing Waters Church. Crops were maturing, and plans were made for harvesting. By early September, it was time to pick cotton. The fluffy seed cotton was plucked from the open boles and put in a large pick sack with a strap around a shoulder and pulled along the ground. Both Jasper and Ellen worked long days and picked as fast as they could. When the amount weighed about 1,200 pounds, a bale was taken on a wagon to the gin in Athens. After ginning, average weight of a bale was a little more than 500 pounds.

After a couple of weeks, three bales had been ginned, and the picking was continuing. Both Ellen and Jasper were working as hard and fast as they could. But, Ellen, for some reason, started not to feel well in a way that she had never felt before. She told Jasper that her bleed time did not happen on schedule--it was at least three weeks late. She said that she felt puffy and kind of big-bellied. Maybe she was going to have a baby. But, she kept picking. She couldn't waste time.

The next morning, she told Jasper that she was beginning to bleed in a way she didn't know about. It was heavy. After a couple of days, Jasper asked Candy, as a midwife, to come by the room to see Ellen. She did. After a brief conversation, she said that Ellen was likely having a miscarriage, or, as she also said, a "spontaneous abortion." She recommended that Ellen rest in bed for a couple more days and see how she felt. Candy did mention the name of a doctor in Athens.

Jasper had to pick cotton by himself. In a couple more days, Ellen was beginning to feel almost back to her usual self but a tad weak and downhearted. No doubt, she had had a miscarriage. After about a week, Ellen returned to picking. She suffered mild depression for a few days. This was something not much was known about in 1864.

During all this, Ellen had a birthday. On September 7, she turned 17 years of age. It was different this year. She was not with Pa or Ma or her siblings. Jasper didn't realize it was her birthday until she told him. He told her, "Happy birth-day," and gave her tender kisses. He found a gardenia shrub blooming near the front of the house and picked a bouquet of three blossoms. They had such a sweet fragrance and helped Ellen adjust to her being away from her family and to get over the miscarriage.

Cotton and corn harvest progressed. Jasper and Ellen wound up with 11 bales of cotton, or about 5,526 pounds of lint cotton. Of everything harvested, Mr. Smith got a third. At 8 cents a pound, the value of the cotton was $442.08, of which $147.36 went to Mr. Smith. Out of the two-thirds for Jasper and Ellen, Mr. Smith deducted the costs of furnish-ings charged to their account since April 1. Ellen and Jasper had lived frugally to keep the costs down. The amount owed was $98, which left them about $197--not much con-sidering all the work they had done--but the amount was in line with what sharecroppers made on other farms.

They harvested 110 bushels of corn, with a third going to Mr. Smith. The corn was stored in a space Mr. Smith let them use adjacent to the corn crib. It would be used for making cornmeal and hominy, helping Ellen and Jasper have food for several months. It would also be used as ani-mal feed.

Mr. Smith asked Jasper to speak with him. He wanted to know if Jasper and Ellen would be there next year. Jasper said yes, if the sharecropper arrangements were the same. They would be. Mr. Smith also said that there would be a little day-work during the winter for which Jasper would be paid. Jasper told him that he really needed the work and, if the job was right, Ellen would work, too.

They found Mr. Smith to be a nice, honest farm man. Some day-work helped them have money for clothing and food. Spring was approaching; Jasper and Ellen began cleaning the fields. This year Mr. Smith let them have four additional acres. So, Ellen and Jasper slightly expanded their farming, particularly their cash crop--cotton.

The next couple of years went routinely. They saved what money they could and began to look for farm acreage they might buy. They wanted a place with a small house and stable or barn.

In the summer of the couple's fourth year in Henderson County, Ellen was pregnant. She spoke with Candy and got suggestions to help avoid another miscarriage. Candy was helpful in many ways. She talked to her about exercise, well-balanced meals, weight management, and the need to avoid stress. She talked about trimesters (something new to Ellen) and preparation for the birth of a baby. Candy explained that the baby would be due 280 days from the first day of her last period. She said that she would help with the birth process and cutting of the cord. She would support the baby's head as it emerged and hold the baby so any fluids in its mouth and nose would drain away. She would make sure the baby was breathing. The baby would be placed on the mother's chest with the cord connected. Candy explained how the cord would not be cut as long as it was pulsating--a sign that the placenta (a fancy word to Ellen) had not separated. She said that separation of the placenta (they called it the afterbirth in Tinnin) usually occurred within 10 minutes after the birth. Candy talked about how she would tie the cord and cover the baby to keep it warm. She also talked to Ellen about how to breast-feed the baby.

The big day arrived. Ellen believed she was in labor. Jasper went and got Candy. Ellen delivered the baby with Candy's help on February 3, 1868. Candy announced that it was a boy. Ellen and Jasper had decided, if it was a boy, to name the baby Ira Jasper Lee. Both parents were so happy with their new baby son. They were proud of the name as well. Having Jasper in the name gave another generation of the Lee surname named Jasper. The name extended over centuries back to England.

Being a mother was something new to Ellen. However, providing for a newborn was not all new to her. Ellen, as the oldest child in her family, had helped her mother with her younger siblings. For her baby, she had made a few items of clothing, diapers, and blankets. Fortunately, there were no problems with the baby or its mother. Ira was healthy and grew well. Both Jasper and Ellen adored him.

But, Ellen had an emptiness. She did not inform Ma and Pa Shepard in Tinnin, Mississippi, about the birth of their firstborn grandchild. In fact, she had not had any contact with them since March 1864, and none was planned. The emptiness also applied to Ma and Pa, who also missed Ellen. They often wondered about what was going on with her, if Jasper was still around, where she was living, and if she had children.

Ellen had additional responsibilities with home, baby, and farm work. Ira was about six weeks of age when the time for major field work arrived. Jasper prepared a small wooden box with a blanket so Ellen could have baby Ira near her in the field for nursing, comfort, and care. After all, they didn't own a cow, and milk was not available at a store; Ellen had to produce the milk for Ira.

Jasper and Ellen had begun to develop a good reputation in the Henderson County community where they lived. They had an open account at Morrison and Greenwood Mercantile. This allowed them to get things for home and farm and pay for them when the crops were harvested at the end of the season. Beginning February 21, 1868, they got a number of things for farming and living on account throughout the spring and summer. Examples included 2 pecks of potatoes, 22 yards of cotton cloth and 4 yards of linen, a wood chisel, a looking glass, a pottery dish, and a 12-pound smoothing iron. The last charge on their account was 60 cents for turnip seed on August 31. This open account was paid off in the fall with the sale of harvested cotton. The couple had figured out how to live and farm without having cash on hand.

Ellen and Jasper continued to pursue their dream of owning a farm. They found a good-size piece of property that seemed right for them. They spoke with Landlord Smith about it and their goals. He said that for their long-term benefit, they needed to find a way to buy it. He would understand if they no longer sharecropped.

In October 1869, Jasper entered into a promissory note agreement with a Randall Odom to buy 200 acres of land. The note was payable in full on January 1, 1871. The approval of Ellen, as Jasper's wife, was not needed for him to enter into such an agreement for property that included a residence where they would live. The farm property was in the same community where they had been living. It had a good location with acreage for row cropping. They used savings to get hand tools and a couple of mules and plows. A line of credit was arranged from a local merchant until crop harvest in the fall. Getting new land into production required extra effort. Some of it had not been row-cropped

LIFE WITH JASPER   87

and grew scattered trees, grasses, and broad-leaf plants. The soil was rough for planting and tillage.

A small house on the land became home for Ellen, Jasper, and Ira when they moved in January 1870. The same day they moved into their house, the home of a neighbor burned in the night. All died in the fire except a 14-year-old girl named Mary. Ellen and Jasper had her to move in with them. In exchange for room and board, she could help care for Ira, who was now approaching two years of age. Ellen could now have a little more flexibility with farm work.

Farm life and work progressed as well as could be expected for Ellen and Jasper. They lived frugally and saved as much as they could. As a property owner, Jasper became more concerned with civic responsibility. He registered to vote in November 1869. Ellen couldn't register because she was a female. That slight always concerned her, as she felt she was equal in most regards to Jasper and other men. Unfortunately, the right for women to vote would not come during Ellen's lifetime.

The crops did well in 1870 considering the nature of the land. They got in 20 acres of cotton, 15 acres of corn, and a couple acres of vegetables, including sweet potatoes. Each of these crops required a great deal of hand labor. Not much animal-powered equipment was available except basic plows and cultivators. Fortunately, adequate rainfall promoted growth and productivity. In addition, they had added chickens as part of their farm. This gave eggs and meat for the family. They were kept in a way that would become known as yard or runabout chickens. A small house was built for the chickens to use as shelter and egg nesting.

In July of that year, an unknown person on a horse came onto the property. Jasper investigated. He learned that the man was a U.S. Federal Census enumerator. Jasper cooperated as the head of household. He described his four-person household. The information was recorded by the enumerator.

Crops matured. Harvest began in late summer. Jasper worked as hard as he could because he had a mortgage payment staring him in the face. He was under even more stress than usual.

CATASTROPHE

Tragedy...many of Ellen's hopes and aspirations came to an end in November 1870.

Ellen was awakened in the early morning of November 15 by Jasper gasping for breath. She tried talking with him about how he felt. He made only a few sounds, but she did understand that he had a bad chest pain. She held his hands and kissed him on the forehead.

Ellen ran to the next house, about a quarter mile away. A young family lived there named Eudy. She alerted the man, Jay, to Jasper's situation and asked if he could quickly summon a nearby doctor. It was some three miles to Athens and the nearest doctor. Eudy quickly saddled his horse and rode off at great speed. In town, he went to the doctor's home and told him. Dr. Pierpont Ponder immediately came in his horse-pulled buggy (typical quick travel mode for a physician in those days when making house calls; it had one seat for two people and a folding cover). Dr. Ponder was an experienced physician. He had tended to a wide range of health conditions over the years. He had sometimes brought good news, other times bad news. Regardless, he was held in high regard for his care and consideration of all patients, regardless of income and social status.

Everything happened quickly. In about 30 minutes, Dr. Ponder was tending to Jasper. He checked for breathing, pulse, skin color, and eye condition. Jasper was breathing irregularly and with effort. He couldn't talk coherently and appeared to be fading in and out of consciousness. Dr. Ponder gave him a small dose of paregoric by mouth. He told Ellen what the solution was and that it contained, among other things, opium. It would relax the body and help relieve pain. It might aid the body in restoring certain functions, such as breathing and heartbeat. He told Ellen that she could watch chest movement and check for pulse on the vein in Jasper's wrist.

Dr. Ponder spent some time with Jasper; he seemed to be stabilizing, and his vital signs were somewhat stronger. Then the doctor had to go. He asked Ellen if she had any whiskey she could give Jasper as a medicinal; she answered, "No." Dr. Ponder said he would come back late that afternoon to check on Jasper and bring a small bottle of whiskey. He asked if Old Dexter Bourbon would be okay; Ellen said it would. (She remembered Dexter as the kind of whiskey her father bought in half-barrel amounts in Vicksburg at Duff Green Mercantile.) As the doctor was leaving, he handed Ellen a small bottle of paregoric and said that if Jasper appeared to be in major pain, she should give him a half-teaspoon by mouth. Interestingly, Dr. Ponder was a physician who cared more about his patients than he did about the money he made in practicing medicine.

Ellen spent the day caring for Jasper. She bathed his face and hands in slightly warm water. She brushed his hair. She tried to give him a little food, beginning with molasses on a small piece of corn pone--something he normally really liked. He ate a little and refused more. He drank a couple of swallows of water. At mid-day he got a little better, and she was able to help him go pee. She thought that at least his kidneys were functioning. Afterward, Jasper fell back asleep on the bed; Ellen was at his side all the time (except when Ira needed attention).

Mid-afternoon Ellen went out to check on animals and things around the barn. All appeared in good order. She fed corn to the horses, mules, oxen, and pigs. She was outside as Brother Yonah came riding by in his wagon. He had no idea that Jasper was gravely ill. He stopped and said hello to Ellen; she told him about Jasper. Brother Yonah asked if he could see him and offer a prayer. Though she wasn't too keen on the idea, she was courteous and invited Brother Yonah to go inside. He greeted Jasper; there was no response except for slight facial recognition. He held Jasper's hand and offered a prayer of healing for him. He said he was glad that he had baptized Jasper. As the preacher left, he said a few words and, honestly, wasn't all that sincere about the well-being of Jasper. He seemed more caring for Ellen.

It was now getting late in the afternoon. Dr. Ponder was due back any time to reexamine Jasper. He arrived before dark and checked his vital signs. Overall, he noticed little change since morning. He asked if another dose of paregoric had been given; the answer was no. Dr. Ponder told Ellen to keep Jasper comfortable and offer him a little water with a bit of honey in it. He handed Ellen the bottle of Old Dexter Bourbon and said that she could give him one or two teaspoons a couple of times through the night. It might be best to mix the bourbon in water and have him drink it. Of course, she could give him anything he would eat, but she should not try to force liquids or solids into him. If he was unable to swallow, the food might be pulled into his lungs, resulting in pneumonia.

Dr. Ponder now had to go. He said he would be back in the morning just after sunrise. In reality he did not think Jasper would make it through the night, but he didn't say so. Knowing that Dr. Ponder would be back helped Ellen feel a bit better, though she was very concerned about getting through the night. Ellen cared for Ira and got him to sleep. She couldn't sleep. All she could do was think about Jasper, check on him, and wonder about what might happen in the future.

About an hour after Dr. Ponder left, Ellen sensed that Jasper was in pain and needed fluids and relief. She fixed a half cup of water with honey and a teaspoon of bourbon. She was able to get Jasper to drink about half of it before he could not swallow. It appeared that he was now sucking the fluid into his lungs. He wheezed, coughed, slobbered, and spit. Dr. Ponder had told Ellen that if Jasper sucked fluids or bits of solid food into his lungs, he would likely develop pneumonia and die. She was careful in feeding him. Things didn't look good. The little bit of bourbon resulted in his going to sleep; Ellen would try to get some rest as well.

The next morning, Jasper had little chest movement. His eyes were mostly closed. He did not respond to questions. His body was still warm, so Ellen rubbed his head and held his hands. She knew Dr. Ponder would be there soon.

Conditions deteriorated by the time of Dr. Ponder's arrival. Jasper was not breathing and had no pulse. His skin color was fading, and his eyes were glazed. His body was cooling. He was dead.

Dr. Ponder told Ellen that Jasper did not live. He covered Jasper's body with a blanket. It was November 16, 1870. Dr. Ponder told Ellen that he was sorry for her loss and wished her well. Ellen told him she would come by his office in a few days to pay the account. He said not to worry.

Tears came to Ellen's eyes. She pulled the blanket back and kissed Jasper's forehead again; she stroked the hair on his head. She asked if there was anything she could have done to save his life. And, then, she asked what caused his death. Dr. Ponder said, "Probably heart failure or maybe a stroke. How was his diet? Had he had chest pains, shortness of breath, or anything like that?"

Ellen wasn't sure. She said, "Jasper was not a man to complain and act sickly. He kept working all the time-- seven days a week. He had a lot on his mind, such as paying the mortgage that was coming due and getting the last of the crops harvested." Dr. Ponder then said something about stress.

As he was leaving, Dr. Ponder indicated that he would notify Mr. Medford, the county coroner, who was also the local funeral director, when he got back to Athens. Dr. Ponder further stated that Mr. Medford would probably be out to the house in an hour or so. He would discuss funeral arrangements and talk about what Ellen wanted. Dr. Ponder said to leave the body covered until Mr. Medford arrived.

Jasper had died. Suddenly. Ellen was 23 years of age with a two-going-on-three-year-old son. She had to make decisions and take action quickly. What was she to do? The decisions had to be ones that she could live with the rest of her life. She had few people she could turn to for suggestions or help as she faced burying her husband

Ellen had shared life with Jasper for six years and eight months. They had many hopes and goals that would have carried them for a number of years. What was she to do? How was she to provide for herself and her son? How was she to settle the estate of her husband? How would she relate to the advances of men who had ambitions toward her? After all, she was an attractive, thoughtful and energetic woman.

The love of her life was gone. Her hopes for the future had been dashed. How would Ellen carry on? She had no contact with family. She was all alone. She really needed support from family.

Ellen began to think about the burial of Jasper. Above all, Ellen wanted a proper burial for her beloved husband. But, she had other things to think about and do. Animals on the farm had to be fed and otherwise cared for. Harvested and yet-to-be-harvested crops had to be managed.

Ellen, first of all, wanted to memorialize Jasper to the extent her means would allow. Mr. Medford arrived and talked about a range of things. Many required a good bit of money, which Ellen didn't have. She had to economize in arranging for Jasper's funeral. She was glad that Dr. Ponder had informed an experienced funeral director. She soon became comfortable with Mr. Medford; he appeared honest and of high integrity. Besides planning the funeral (something she had never done before), she needed help in arranging for a burial plot in Smith Cemetery.

Overall, Ellen found Mr. Medford to be sympathetic and understanding of her situation. Together, they worked out the details of an order of service.

Memorial Service
Flowing Waters Church

Brother Yonah, in charge

Jasper H. Lee (Born on March 27, 1827; Died on November 16, 1870; age 43 years and 7 months)

Service:
Purpose of gathering and brief summary of the life of Jasper by Brother Yonah
Short prayer by Brother Yonah
Song by those gathered: "What a Friend We Have in Jesus"
Scripture reading: Psalm 23
Short message by Brother Yonah
Song by those gathered: "Amazing Grace"
Ending prayer by Brother Yonah

Interment in Smith Cemetery.

Casual covered-dish dinner by members of Flowing Waters Church.

Now all Ellen needed to do was work out the details with Brother Yonah. She needed Brother Yonah to deliver a short eulogy and conduct a memorial service in tiny Flowing Waters Church. She would ask him about the order of service that she and Mr. Medford prepared. She hoped the preacher would accept it.

Mr. Medford placed a velvet-lined pine casket he had brought with him beside Jasper's body on the bed. He was going to take the body back to the funeral home for preparation and then bring it to Flowing Waters Church, but Ellen had other ideas. She wanted to bathe, dress, and groom the body in their home. She had a new black jacket, as well as pants and shirt, for dressing the body. She wanted Jasper to lie in repose in the house where he had lived about a year. It was also the house that held a lot of dreams about his and Ellen's future together.

Mr. Medford went by Flowing Waters Church on his way back to Athens and told Brother Yonah what had happened. Brother Yonah quickly went to see Ellen. They talked. He hugged Ellen and Ira. Ellen asked him to conduct the memorial service. She also asked him to keep it simple and sophisticated and not to deliver a "come to Jesus" sermon. A burial site was arranged in Smith Cemetery through one of the members of Flowing Waters Church. This cemetery was just across the road from the church. Two church members volunteered to dig the grave.

Ellen was surprised at how comforting and supportive Brother Yonah appeared. Was he sincere? He was normally self-centered and ready to condemn the "sinners" around him in the world. She likely had some sort of thoughts about a few dollars being passed to the preacher for the service. Was he promoting his own financial well-being at the expense of a newly widowed young mother and son? Or, since he was living as a single person, was he viewing Ellen as a potential preacher's wife? Those questions were never uttered aloud.

The time for the funeral was two days after Jasper died. Ellen asked the funeral director to assist in managing the casket for viewing the body in her home. The casket was placed in the front room of the house. It was located with one end on one homemade table and the other end on another homemade table. Both tables had been built by Jasper from local wood. People could enter from the porch. He had a slight smile as he lay dead in the casket. Ellen and Ira were so sad. They kissed the body's cold forehead and said goodbye in a way only a loving wife and son could do.

Ellen prepared a casket arrangement of holly with red berries and magnolia leaves. She and Ira picked the holly from a couple of small trees at the entrance to the barn. The magnolia leaves came from a tree in the edge of the woods. Several people came by the house to pay their respects to Jasper. Each would linger a bit, view Jasper's body, and offer condolences. Most would offer assistance to Ellen, but she, being an independent person, was reluctant to ask for help. A few people brought dishes of prepared food for Ellen and Ira. Brother Yonah came by four times--he wanted to be sure to provide "comfort" in this time of loss. He was also quite willing to eat some of the food that had been brought. An hour before the funeral, the casket was moved from the home to Flowing Waters Church in the back of a wagon by Mr. Medford. It was taken inside and placed at the front of the church by the pallbearers. Six local men from Flowing Waters Church served as pallbearers. Ellen was so grateful for their help. She had no family members to turn to in this time of grieving.

A few local neighbors attended the service. There were no family members present, as none had been informed (the family divide caused by the marriage of Ellen and Jasper continued). Some people brought small bouquets of fall flowers picked from their yards. Sweetest of all was a bouquet of red camellias, which reminded Ellen of the bouquet Jasper brought her years ago in Tinnin. Brother Yonah delivered the eulogy much as the service had been planned. Burial followed in Smith Cemetery. Ellen gave Brother Yonah two dollars afterward in appreciation for his help.

An engraved stone marker was installed by Mr. Medford a couple of weeks later. It had the inscription: Jasper Henry Lee, Born March 27, 1827, Died November 16, 1870. Father of

Ira Jasper Lee. After the marker was up, Ellen and Ira rode in their horse-drawn wagon into Athens and went by the funeral director's office to pay the changes. Mr. Medford kept costs to a minimum, and Ellen was able to use grocery money to pay.

One family provided particular support. The Bell family had moved to Henderson County from Mississippi a few years earlier. The family had several children. It settled near where Ellen and Jasper had bought the farm land. A young man named Walter Nelson Bell was quite helpful. Nelson, as he was called, was about two or so years younger than Ellen and could sense some of the difficulty she was having. He knew that Ellen and Ira would have to move from the farm house they had lived in by late December or, at the latest, early January. The mortgage was due January 1, and money to pay was not available. Maybe she could have a little grace time in paying, but delaying time for payment wasn't the reputation of the man who held the mortgage. Bell and his aging parents agreed to provide a place for Ellen and Ira to sleep when time came for them to move from the farm house. In exchange for work in the home and on the farm, food would be provided with the regular family meals.

Other things were already happening. These were things that failed to recognize the memory of Jasper. Men appeared to come out of nowhere. Some wanted various things from Jasper's estate; others wanted Ellen! But, Ellen was strong...she knew right from wrong, and she would speak up for herself and her son Ira.

After Jasper's burial, settling the estate was of first order. Ellen asked Mr. Medford for guidance. How would the estate be settled? What would be the outcome? Ellen and her son, Ira, had little-to-nothing to live on. How would they have food? Clothing? Shelter? Many challenges lay ahead.

Answers were not easy. The mortgage was due. The house they had lived in was included in the mortgage agreement. The court needed to settle the estate of Jasper Henry Lee. Ellen, as a female, had few if any rights. Harvest of crops had not been completed at the time of Jasper's death. Many challenges lay ahead.

Ellen could not turn to her parents in Tinnin, Mississippi. They had pretty much cast her away; she had pretty much cast them away. But, parental love is greater than relationships in human life. She had married outside the approval of her family. What would be the result? Now, the love of Ellen's life was dead. What would happen?

Where was the good work of Flowing Waters Church during difficult times? Most of the time, Brother Yonah was not to be seen. Some church members jokingly said that he was probably preparing frightening sermons. As a preacher, he could be counted on to baptize, preach fire-and-brimstone sermons, and do funerals. But, when needs arose, he didn't seem to be around. When he was around, he did not appear very sincere. Supposedly he was in hopes that members would provide support to those in need. Maybe some of the trusted members of the church were also individuals who tried to "beat" Ellen out of the proceeds of Jasper's estate. Brother Yonah had earlier lived with a wife, children, and church congregation in the mountains of Northeast Georgia. He was able to observe great cruelty to slaves and native Americans. He deserted all this for a new life in Henderson County. But, was he still married to the mother of his children (the wife who worked for gold-miners and loggers in bars and cheap rental rooms)?

Brother Yonah appeared to give Ellen and Jasper special attention. Maybe he suspected some vulnerability. He visited Ellen at her home shortly after the funeral...always very nice, willing to eat, and appearing sincere in expressing sorrow and offering support. He reminded Ellen that the church Thanksgiving meal was coming up and invited her and Ira to attend. Maybe she could bring a dish of some type if she could afford it. Ellen and Ira did go. She prepared and took sweet potato casserole using sweet potatoes she and Jasper had grown. Those at the dinner were a nice group that offered support to Ellen inasmuch as they could.

In early December, Brother Yonah went by to see Ellen and Ira. He offered help as needed. He said he could get church members involved helping her. He asked her to come see him if she got lonely. Nice, but not the kind of help she wanted. She wanted sincere interest and help.

The next week, Brother Yonah again visited. He told of the Christmas program and dinner coming up at the church and invited Ellen and Ira to attend. He said he would come in his wagon and transport them to the church. They went along. It was good to get better acquainted with people in the community. Brother Yonah arranged the Christmas dinner seating so that he would be next to Ellen. Was he trying to "move" on Ellen and doing so too fast? He appeared to be after friendship beyond routine for an older and most likely married preacher who was attempting to help a grieving young woman and young son.

Ellen made one of her special dishes: Mama Tinnin's Apple and Cheese Casserole. She got red-wax, yellow hoop cheese, and other needed ingredients at the mercantile store in Athens...a special and extravagant thing for her to do. She used apples she had picked earlier from a wild tree on the Lee farm. Brother Yonah bragged on how good the casserole was and went back for a second serving. Other people liked it too; the dish was scraped clean.

After the meal, there was a short program. Brother Yonah made himself to be Santa and gave all the little children (only six were there) a small candy treat. He hugged each child and offered admonishment to behave or there would be no gifts on Christmas eve. The program ended with the reading of selected verses from Luke 2 in the Bible and a short prayer. Somehow, Ira wound up with two pieces of candy...probably the doings of the preacher to gain favor.

Brother Yonah would sometimes come by and help with light farm work, such as tending animals and cutting a few pieces of firewood. He now usually chose not to eat with Ellen and Ira. Ellen shared her mortgage situation and that she was having to move out before the end of December. She said that the Bell family had invited her and Ira to stay at their home until they got their situation worked out. On moving day, Brother Yonah helped Ellen and Ira pack. He brought his wagon to help in moving the few things that were taken to the Nelson home.

Ellen left some big things in the house and on the farm. The place was being foreclosed. The mortgage payment could not be made on January 1. She did take a few house-hold items, a horse, a light one-horse wagon, and some corn for feed and grinding.

On one of his visits to comfort Ellen, Brother Yonah told her that if living with the Bell family didn't work out, she and Ira could live at his home. That statement was a sur-

prise to Ellen. She wasn't ready for anything other than security and safety. She was still grieving for Jasper. Fortunately, she was able to make things work living with the Bell
family. The Bells had been very nice to her.

Ellen and Ira went to Sunday services at the Flowing Waters Church. The congregation sang hymns and listened to
the sermons by Brother Yonah. Each Sunday he would give
Ellen a special goodbye hug and say that he would be by to
see them during the week. Attending the services allowed
Ellen to meet and talk with people and allowed Ira to have a
few friends for playing. But, something seemed out of place
about the relationship the preacher was trying to develop.

Ellen talked quietly to one of the church members about
the nature of Brother Yonah. That individual didn't know
much about his past; she didn't think any church member
would know. Ellen learned that Brother Yonah showed up
one day and got access to an old out-of-service church
house and started Flowing Waters Church. He cleaned and
fixed up the place a bit. He visited families, asking them
to come to the new church he was leading. He always had
prayers about church and God.

Brother Yonah developed two slogans for the church:
The first, "Quenching the Fires of Hell--QFH," was meant
to strike fear in the hearts of the congregation. (Every time
Brother Yonah got into a heated sermon on sin, guilt, and
QFH, Ellen would think back to the delightful Presbyterian
Church in Brandon, Mississippi, where she met Jasper.) Also, if Brother Yonah was preaching loud and fast and had a
lapse in thought, he would say "QFH" once, twice, or however many times he needed to get back on track. The other
slogan, "Opening Heaven," was meant to offer hope in the
hereafter to church members if they did what HE said.

Brother Yonah never told the church folks much about himself other than that he was from the mountains of Northeast Georgia (of course, he once confided a few details to Jasper and Ellen). In fact, he never told them if he was using his real name, his age (he appeared to be in his late 50s or early 60s), or about his education or lack of it. He never told them about his wife and five children. He just pretended he had never been married or fathered children.

Brother Yonah owned the church and marketed it well. He was able to attract enough people to come to the church to make it successful. He could get the people who came to give money from their meager amounts. Most of the contributions went straight into his pockets. He had the ability to create guilt in a person who did not show up on Sunday by frequently preaching about sinning and the fires of hell. He would also tell those who did attend to tell those who didn't when they saw them during the week that they were missed on Sunday. He also told them to say that Brother Yonah prayed for you. It probably helped that there were no other churches in the community.

Flowing Waters Church doubled as a community center for selected social events, including weddings and seasonal dinners. So, was Brother Yonah a true believer? Was he sending a little money back to Northeast Georgia for the family he had apparently deserted? Was he investing money in a business enterprise that he might one day go into on a full-time basis? Once, in the passion of a fiery sermon, the mention of a tiny desert town known as Las Vegas slipped out of his mouth. He quickly refocused and never mentioned Las Vegas again.

Brother Yonah came by the Bells to visit Ellen like clock-work. He didn't miss, nor was he late. The Bells were kind of amazed at the goings-on. One day he asked if Mrs. Bell would keep Ira while he and Ellen went for a walk in the woods. Ellen heard the question and refused to go walking. She simply could not assess all that was on Brother Yonah's mind. His intentions might have been something that would have compromised the lifelong commitment Ellen had made to Jasper.

This mid-January visit by Brother Yonah was no different from recent ones. He brought a small bouquet of early-blooming daffodils. He reached and grabbed Ellen's hand and raised it to kiss it. Another time he reached and held her hand and pulled her toward him for an embrace. The preacher was being open about his desire to build a roman-tic relationship. He did not know about past times when Ellen extricated herself from embraces of men, as with the powerful elbow to the gut of Private Cason on the porch of the Shepard home or the similar defense against the booz-ing customer of "The Spoon" saloon in Athens. All men, in-cluding preachers, needed to beware of Ellen.

Brother Yonah returned a couple of days later. Ira was taking a nap. Mrs. Bell was home, but everyone else was out working to get the fields ready for spring plowing and planting. He calculated that this would be a good time to try to "connect" with Ellen. He told her that he needed her help at Flowing Waters Church in arranging the pulpit for a special service that was to be held on Sunday.

Brother Yonah quickly seized on a weak moment in Ellen's defense against his advances--maybe what he had in mind didn't register with her. They rode to the church in the horse-drawn wagon. When they arrived, he jumped out and went around to Ellen's side and lifted her out of the wagon and to the ground. He said, "See, I am strong. My strength is greater when I am around you. I think you are a beautiful woman of God. As a man of God, I need you to help arrange chairs around the pulpit." They went inside the church and walked to the pulpit. Ellen noted that there were no chairs to arrange.

They got to the pulpit and sat down on the edge. She said nothing. He reached over and grabbed her around the body and whispered, "Praise the Lord." By then Ellen had had enough. She wanted no more advances from a preacher...a fake preacher at that. She remembered the success of elbow throws and promptly delivered one into the preacher's mid-gut with such power than he fell over onto the pulpit. "Holy crap!" he gasped. "What have you done to me as a man of God? You made me say bad words." Ellen quickly ran out of the church and jumped into the wagon, grabbed the reins, and rapidly drove the horse and wagon back to the Bell house. The preacher, once he got over the blow and fall onto the pulpit, would have to walk back to retrieve his horse and wagon.

Brother Yonah made no more advances toward Ellen. He became somewhat of a recluse around her, even though Ellen and Ira still went to Flowing Waters Church occasionally. Obviously, his niceness to Ellen had little to do with sincerity toward her in time of grieving.

Ellen was a good mother and tried to continue raising Ira just as Jasper would have wished. She continued to nurse him well past two years of age. Following Jasper's death, nursing provided some security and bonding for both Ellen and Ira. Of course, he was eating some chewed solid foods from the table (Ellen chewed and spit out the food for feeding with a spoon).

Ellen was appealing and, some men figured, available. Men tried to take advantage of Ellen. One was the traveling Rawkins Products salesman. He went house to house selling liniments, flavorings, baking products, and the like. The first day he stopped at the Bell house he somehow determined that Ellen was a widow. He immediately set about talking and trying to show her how to apply liniments to various places of the human body; she didn't fall for it. Another time he wanted in the house to show her how to use the flavorings in cooking. Each time as he left, he said he would be back soon. Another man that appeared to have intentions was the itinerant horse-shoer. He was regularly by the house trying to generate business but mostly to talk about and showing various stages of horse shoe wear in a somewhat hidden location of the horse pasture. She was smart; she didn't fall for this sort of thing. She was also defensive and avoided situations that could lead to unwanted consequences. Some people thought that she was flirtatious; others thought that she was just personable. Maybe she was not sufficiently appreciated. We shall see.

Just as bad things can happen to good people, so can good things. Such was the case with Ellen. Though there were men who stole from the estate and otherwise tried to take advantage of her, there were also people who reached out and helped her in this difficult time.

Ellen and Ira managed with life in the Bell home. They certainly appreciated the Bells' generosity; they were nice folks. All the Bell's children were gone from home except Nelson. This made a little more space. But, Ellen did not know how long they could stay. She would frequently mention to Mr. and Mrs. Bell how much she appreciated staying there and when she and Ira could they would move out. She tentatively set moving out as being the time when Jasper's estate was settled.

Unfortunately, Mrs. Bell became quite ill in late January and died after a couple of weeks. No one knew much about her illness. She appeared to be in declining health for a while...maybe breast cancer. She was in quite a bit of pain. So, Ellen was in just the right place to help a grieving family. She could help maintain the household.

Just how "things" developed between Ellen and Nelson is unknown...probably nothing more than friendship. She supported his grieving in the death of his mother. She probably also confided in him and told him the story of her love, marriage, and life with Jasper and her despair after his death. She, no doubt, told him about her family back in Mississippi that she hadn't seen or heard from since March 1864. And, she made no effort to contact them, though she needed support in coping with life.

Nelson talked a little about his growing-up years. He told about life in south Mississippi before he and his family moved to Texas. He told how his family had experienced Confederate troops on their property during the U.S. Civil War. As was the case with Ellen's family, his family was fearful when the troops passed through. He mentioned a young adult goat that was a pet of the family and how the troops seized it, killed it, and prepared barbecue. Ellen could identify with so much of what he said. Maybe she experienced a slight internal pull toward him, but she knew not to let that take charge of her life.

Here was single Ellen, a smart, good-looking woman in her mid-twenties. She was temporarily living in the same house as a single young man. Several men in the community eyed her. Maybe she stayed in Texas because of possible romance with one or more of them. But, at least until 1875, she stayed to honorably probate the estate of her deceased husband. During this time, she kept thinking to herself, where did all the men come from after Jasper died?

THEFT AND INTEGRITY: ESTATE PROBATE

It was a tragic day in 1870 when Jasper suddenly died. Ellen was now left alone with a small son. She had shared life with Jasper for six years and eight months. Together, they had experienced much happiness and many hopes and goals. The time was cut short--way too short in her opinion.

After what Ellen considered to be a proper burial in Smith Cemetery (that was affordable), settling the estate was of first order. How? What would be the outcome? Ellen would need to provide for herself and son, Ira. They had little-to-nothing to live on. How would they have food? Clothing? Shelter? Some of her issues were further compounded by the advances of adoring men who had ambitions toward her. It wouldn't be easy to take care of matters without unwanted attention from certain men. After all, she was a smart woman, only 23 years of age, but still grieving from the loss of her Jasper.

People appeared to come out of nowhere to take advantage of the estate Jasper left. He didn't leave much but they wanted it and they wanted it without paying full value for it and, in some cases, nothing. Steal? Yes, steal from a widow with a son! Some folks might remember Ellen as relatively new in the community having moved from back east of the Mississippi River and, as a refugee of the U.S. Civil War, was a Southern belle. Maybe they thought that Ellen was weak and would not stand up for herself. But, Ellen was strong and she knew right from wrong. She would speak up for herself and her son.

Among the first whose advances she had to fend off was that of Brother Yonah, the preacher of the Flowing Waters Church she attended. Can you believe it would be a preacher? A supposedly married preacher was possibly trying to take advantage of a young widow. Ellen was not ready to begin thinking about another man in her life. After all, she had made a lifelong commitment to Jasper. Maybe she really didn't want another man. Her moral character was not that of a women who would carelessly run around with men who lived in the community or were passing through on their way to another home.

After the last defense of her very being to protect herself from the preacher, he left her alone and seemed to become sullen if anywhere near her. It seemed, though, that if the preacher couldn't have her, he was not going to make life any easier for her. There would be numerous times when Ellen would need to defend herself and her son against other men. She was smart and somewhat aware of local government operation, but she didn't know much about estate laws of Texas in the 1870s. Thus, she couldn't prepare herself for all the related situations that would arise. She could also be defensive and protective of what was hers. She was a good mother and wanted to be even better. Maybe she was not sufficiently appreciated by the people in the community where she lived. She wanted to live in a supportive community with people who would not take advantage of her new-widow situation. The death of her husband was not something she could have prevented.

Answers were not easy. Many challenges lay ahead. Ellen made up her mind that she was going to be up to the task. She recalled something said by one of her past preachers to the effect that the Lord would give her no more than she could handle; sometimes she wondered why the Lord thought she could handle as much as she had been given. She was quite capable, but she needed a lot of time to think, meditate, and learn. In addition to a concerted effort to properly settle the estate, a little luck would be beneficial.

Ellen, as a female in the 1870s, had few if any government-granted rights. She could not own property nor sign contracts. She could not vote, file law suits, nor have her own money. Though she worked on the farm, she had no role of consequence in managing it or seeing that the mortgage was paid. Animals on the farm at the time of Jasper's death needed to be looked after until they could be properly under the care of the next owner. Harvest of crops had not been completed at the time of his death. There was work to get done and things to take care of on the farm.

The mortgage was due on January 1. Jasper had all plans in place to pay the mortgage, but he did not do so before his death. Many situations were in play. The house they lived in was included in the mortgage agreement. The estate of Jasper Henry Lee needed to be settled in a timely, honest, and legal manner.

Fortunately, the Bell family had invited Ellen and Ira to live with them until Ellen could get her situation worked out. She and Ira moved in before the first of January 1871.

Ellen thought probating the estate would go quickly, but she had no experience with such. She thought she could move on with her life once that was done, but it went slowly. Where she grew up, something that moved slowly was said to go "at a snail's pace."

Ellen could not turn to her parents in Tinnin, Mississippi. She had pretty much moved on with her life without them; they, too, had moved on, realizing that the choice she made for a man was now beyond something they could do anything about. At the time of her marriage to Jasper, Ellen wanted to share her life with the special man named Jasper. She had married outside the approval of her family. What would be the reaction of her parents now? Ma and Pa Shepard did not know that Jasper was dead, and this would have changed the dynamics of the situation. Since, parental love is often greater than most other relationships, Ellen thought that her parents might be more accepting of her.

The settlement of the estate was not going to be easy. Jasper did not have a will. Without such, there was no legal statement of his wishes for the disposal of his property upon his death. Texas laws granted a husband certain rights relating to his wife's separate property as well as to their community property, but women had few property and legal rights in 1870. Mostly, women couldn't own property, nor could they make many decisions on their own about property. Not having a will was a big disadvantage. So, Ellen set about to defend Jasper's estate against theft and other bad actions and to assure that what was done would have met with Jasper's approval. Settling was going to be challenging, to say the least. Fortunately, she could usually quickly assess human behavior. She would take steps to defend the proceeds of the estate as best she could under laws at that time. She also wanted to move ahead quickly and fairly to settle the estate.

Ellen needed an administrator to handle the matters related to the estate. She knew she did not want the attorney who had been involved in drafting papers related to the Lee property and mortgage. She asked around in the community about the probate process. She particularly asked the people she knew and trusted at church (Brother Yonah was not one of them). Rural Henderson County did not have many attorneys or professional people. She got several suggestions. Some of those suggested were touted as good people who would be honest and fair; others were said to be experienced as administrators and know their way around Henderson County.

A major recommendation that made good sense to Ellen was that she become informed about the probate process. So, in early December, Ellen harnessed her horse to the wagon, took Ira with her, and drove into Athens to the County Clerk's office. She learned that an estate is composed of the assets and liabilities a person has upon death. Probating is the legal process used to settle an estate and includes the business affairs of the person who has died. The dead person is sometimes referred to as the decedent or testator. Legal notification of the death of an individual is needed to assure all people with claims have the opportunity to get what is due them such as an unpaid debt. Notifications are posted on courthouse walls, published three consecutive times in the weekly newspaper, and announced at public gatherings, such as a meeting of the County Commission.

Creditors and others with interest in an estate are paid first. Heirs receive any assets that remain. These assets are divided among heirs based on their legal rights to them. Ellen learned that she, as the surviving widow, was the heir to Jasper's estate. She was told in the Clerk's office that the process for her would be rather simple but would require an administrator. She was told that the administrator should a capable person who could accurately identify and collect the property; pay all debts and other claims, such as taxes; and transfer the remaining property to her as the heir. She learned that the property might be sold by the administrator, the costs of doing the administrative work deducted, and the balance then given to her. This required an administrator who could keep detailed and accurate records. She was assured that any administrator sworn under oath by the County Clerk would be of high integrity.

The assistant in the Clerk's office suggested that a Mr. W. G. Price would be a good person for her to consider. He was a person the Clerk noted as experienced in probating estates. Ellen was told that he ran a small store across from the courthouse, so it was easy to find him. She wanted to talk with him and assess how well he could relate to her and represent her in settling Jasper's estate. After arrival at the store, she introduced herself and told her purpose. Mr. Price readily indicated that he might be able to help. He mentioned other estates he had done. He and Ellen, along with Ira, went into a small back room for discussion. The room kind of doubled as an office and storage area. Ellen was businesslike. She came to the conclusion that Mr. Price might be a good administrator for Jasper's estate. Outwardly, he appeared to have high integrity and be someone that she could trust. She felt he might be able to offer suggestions and be a person who would listen to her concerns as a woman and mother. Did she misjudge him? She also thought in the back of her mind that she might later need an attorney.

Discussion of the procedures in settling an estate intimidated Ellen a bit. She realized that she needed the help of an administrator. Ellen and Mr. Price discussed, in general, contents of the estate, family and heirs, general procedures in Texas, and costs. It was agreed that Price would be the administrator. He had never met Jasper and didn't know much about the farm and Jasper's belongings. Anyway, Mr. Price told Ellen that she could just call him Price (this made her wonder what he might be up to).

Ellen indicated that she wanted Price to come to the farm so that she could help him develop an inventory of the contents of the estate. She also wanted to help him estimate the value of the items by telling him what they paid for them when purchased or what she thought they were worth. Price did come to the farm and develop a detailed list but paid little attention to the statements Ellen made on property values...maybe he had his own approach to valuing estate items. She wanted to be sure that Price knew that she wanted to move ahead expeditiously. She did not have the money to post the needed bond with the Clerk's office, so Price did it. Ellen would eventually give Price a power of attorney in probating the estate.

On December 10, 1870, the Texas District Court for Henderson County, with Jeff E. Thompson as clerk, recorded the following document:

Now comes W. G. Price, a person of good character residing in the County of Henderson and State of Texas, and respectfully applies for letters of temporary administration pro tem upon the Estate of Jasper H. Lee, dec'd late of said county, and respectfully states that Jasper H. Lee of the County of Henderson and State of Texas and domiciled therein died *on the 16th day of November AD 1870 and leaving no will to the knowledge of this applicant and leaving a surviving wife, Ellen S. Lee, and one child, Ira Lee about 3 years of age, and a personal estate of the value of seven hundred, thirty-two dollars as estimated according to law and which needs immediate attention...*

I do solemnly swear that I will well and truly perform the duties of temporary administrator of the Estate of Jasper H. Lee, deceased. Signed W. G. Price

Subscribed and sworn to before me this 10th day of December AD 1870. Signed Jeff E. Thompson, clk, District Court Henderson County

Most people felt that Price had markedly undervalued the estate in this sworn oath. The amount of $732 was far below actual value; Ellen knew it. She began to realize that the administrator she chose was likely a mistake and it was now a little late to be reaching that conclusion. She also began to inquire about an attorney to represent her interests. There was a lot more she needed to know. There were several new terms that she tried to understand and relate to the probate process: District Court, judge, term of court, order, hearing, deposition, summons, subpoena, and ruling. Ellen was learning fast!

Shortly after Price had sworn under oath that he would "well and truly perform the duties of temporary administrator," he was reported to have been out in the community talking about his role as temporary administrator of Jasper's estate. It appeared to Ellen that he had purposefully set a low value on the estate so he could offer to sell items well below their value to his friends. Ethically, this was not the thing he should do. He was overheard to tell a couple of men at his store about some of the contents of the estate--"excellent oxen, horses, and mule and an assortment of well-kept tools." He went on to talk about Jasper's young, good-looking surviving wife. He said that she might soon be looking around for another man and that she probably would be a pushover when it came to the estate. (He didn't know Ellen!) Items could be bought at low prices...just see him! As retold by people, the notions of deals probably got bigger and bigger.

If Ellen had heard this, she would have let him have it! Not only was it disrespectful of her, but it encouraged dishonesty with the items in Jasper's estate. Ellen had grown up in a family with a "good farm business sense" in Mississippi. She knew a lot about values of farm land, crops, and animals. She was not going to be a pushover!

The first filing of estate matters in the Texas District Court was on December 17, 1870. Clerk Jeff E. Thompson, District Court, Henderson County, Texas, prepared and filed the documents on behalf of the heirs of Jasper H. Lee. W. G. Price was earlier appointed to serve as temporary probate administrator and had made a bond and signed an oath related to fulfilling the probate of the estate according to Texas laws.

Price continued to tell friends and acquaintances about "good deals" that could be had with items from Jasper's estate. Just see him. Some of the individuals he told were W. S. Crowson, J. T. Straite, and J. V. Sheldon. They apparently did "see" the administrator and wound up with some items from the estate in their possession. Did they pay or not for the items? Little did they know that Ellen was keeping a close eye on them and would likely later see them in court.

Through a friend at Flowing Waters Church, Ellen got wind of what was being discussed. It seemed to her that she was going to be cheated if she didn't stand up for herself. To prove that dishonesty was going on would take some time. So maybe something good did come out of getting involved with the church.

Ellen began to discretely inquire about an attorney to represent her interests and those of her son, Ira. She settled on Farrell, Eaves, and Keith Attorneys at Law from the not too distant city of Austin, Texas--the State Capital. She made a smart choice. They were there to defend her and protect the estate. Her lawyers followed progress through the court and filed needed papers in Ellen's best interests. But this didn't keep legal matters from dragging on.

Price made attempts in December to move ahead with some of the estate. Cotton has value only when harvested! As a cash crop, it would be important to the value of any estate, but particularly to a small one, such as Jasper's. Fortunately, people were found to pick it this late in the year. Price kept some receipts and records. Evidently, some of the cotton "got lost" after harvest and ginning. Some items of farm equipment and tools kind of "went missing," too, in the vouchers filed with the court.

Among estate items, there were 2 horses valued at $75 each, 2 yoke oxen valued at $40, 20 head of hogs valued at $40, 1 mule valued at $100, and 1 double-barrel shotgun valued at $8. Many other miscellaneous farm items and tools were included, such as saddles and saddle bags, carpentry tools, and hoes and shovels.

The animals required care. They needed feeding and watering. This meant that Ellen had to have feed available and tend to them each and every day until they had new owners or at least someone else to take care of them. Ellen appreciated animals too much for there to be any mistreatment or failing to provide for their needs. The feed was corn grain and some fodder that had been harvested on the farm. Ellen was hopeful that Price could move the animals before the end of December, and he did.

Progress was slow. Some of the animals were being sold at very low prices. These amounts did not reflect well on the overall value of the estate. Ellen got to keep one of the horses and a single-horse wagon for her personal use. She was able to use a stable at the Bell's farm after she had to move.

Ellen wanted faster progress. Every week or so, she harnessed her horse and wagon and headed into Athens to meet with Price or to go by the courthouse. Sometimes Ira would ride with her; other times Nelson Bell might keep him. While there, she would occasionally go by the mercantile store to pick up needed items.

In March 1871 additional papers were filed in the District Court. The result was to remove the word "temporary" from Price as estate administrator. Ellen wasn't too pleased with this move but little more could be done until the judge had heard from the administrator and issued a ruling on the estate. Part of the document reads as follows:

The State of Texas, County of Henderson,

Know all men by these presents that I, Ellen S. Lee, of said County and State as such surviving wife do hereby authorize,

appoint, and constitute W. G. Price of said County my attor-
ney in fact and in my stead (hereby waiving my privileges) to
apply for and obtain letters of administration upon the estate
of my late deceased husband hereby certifying his action in
the premises. As witness my hand this 6th day of March AD
1871. Signed Ellen S. Lee

Ellen's signature was witnessed by Clerk Thompson.
Stamps were added to show that this was an official legal
document. Price was no longer the temporary administrator; the word, temporary, was now gone.

Ellen soon observed that Price was not able to gain a
quick, forthright settlement. Some items in the estate disappeared or were sold by the administrator at very low
prices to friends and relatives. The administrator made a
number of questionable charges, such as the daily charges
for collecting property, hiring hands to pick cotton, and
advertising property for sale. Daily charges were made for
weighing cotton as late as March 10, 1871. Cotton harvest
is normally completed by the middle of December, but circumstances had extended the harvest a bit. Delaying cotton harvest runs the risk of rain on the open bolls; wet cotton may turn gray and lose its white, high-value grade. The
court, as an interim step, provided Ellen with a little money,
such as a one-time amount of $10.93 to buy coffee and salt.
It is a good thing that she had a little money she had saved.
She was frugal with what she had.

Progress was slow. Were flagrant attempts being made
to cheat Ellen and Ira out of the cotton (their major source
of cash)? Most likely. Ellen began to think that something
wasn't going as it should. So, not being a person to roll over
and allow others to take advantage of her, Ellen went in-

to court against the administrator of the estate. Price now also had an attorney, P. T. Tannehill, to help him defend himself against charges of improper conduct. Ellen had the services of a legal firm to represent her. The relationship between Ellen and the administrator had become somewhat contentious.

In the March 1871 term of the District Court, papers were filed to gain payment for Dr. Pierpont Ponder. Ellen had told him in November 1870 that she would come into Athens to his office and make the payment, and Dr. Ponder seemed to indicate that there was no rush. On March 13, 1871, Judge J. H. Skinner awarded Dr. Ponder the sum of $10.65 from Jasper's estate. This was for visits to Jasper when sick and for medications, including quinine, paregoric, and medicinal bourbon. Price was the intermediary in gaining payment for Dr. Ponder and would be responsible for seeing that he was paid from proceeds of the estate. Now, this seemed reasonable to Ellen. However, her feelings were hurt because she was going to pay the amount, but Dr. Ponder had discouraged her. Ellen began to think: "Just about everything is stacked against women. If I were a man, it wouldn't be this way--not even in Texas." Two judges were involved: the Honorable J. H. Skinner and the Honorable G. Scott. Both judges heard some of the testimony but they did so on separate occasions. Could it be that the slow movement of probate occurred because no one single judge was in charge?

More action occurred during the July 1871 term of court. The presiding judge was the Honorable G. Scott of the Texas District Court serving Henderson County. Ellen was present to observe progress. Her attorney was there to represent her best interests in court proceedings. Price presented the court with a partial listing of items and values in the estate of Jasper H. Lee. He also petitioned the court to reimburse him certain expenses he had incurred as administrator of the estate. Price requested $17.88 he had paid for taxes on the land for the 1870 tax year. Jasper had only had title to the land for a little over one year between its purchase in late 1869 and foreclosure a couple of months following his death. For the tax expense, he had a receipt. He then submitted receipts from two individuals totaling $15 for hauling six bales of cotton to the gin. He also had a receipt for $19 that had been provided to Ellen S. Lee. He requested $2 reimbursement for two bushels of corn fed to the team that pulled the wagon loaded with cotton. He requested permission of the court to sell three bales of cotton for supplies for the surviving wife and child. Overall, property valued at $730 had already been sold. Numerous charges were made against the income. One charge of particular interest was a payment to Dr. Pierpont Ponder in the amount of $10.65, which was for attending to Jasper in his final two days. This had been approved for payment in the previous March term of Court but had not been paid. It appeared that Court action might be needed more than once for payments to be made, such as medical payments to Dr. Ponder. Price frequently sought approval by the court for himself to receive several payments but he was not punctual in paying others court-approved amounts. Ellen wondered if these were honest and fair, but she stayed quiet for now.

Judge Scott of the Texas District Court serving Henderson County, made some other important findings in the July 1871 term of court. Though administrator Price stated that the value of the estate was only $732.00--well under its actual value--Judge Scott considered additional evidence of estate contents and value. He found that the estate was worth $4,200. Encumbrances and liens amounted to $2,200. The husband left no homestead for his surviving wife and son. The judge ruled that the estate was not of sufficient wealth to be subject to administration. He ruled on errors in submissions by the individual who had earlier and in error been appointed administrator, W. G. Price. Since Price was well into the administrator work, the judge allowed Price to continue. Maybe the judge was going to closely monitor what Price was doing. There is also the possibility that a judge or a close associate or family member could have been in on receiving benefit of some sort from the property. Some folks would think that Price should have been removed and a ruling issued that the estate was not of sufficient value to be subject to administration. Some of the receipts and other financial matters had been the subject of earlier court action.

Price attempted to justify the work he had done. The situation was now quite entangled with court activity, administrator "doings," and surviving wife needs. Price had made regular but sometimes half-hearted attempts to move ahead with his role as administrator of the estate. Some work was sloppy to the extent that it might have purposefully been done that way to defraud the estate. At one point, the judge decried the poor writing used to record estate items and disposals. The indication was that some written names and descriptions were not decipherable. The judge admonished that records be kept with neater penmanship. Further, the judge specified that accuracy and fairness were extremely important.

Court action was continued and dragged on for another few years. Ellen was issued a subpoena to appear in court on November 4, 1872. In court action that day, Ellen Lee became a plaintiff against W. G. Price, defendant. Three other individuals were also named as defendants: W. L. Crowson, J. T. Straite, and J. V. Sheldon. Summons were issued to these men indicating that they were the subjects of a lawsuit to protect the property and rights of Ellen S. Lee. Yes, that is what a summons does: it informs a person that they are being sued. By and large, these men ignored summons; they said they weren't going to show up in court with complaints by some woman. Due to their failure to appear, the court issued subpoenas that were served on them compelling them to come to court to account for their roles in the probate of the Jasper H. Lee estate.

Ellen could sense that she was continuing to be short-changed. She was a gutsy woman to take on the court-appointed probate administrator, but she did. Her attorney from the firm of Farrell, Eaves, and Keith was quite helpful in this regard. In short, the administrator was making false claims and not offering full accounting of the items in the estate. Maybe his vouchers reflected on what was good for him and his buddies.

About two years had passed since Jasper's death. The estate wasn't settled. Ellen made up her mind; she wasn't going to be swindled any more. Her attorneys helped her file court challenges. On November 7, 1872, court action was initiated to challenge the financial records and proposed settlement previously filed by Price. Ellen had been cautioned about being too insistent on getting things properly done as there might be someone who would "try to get even" by physically attacking her. Fortunately, this never happened.

Four major challenges were introduced into the court. In summary, these were: Price did not turn over money from the sale of cotton; records could not be comprehended because they were so poorly written and kept; Price paid himself without filing vouchers; and Price was erroneously claiming that the estate still owed him money.

Altogether, 14 bales of cotton were involved in the dispute. Court documents show that the bales were valued at well over $100 each. Additional court documents show that Price took possession of farming tools. Court records also show that some items were sold far below value, such as two yoke of oxen for $25, when they would have been worth at least $80. The same situation existed with 2 horses, 40 head of hogs, 150 bushels of corn, and many other items, such as a shotgun, pistol, and saddles and saddle bags. Ellen was fuming over the treatment she had received at the hands of the estate administrator.

In that November 7, 1872, court session, Ellen's attorney presented a compelling case about the apparent flagrant disregard of honesty and integrity of the estate administrator. After all evidence was presented, the attorney asked that "the said administrator, W. G. Price, be held in contempt of your honor and the Court for failing to file receipts and vouchers as required..." The judge delayed any action until later in November. It seems that court hearings sometimes resulted in very little progress.

Court action continued in the November 23, 1872, term with the filing of papers in the case of Ellen S. Lee, surviving wife of Jasper H. Lee, deceased, vs. W. G. Price, administrator. One claim in court, that was thought to have been settled in the March 1871 term of court, was that of paying Dr. Pierpont Ponder for services and medicines for Jasper H. Lee shortly before his death. The total amount billed was $10.65. A receipt signed by Dr. Ponder in July 1871 was presented as evidence in court proceedings that this had been properly handled. Could it be that Price was trying to get two payments for Dr. Ponder? Price defended his other actions in administering the estate, such as delaying payments, and promised to move ahead honestly and fairly. Further decisions were delayed until the March 1873 term of the court.

This estate administration had dragged on so long. Ellen was becoming weary and disillusioned with the process. She was concerned about whether, in death, her Jasper would ever receive justice. Jasper had worked hard to gain the few possessions he had and she did not want them stolen. But, more was on the way--some through court action and some through confidential conversations of her with friends.

Friends continued to tell her of the "good deals" that people in the community got when they dealt with administrator Price to acquire items from Jasper's estate. In some cases, they insinuated that he would cut a price far below an item's true value if he was given the equivalent of a bribe by the buyer. Others had different experiences. All of this broke Ellen's sense of the decency about humans. She and Jasper had lived in poverty, worked hard, and been smart in order to acquire what little they had. It was sad to Ellen.

It would soon be time for the March 1873 term of the court. Summonses were issued to certain individuals, one being W. L. Crowson, to appear as a witness in the March 1873 term of court. The court date was set for the 2nd Monday, March AD 1873. Court records include the following:

The State of Texas
County of Henderson
Ellen Lee, surviving wife of Jasper H. Lee, deceased

vs
Wm. G. Price, Administrator

Now at this term of the Court comes Wm. G. Price, administrator pro tem of the Estate of Jasper H. Lee, deceased, by his attorney and the attorney for said Estate--leave of the Court being first had and obtained--and amends his answers and reports in answer to the execution filed...The cotton has been sold and thus he is ready to verify...He denies exception...is ready to prove the facts alleged...and asserts that he has complied with the requirements except for receipts...That...in or about July 1871...he delivered all property of said Estate then in his possession or under his control to said surviving wife and that she willingly signed a receipt for it...All property in his possession as administrator has been delivered to said surviving wife...All property not sold remained in the actual possession of said surviving wife and family for their use and benefit and was exempt from forced sale...

Other court hearings were needed to get at full and accurate truth about the estate of Jasper H. Lee. Why did it take so long to sell ginned cotton? Cotton is usually sold in days or weeks at the most but not years! Ellen was always present, always thinking and defending herself and son, Ira, as best she could without a legal background. And, finally...

The probate of the estate was completed on February 25, 1875, in the District Court of Henderson County, Texas. From the original honest and relatively accurate itemization of the estate value at about $4,200, only a few hundred dollars were left. What happened to the value, and why did the process take so long? How did Ellen and Ira survive? Ellen had to pay costs of her legal representation, which she at first thought she wouldn't need, but later found that some people weren't as competent and/or trustworthy as they should have been even when under court oath. Failure of a sworn administrator to accurately keep receipts and submit vouchers for reimbursement of expenses contributed to failure. And, it will never be known how widespread dishonest practices were in settling the estate.

Fortunately, 23-year-old Ellen (she was about 28 years of age at settlement) stood up for herself and Ira and demanded fairness. She was able to keep the horse and wagon she had used since Jasper's death in November 1870--that was her transportation. Court records show that the full and complete transcript of orders were issued on July 17, 1876--five years and eight months after Jasper's death. Some of the delay is attributed to lax efforts by court employees to see that what was needed was done in a timely manner. Maybe court action occurs "at a snail's pace"! Not moving ahead certainly delayed any plans that Ellen might have made for her life after Jasper.

Why was the value of the estate so depleted? Some, but not much, of it had been granted to Ellen and her son for living expenses. Some was taken by creditors, such as the holder of the mortgage on the farm. Loss occurred through undervaluing items that were sold, including animals, equipment, and tools. And, it was reported, some items were taken by the administrator. Ellen sometimes wondered why people were so corrupt and dishonest. Why couldn't people be honest and fair in life? Why couldn't people treat others as they would like to be treated? This was especially true when grieving over the loss of a loved one.

Ellen continued to focus on raising her son and on reacquainting herself by mail with her family in Mississippi.

And, getting reacquainted with her family is another story that was playing out during some of the court actions to settle Jasper's estate. She and Ira continued to live in the Bell house. Both Mr. and Mrs. Bell were now deceased. Ellen was about exhausted from the long probate in the District Court of Texas. Maybe she had now reached a point in life where she could think beyond estate settlement.

An observation of Ira's development was that he needed a man to teach him about manly things--how to be moral, honest, personable, courteous, and genuine. Of course, Ellen also thought that Ira needed to learn how to be kind and loving with a wife he might some day take. Ellen worked on this a little; so did Nelson. She also noted that Ira needed to be taught skills associated with life on a farm, particularly as he got a little older. She thought that he needed to know how to lay out straight rows in a field, plant sweet potato slips and harvest sweet potatoes with a plow, and butcher a pig. Other skills Ellen thought Ira needed to develop were how to gather honey, sharpen a plow point, and operate a smokehouse to assure that meat was properly preserved and seasoned.

In each of these needed skills, an experienced person would be the best teacher. She felt that neither Nelson nor she was qualified for this. She felt that Ira needed a stronger, more credible teacher. And, that teacher should be Pa!

SISTER REUNION

Do the right thing, and situations will turn out to the good. Such was the case with Ellen. Though there were men who tried to steal from the estate and otherwise take advantage of her, there were also people who reached out to Ellen and helped her in this difficult time. You would think that those who reached out were very much a part of Flowing Waters Church. Not so.

Most supportive of all were the Bells. The family provided Ellen and Ira with a place to stay and food in exchange for Ellen=s work in the home and on the farm. Adult son Nelson Bell was particularly helpful. Unfortunately, Mrs. Bell soon died, and then Mr. Bell. This left Ellen with an important role in the home, where Nelson had become the head of household.

Ellen missed and needed her family, yet she made no attempt to contact them. This was not like Ellen, because she loved people and valued family. Maybe she was waiting until the right opportunity to make contact with her parents and siblings came along. Maybe she didn=t realize that the death of Jasper would result in a change of Pa=s mind toward her.

Nelson decided that he would try to build a bridge. It would be a bridge to connect Ellen with her family. While wanting to help Ellen, Nelson was also aware that she had younger sisters, one of whom might be about ready for taking by a manCmaybe he might be that man. He certainly knew that Ellen had a lot of desirable qualities, and her sisters were probably much like her. Nelson did not know that those young women were searching for romance and good men. They lived hundreds of miles apart. Would Pa approve of his daughters in their romancing of Nelson? How would Nelson respond? What did Ellen think?

Nelson asked Ellen if he could write to her parents with information about her, telling where she was and her situation in life. He explained that her family would want to know her whereabouts and how she was doing. Ellen agreed, though she did not know how the letter might be received. Ellen provided the mailing address, and Nelson wrote the letter in 1872 during major probate hearings. George and Sarah Shepard (Pa and Ma) in Clinton (Tinnin), Mississippi, received the letter in a few days. In the letter, Nelson introduced himself and told of Ellen=s whereabouts in Henderson County, Texas. He told about the birth of a son, Ira Jasper, in 1868 and about the death of Jasper in 1870. He told of efforts to settle the estate and of the loss of income, home, and farm upon Jasper=s death. He also said that Ellen and Ira had a place to live and that they were okay.

The death of Jasper probably created at least a little sympathy with Pa and Ma, particularly Pa. Though he did not like Jasper, he had immense love for his oldest daughter. He wanted a good life for her. Upon receiving the letter, Ma immediately wrote back. She and Pa were sympathetic to their daughter, Ellen. Ma told of events in the family in the eight years since newly married Ellen left with Jasper. She wanted to see Ira Jasper, her and Pa=s four-year-old grandson, whom they didn=t know existed until Nelson wrote. Ellen=s sisters also wrote back. They had missed Ellen so much. She was the older sister and a person looked up to by all her siblings.

Ellen continued to focus on raising her son, living in the Bell home, and communicating with her family in Mississippi. It was hard for Ellen to get her thoughts organized around her family and a return to Tinnin.

After a couple of exchanges of letters with family, her sister Georgia Ann Shepard began planning travel to Henderson County. For a young woman (age 20) who hadn=t been much of anyplace, this would be quite a trip.

In April 1874, Georgia Ann began her trip to visit her sister, Ellen. She, along with Pa and sisters Rachel and Mag, traveled to Vicksburg on the car (train). Georgia Ann=s plans were to cross the river on a ferry and get another train from Tallulah, Louisiana, on to Shreveport and Athens. A big problem presented itself--the Mississippi River at Vicksburg had flooded extensively over the delta area. The flooding stopped train traffic from originating at the nearby depot in Tallulah. Floods such as this usually resulted from heavy snow melts in the upper Midwest and rain along the river. Levees and other flood-control structures had not been built.

Plans had to be altered. Georgia Ann asked if she could travel much of the trip by boat. The answer was yes but that this would take two or more weeks. The travel involved going south on the Mississippi River and back to the northwest on the Red River to Shreveport, where she could catch a train. She was told that the operator of the boat would assure her safetyCno men would be harassing her. (Like her sister Ellen, she was good looking.) The cost would be $18. She had the money to pay. Georgia Ann went; Pa and her sisters returned to Tinnin. But, they feared for Georgia Ann. What if there was a problem?

Here is an excerpt from a letter written April 12, 1874, to Ellen in Texas by her sister Mag Shepard:

My dear and affectionate sister,

I this cloudy evening take the pleasure to write you a few lines. We are all well at present. Sister Ellen, Georgia Ann has started to Texas. Pa, Rachel, and myself went with her as far as Vicksburg on April 6. We went with the intention of going across the Mississippi River with her and seeing her on the cars but the river was too high. The cars could not run any ways close to the river so there was not chance for her to cross unless she had gone a long ways in a skiff and there was several told us that it would be dangerous to cross that way. I never saw so much water in all of my life.

The letter continued. It explained that Georgia Ann very nearly backed out on the trip. But, as any of the Shepard girls would have done, she worked out the trip to see her sister Ellen. More from the letter of April 12, explains:

Georgia Ann came very near coming home and waiting for the river to run down. Mr. Green, the gentleman who sells tickets, persuaded her that if she wanted to go to Texas to go on a boat by all means. He said that the next boat would be on Wednesday, April 8, going to Shreveport. He explained the route as down the Mississippi and back up the Red River. He told her that she could get on it at Vicksburg and wouldn=t have to change a tall until she got to Shreveport. She would then get the car (train) in Shreveport to complete the trip.

Amazing! Georgia Ann was a brave 20-year-old woman with virtually no travel experience. Yet, she had little reluctance to change travel plans because she was dealing with people she trusted. Trust was based on how the people presented themselves to her. Personal relationships were very important. Getting to know ticket agents and others involved with travel helped her have a feeling of confidence.

The letter of April 12 continued:

There was a lady who also persuaded her to go on a boat. She concluded that she had better go on a boat. We left her in Vicksburg in care of Mr. Green and Mrs. Burgess. Mr. Green said he was well acquainted with the captain and he was a perfect gentleman. He said he would put her in the care of the captain. He said he would sell her a ticket to Shreveport for 18 dollars. Ma received a letter from Georgia Ann written Wednesday morning indicating that she expected to start that evening if the boat came, and I guess it came for she said if it didn=t she would come home. She hasn=t come and we know by that she must be gone. Georgia Ann wrote in that letter to Ma that there was a gentleman staying at the same place where she was staying and going on the same boat rite to Shreveport. He said he would assist her all he could. There was some lady expected to take the same boat so I recon she will have plenty of company.

Ellen received a letter from Georgia Ann one day before she was due to arrive. This alerted Ellen when to be at the depot in Athens. Now, if the train carrying her sister would just get there on time, Ellen would be fine.

After several days of travel by water and land, Georgia Ann made it to Athens. She was met at the depot by Ellen and Ira (now six years of age). What a glorious reunion of sisters! What an introduction of Ira to his Aunt Georgia Ann! There were many things to talk about. Ellen told her about Henderson County and the family with whom she was staying. She told about all of the effort in settling deceased Jasper=s estate and that the effort was still underway. Ellen didn=t say much about the administrator trying to steal value from the estate.

Georgia Ann told Ellen about some things and people in the Tinnin, Mississippi, vicinity. The farm continued with

Ma and Pa and children adjusting to doing more work now that the slaves had been freed. Crops had been doing well, but acreage was reduced, since it was no longer necessary to produce foods for the slaves, particularly the pinda (the name brought from Africa by slaves for a popular food known as the peanut). Ellen in particular asked about the two dogsCBummer and Ritz. Georgia Ann said that Bummer was still his usual loud-barking, one-eyed watchdog self and that Ritz had died when he nipped at the heels of a mule that subsequently kicked him in the head. Ma and Pa had discussed getting another dog but had not yet done so. They thought that Bummer might not be around much longer, either.

Georgia Ann said that some of the slaves stayed close around in Hinds County; others worked as sharecroppers; most left for places unknown but likely big cities in the North, such as Chicago and Detroit. Ellen interjected that Pa was kind to and never mistreated his slaves. Georgia Ann said that once freed, they had good regards for him. They never did harm to him, his family, or his property. But not so elsewhere. Sometimes fearful and dreadful things happened in the community and the nearby town of Clinton.

Georgia Ann told of relationship issues between whites and blacks (freed slaves) in Hinds County. She told of how black males had joined the Republican Party and began voting in 1867 (females couldn=t vote for another half century). Even though Mississippi did not return to the Union until 1870, the State held elections to select people to operate State Government during the reconstruction. Some people referred to this as carpetbagger government because most elected officials were from northern states. These carpetbaggers were also known for taking reconstruction money for themselves without considering the needs of the people who had endured the U.S. Civil War. Both black and white Republican organizers would come through the community and promote registration and voting. Black officials were elected to several offices at state and local levels. She said Pa had told her that skin color didn=t matter as long an elected official did his (only men could be elected) job properly.

Occasionally the activities of the organizers promoted unrest. Georgia Ann said that she and the family didn=t go out much and sought to avoid public areas. Probably more than anything, some of the whites knew that their pa, George, had voted the Union ticket before the Civil War, and they didn=t like it. Some white people feared the rising power of black men. A few whites formed marauding vigilante groups that went around the countryside shooting, hanging, and otherwise being violent in mistreatment of black people. A riot/massacre situation in Clinton was a particular issue.

Georgia Ann said that Pa did not like what was going on among some people. He wanted them to get along and live in harmony. He was also fearful and did not like violence. He also did not like the stance taken by Mississippi politicians after 1870 to subject black people to further discrimination and a life of hard labor. A few times he said he regretted moving to Tinnin from Indiana. But, when pressed, he would say that, overall, things had worked out to the good.

Ellen drove the horse-pulled wagon out to the Willow Springs community. They went to the Bell home, where Georgia Ann was introduced to Nelson Bell. Nelson agreed that she could stay temporarily, as long as Ellen and Ira were there. Space was available because the older children had moved out of the house. No one knew how long Georgia Ann would be there. She had no return travel plans nor money to pay for travel back to Tinnin.

The first order was to get Georgia Ann settled in a living area. She got a small room just across from Ellen=s. It had things in it similar to what she had back home, including a small bed with cotton-stuffed mattress, a stool, and a couple of shelves on the wall. A small looking glass was on one wall. A medium-sized shuttered window with hinges and a latch was on one side; it could be opened as desired to let light in and control entry of outside air. A slop jar was under the edge of the bed. It was for night or bad day use and had to be emptied each day. She was shown a two-holer out back. Water was brought in a cedar bucket from a nearby spring.

At the Bell home, Georgia Ann was also introduced to the guard dog named Bite and the gentle milk cow named Three Teats (a quarter of her udder had been injured; the teat shrunk and did not produce milk). Bite was to be respected. He more often growled than barked. He was large enough to attack about anything that appeared on the farm that he didn=t know or like. He had been known to destroy animals that ventured too close to the house, including a skunk a few months earlier. Three Teats was a calm and easy-to-milk cow; she was aging and probably would soon be replaced, particularly if more milk was needed.

Next would be to find some kind of work Georgia Ann could do. She and Ellen could work together around the Bell house and on the farm. Georgia Ann was good with animals. She liked caring for them. She would help with the birth of animals and getting newborns to nurse. She would also provide care for an injured or sick animal. (Her reputation for this soon spread to other animal owners in the community.)

The sisters were happy to have a reunion. Ellen found it nice to have a sister to talk to and from whom to get news of back home. It took a while to make up for eight

years. They were careful not to get into controversial subjects where differences of opinion could create friction.

Georgia Ann, now 21 years of age, was born to George
and Sarah Shepard five years after Ellen. There were two
sisters between Ellen and Georgia Ann, both of whom were
still single. Their parents generally opposed every man
their daughters brought around. But, by age 21 in the 1870s,
most young women were beginning to seek out in desper-
ation for fear of not finding a man who had desirable qualities. No woman wanted to be designated an Aold maid,@
but that might not have been so bad if a desirable man was-
n=t around. Many men had drinking problems that often
led to wife abuse. After all, what is so wonderful about living around a cranky, abusive, and disagreeable old man?
And now, Georgia Ann, like some of the other sisters,
wanted Ellen to help her find romance. She didn=t have to
go far. Nelson and Georgia Ann locked eyes when they were
first introduced. Romance began to sparkle. Nelson and
Georgia Ann seemed a good fit. Nelson was always so gentlemanly toward Georgia Ann. Of course, she wrote back
to family in Mississippi that she had found this really nice
man. Maybe she called him sweetheart and hinted of marriage in letters sent in late 1875. This probably puzzled Pa,
as he wasn=t around to make an assessment and offer his
opinion on this particular man.
Nelson and Georgia Ann were married in early 1876. They
got a marriage license from the clerk=s office at the courthouse in Athens. The wedding was quite simple at Flowing
Waters Church. Only a few people were there. Brother Yonah performed the ceremony. He was very traditional and
preachy. He spoke of the subservient role for a wife to her
husband and that a wife should submit to her husband. This
kind of thinking irritated Ellen. After the ceremony, he approached Ellen as if nothing had ever happened between

the two of them. He seemingly wanted to patch up their relationship. He said he wanted to offer the church=s special blessing privately to her sometime. What did he have in mind? Ellen was cordial but coolCshe didn=t want anything to do with this creepy preacher.

When the new Mrs. Bell and Nelson got back to the Bell house, she moved her limited possessions into his bedroom. They were so happy together and seemed to be a near-perfect couple. They continued to live in the Bell house (as did Ellen and Ira). The marriage, however, did somewhat limit the relationship of Ellen and her sister. They talked less and spent less time together. Georgia Ann was now committed to Nelson, just as Ellen had been strongly committed to her man, Jasper. Anyway, Ellen had her eight-year-old son, Ira, as a source of energy and joy.

Nelson was a game hunter. He was a top marksman (different from anyone in the Shepard family in Mississippi). He could harvest the smallest bird, rabbit, or squirrel. Game meat was about the only meat the four residents of the Bell home had to eat much of the time. Ellen used the game meat as she prepared a meal for the wedding night. The menu did not include just foods she and Georgia Ann had grown up with in Mississippi. She fixed a couple of new items, including buttermilk cornbread and quail with pepper stuffing. Also among the dishes were squirrel dumplings, roasted sweet potatoes, and apple cobbler. They had a little cider to drink, which Nelson made from apples that grew on the farm. Overall, it was a nice dinner within budgetary and customary confines.

Ellen sent a letter to Ma and Pa. She said Nelson was a nice-looking and considerate young man and that he owned a farm in Henderson County. Ellen was certain that Nelson would be a kind, loving husband for Georgia Ann. She told about the wedding and the dinner. She said that

Brother Yonah conducted the ceremony. A few people were there. She described the dinner she prepared and how everyone seemed to enjoy it. Of course, Pa and Ma viewed the marriage as another daughter lost to some man they didn=t know much about and had never met. At least, he was about Georgia Ann=s age and did not have a questionable background of coming from back East some place like her Jasper.

As was often the case in the 1870s, pregnancy didn=t wait long after marriage. So, Georgia Ann was soon expecting the couple=s first child; Nelson was so happy. The pregnancy progressed without complications. Ellen introduced her sister to midwife Candy Smith, who had helped with the delivery of Ira. Early on February 1, 1877, Georgia Ann thought she was going into labor. She sent Nelson to get Candy, who came quickly and confirmed that the birth was likely an hour or so away. All went well that day as Nelson and Georgia Ann became the parents of a healthy baby daughter, who they named Sarah Ellen Bell. They chose a name that recognized Georgia Ann=s mother, Sarah, and older sister Ellen.

Ellen helped Georgia Ann with the baby and taught her a few things about Amothering@Chow to hold a baby, nurse it, change its diaper, swaddle it for sleeping, and keep it warm in the coolness of February. Of course, Georgia Ann wrote her mother and sisters in Mississippi about the birth of her baby, Sarah Ellen Bell. Little Sarah grew and developed into a charming baby girl.

By now, there was regular correspondence with the Shepard family in Tinnin, Mississippi. They were kept informed about their daughters, son-in-law, and grandchildren. But, none traveled to Henderson CountyCEllen didn=t have any promising men to suggest to her younger sisters. The sisters were finding a few men without leaving home to do so. Some were less than promising Amarrying material,@ and the sisters admitted it. In a letter, one of the sisters described another sister=s man as Aa whisky-drinking crippled fat man who used a wooden leg, which restricted his activities quite a bit@ (she didn=t elaborate on activities)Cnot exactly the best of men in terms of what the sisters wanted. Pa did not like him. And as things went, he was soon sent disappointedly on his way.

Ellen knew that there was a Presbyterian Church in Athens. She remembered that the Presbyterian Church in Brandon was where she met Jasper. She decided to take Ira and visit there for services on a Sunday morning. Everything went well. The people were nice. The pastor had a sermon about the love of God and inclusiveness of the churchCsounded good to her. It was so different from Flowing Waters Church and Brother Yonah with his scary Ahellfire@ sermons. Ellen thought that maybe she and Ira should continue going to church there.

Ellen sought to learn more about the church. She asked the pastor, Reverend John McIntosh, if she could talk with him about the church. He said yes and agreed to come to the Bell home to do so. She learned that the congregation was organized in 1855 (one year before Athens was incorporated as a town). At first it met in a home, then in a schoolhouse; and, when it continued to grow, constructed a church building. A couple of different pastors served the congregation on an interim basis until 1869, when he (the current pastor) was called. He was a seminary-trained man who came from Boston but had spent some time studying for the ministry in Edinburgh, Scotland. Reverend McIntosh had a wife and two children. He told Ellen that the love of God was supreme and that his church focused on seeking thoughtful solutions to the challenges we face. Pastor McIntosh talked about peace, grace, and love and that the church should be for all people and accepting of people who may be different. He talked some about Jesus Christ. That topic always confused Ellen a little; she thought, AWhy not deal directly with God?@ Overall, Ellen really liked McIntosh=s approachCsteady, calm, and educated. He was very respectful of Ellen and didn=t Ahit@ on her or in any way show disrespect for women.

Ellen and Ira continued to attend the Athens Presbyterian Church to decide what they would do. They participated in several activities, including potluck meals. Ellen found those meals interesting, as some of the foods were a tad more western than she was accustomed to in Mississippi. Of course, she took some of her comfort foods for the congregants to enjoy. She met and became acquainted with several of the women in the church. Ira developed some childhood friendships that lasted for several years.

Ellen decided to leave Flowing Waters Church and get involved at Athens Presbyterian Church. She was not quite ready to join this church, because she still had memories of Mason Chapel in Tinnin. Ellen did not right off tell Brother Yonah of Flowing Waters Church about her decision. Additionally, she asked Nelson and Georgia Ann if they would like to go with her one Sunday. Of course, Ira would go, as well as the Bell=s daughter, Sarah.

It was now, mid-1878. Georgia Ann was pregnant again. Her pregnancy went well; she did not know of any problems. She had not seen a doctor or done anything special during the pregnancy. Nelson and Georgia Ann were excited about the soon-to-be new family member. They had chosen the name for the baby. If a boy, his name would be Calvin Jasper; if a girl, her name would be Anna Rachel.

Georgia Ann and Nelson had thought about letting Ellen assist with the delivery and saving what they would have paid a midwife. When they asked Ellen, she didn=t like the idea and smartly said so. The due date was now rapidly approaching. Georgia Ann went into labor. Midwife Candy was quickly brought in to help with delivery, as she had with the birth of their daughter.

Things with Georgia Ann and giving birth didn=t seem right to Candy from the beginning that day. The baby was in a breech birth presentation. The head was not appearing in the birth canal; its buttocks were beginning to appear. Candy worked feverishly to reposition the baby for delivery. She was not successful. She urged Nelson to go quickly into Athens and get Dr. J. B. Bishop, a new doctor in the area, to come there and assist with the birth. He was said to be well trained in delivering babies and had generally taken the place of Dr. Ponder in that area of medical practice.

Dr. Bishop came as hastily as he could to the Bell home-Cwithin an hour. He examined the situation and said that there were problems. He used forceps to try to reposition and deliver the baby. That did not result in a good outcome. The baby boy was finally delivered dead; Georgia Ann also died at the time. No definitive explanation is known about the cause of death, though Dr. Bishop said it was likely a combination of high blood pressure and excessive bleeding. This day in late 1878 was a sad day for Nelson and Ellen. Sarah Ellen lost her mother and baby brother, but she was too young to know the meaning of these things.

In the 1800s, for women to die in childbirth was far too prevalent. They and their partners did not know that they could prevent pregnancyCmaybe they didn=t even understand how it happened. Prenatal and other medical care wasn=t that good, if at all. Babies were often born in homes with midwives present. Medical doctors might not be available. Women might have 8 to 12 babies during their married lives. With that number, a complication is unfortunately likely to occur. Some women continued to have babies until giving birth resulted in their deaths or in the destruction of body organs so that they could no longer conceive.

The situation with Nelson Bell was quite somber. He had lost his wife and his son. He had a one-year-old daughter to raise. Of course, Ellen stepped forward to help.

Brother Yonah got word of what had happened. He came to the house to console Nelson, hug Ellen, and offer to preach the funeral. He never missed preaching if a dollar or so might change hands. It was at this time that Brother Yonah was told that they were now attending another church. When he heard this, he scoffed, AAfter all I have done for you, how could you do this?@ He then uttered a couple of choice words normally not openly used by preachers and left in a hurry with his horse kicking up a great amount of dust. Ellen=s mind flashed to those times when he had tried to take advantage of her. She realized fully that she didn=t owe him any favors. Good riddance!

Arrangements for Georgia Ann and son (who was to be named Calvin Jasper Bell) were handled by a funeral home in Athens. Georgia Ann=s body lay in state in the Nelson home and was moved to the Presbyterian Church in Athens for the memorial service. The service was led by Reverend McIntosh. In his remarks, he talked about Georgia Ann as devoted to family and God. He further spoke of the nature of Georgia Ann in word and deed and her love of life and nurture of family. He spoke so kindly and sincerely; it was comforting. Burial was in Smith Cemetery, which is the same cemetery where Jasper was buried.

Ellen, just as always when times were tough, gave extra effort. She pitched in to care for one-year-old Sarah Ellen. Of course, Ira was now 10 years of age and capable of doing some good farm work, which he did, and he could do a little looking after the baby. He didn=t go to school but learned simple reading, writing, and arithmetic from his mother. Athens, the nearest town, was fairly new, having been chartered in 1850 and then, mysteriously, unchartered. A few years later, it was incorporated. Its population was increasing. This brought a few stores, services, and an improved school to Athens.

Ellen sent a letter back to her Mississippi family telling them about what happened. Sad. No one in the family traveled to Texas, though several sympathetic letters were sent. Ellen still had to be strong, wise, and motivated with life.

Ira and Ellen continued to live in the home with Nelson Bell. Nelson had to work hard to care for the farm and provide needed income for himself and baby Sarah Ellen. Of course, Ira was now old enough to help in a serious way as a farm hand. Folks in the community were somewhat aware of the situation.

Some of the attention Ellen received was not always what she liked. Being pursued by men had gone on since Jasper=s death, and some were married men. She wasn=t the kind of woman who had to have a man around. She thought that if the opportunity was right, she would marry again. She had been married and she had a good relationship with her husband. There was never any evidence that he had involvement with another woman after their marriage. She had given major commitment in the marriage to the man she loved and remained faithful to him. She felt that women could achieve goals and be successful without men, though that was not always easy in a society that valued the role of men and had laws restrictive of women. These laws and customs bothered Ellen, as particularly evident in the probate of Jasper=s estate.

Amazing things happen! Cousin Susan Ratliff was now not far away. This is the cousin that got Ellen to go to Brandon in Rankin County in 1863, where she met Jasper at a barbecue and singing at the Presbyterian Church. A couple of years later, Susan married John P. Walston, and they had moved to the Lovelady Station area of Texas. Somehow, maybe through shared family connections in Mississippi, they had heard of Ellen=s whereabouts. So, John Walston wrote a letter to Ellen. He intended it to be a letter of encouragement and with an uplifting future. The letter John sent to Ellen read, in part, as follows:

We heard that you were in Henderson County. Ellen, that is a poor county. You had better come down here. The land is good and we have all lived in good health here these past six years. You can get to Lovelady Station in three hours. We live nearly in sight of the station.

With Ellen=s situation in life, this was a compelling statement. There is no evidence, however, that she ever went to Lovelady Station. No doubt, she thought about it. Was Texas going to be her home for the rest of her life without Jasper?

Letters from back home in Tinnin kept pulling at her. She was intrigued by what was going on. She even gave some thought to returning to Tinnin. But, she did not go. She regularly wrote Ma and Pa but did not inquire about the possibility of her returning to Tinnin. She also received word about unsettling conditions in the area near her Tinnin home.

One of her sisters sent a letter about a race riot in Clinton. She described it in some detail. She said that some folks called it a massacre. It happened in 1875. The Republican Party planned a rally in Clinton on September 4, with the goal of continuing to expand the role of freed men in the political process. Some 2,500 people gathered and enjoyed an afternoon of picnicking and politics. Amazingly, some 75 whites were present. Some Democratic Party candidates showed up and were given the opportunity to speak. Heckling of the speakers soon got out of hand. Violence erupted. Her sister continued that a group of white-liners came with the intent of storming the town. They went about shooting at black people Ajust the same as birds,@ she said. Some of the people were from northern states; this didn=t calm the white southern hard-liners. Her sister went on that some of this was from hard feelings over Areconstruction@ efforts in the area. Before it was over, the letter continued, more than 50 people had been killed in a day or so.

Amazing! Clinton was considered the top town in Mississippi educationally, with two institutes of higher learning (colleges). One served women (Institute for Women and later known as Hillman College), and the other served primarily men and known as Mississippi College. The one serving men let a few women enter early in its existence. To this day, Mississippi College advertises itself as the first coeducational college in the United States to grant a degree to a woman in 1831. Being separated by gender may be a clue to failed opportunity. Further, these institutes were run by, at first, progressive people and later by conservative religious organizations. The town had a collection of relatively well educated scholars and religious leaders. Where were they in seeking peace and human love in postBCivil War race relations? They were about gone; destroyed and chased away by war. Most people suspect that these institutions were established to serve only white people. Were any blacks or Native Americans enrolled? None appeared to have been.

A few people felt that the institutes of higher learning actually carried out discrimination against blacks and Native Americans. They failed in a wonderful opportunity. It was about a century later before Native Americans were visibly enrolled and another quarter century before blacks. Certainly, different leadership roles would likely have served the community well. How did the roles these institutions took serve to further principles of religion and human decency?

All of this frightened Ellen. She thought it would be risky to go home at the present time and into such possible violence. She thought that people who have different traits need to find a way to get along and live in harmony. Questions arose: Why would she take her son into such a situation? How could she live there until things settled down a bit? How could she make a living?

Maybe Ellen would be taken by her parents back into their home. If so, she didn=t want to be treated like a small child. She wanted to be an equal who did her share of the work and contributed to the well-being of the family. Though she was continuing to grieve from the death of Jasper, the attachment to him was seemingly getting smaller. If she did return to her parents home, she would need to be careful how she grieved for Jasper. Pa would not like an outward expression of grieving for a man he did not approve of as Amarrying material@ for one of his daughters.

Sweethearts and Traditions

Ellen didn't really understand how much her siblings loved her. As their older sister, they viewed her as their leader and a role model. They always looked up to her. This didn't appear to change when she left home in March 1864. For years, her siblings had such special memories of her. They wanted her advice. Could Ellen help her sisters find romance?

Through the efforts of Nelson Bell, Ellen reconnected with her parents and siblings in 1872. Special bonds quickly redeveloped. Of course, Ellen's sister Georgia Ann had made the trip to Athens in the spring of 1874--10 years after Ellen had left her home. Unfortunately, Georgia Ann died in childbirth in 1878. Ellen now filled a more important role in caring for her niece, Sarah Ellen Bell.

Whatever direction Ellen might take in the future, she would choose among directions torn by emotion. She would have the sisterly love and loyalty to care for the surviving child of Georgia Ann. She would also have the pull and desire to return to her childhood home in Tinnin to see her family. At times, she thought an acceptable man might emerge in Texas. If so, she would stay there.

Ellen was a smart, widowed, good-looking woman. As has been said, men in the community eyed her. Maybe she stayed in Texas because of possible romance with one of them. But, at least until 1875, she stayed to honorably probate the estate of her deceased husband. No romance emerged.

Just as Ellen was noticed by men in the Henderson County community, her sisters back in Tinnin received plenty notice of their own. It seemed that men always paid attention to the Shepard girls as they reached adulthood: Rachel, Mag (Margaret), Georgia Ann, Sarah, and Naomi. And, not surprisingly, the girls sometimes took notice of selected men. Pa and Ma, particularly Pa, tried to keep them reasonable and of high standards. Maybe Pa understood the motivation of men a little better than this group of young women. He generally didn't feel that some of the young men his daughters had brought around would make good "marrying material." He wanted the very best for his daughters.

Most men in Henderson County were farmers, farm laborers, or workers in similar important vocations. A few worked jobs for the county government; a few others worked in local stores and offices; some worked in the cotton gin, but that was seasonal. A small number of men were wanderers and lived with only occasional day-work and scavenging from the land. They would move on to the next town after a short while. Ellen never knew when a man was eyeing her.

On a mid-October day, as the sun was beginning to set, one of the men who worked with county government stopped by the Bell house to see Ellen. She didn't know him but had seen him about. He introduced himself as Sam Johnson and told about his work with the county. He said his wife was dead; she died in childbirth. He told Ellen that there was a traveling carnival coming into Athens by railroad and he wanted to know if she would go with him. It was setting up for the weekend near the courthouse. He gave some details about himself and promised to pay all expenses. He told about the midway of the carnival and that it had food, games, and activities. He told her that there were a couple of side shows she might like: one featured magic, and the other was an old-time fiddle-music show. He told her it would be his great pleasure if she would accompany him. He would call for her at her home in his carriage, they would take in the carnival, and he would safely return her home before midnight that evening. It caught Ellen a little by surprise; maybe this was a good opportunity, or maybe it was a setup for a bad ending. Sam was a good-looking, courteous man, who had a job. Ellen thought about possibilities while talking about herself. She decided that she would not go, as it might have been much too risky. She thanked him for asking her and said goodbye.

Women rarely worked outside the home or away from a family farm except the few who lived "town" lives. The attainment of formal education was low among both men and women. Often, a mother or sister (and sometimes a father or brother) would teach younger children the fundamentals of reading, writing, and arithmetic. That had been the case with Ellen's family.

Maybe some of Ellen's notions were tempered by the values of her father; his roots were in the Midwest and reflected greater appreciation of formal education. Some people asked why he moved to the South with his background. Remember, it was opportunity in the land available as a result of the Choctaw cessation and the potential returns from cotton as a cash crop.

Ellen and Ira were resting on the front porch late in the afternoon of a busy day. Ira was sitting on the floor and Ellen was sitting in a rickety rocking chair. For some reason out of the blue, Ira said to Ellen, his mother, "Mama, tell me about my Papa." That caught Ellen by surprise and got her attention. She replied, "What do you want to know?" Eight-year-old Ira paused a moment and replied, "Why did Papa die? What was he like? I don't remember anything about him." This gave Ellen the opportunity to tell Ira a little about his Papa.

She said that she didn't know why he died and continued, "It was rather sudden. Dr. Ponder examined him and treated him three times with medicines that he brought. He just couldn't breathe. The doctor was never real sure about his death. Your Papa was 43 years of age and you were going on age three at the time. He wanted to have you in his arms until his last breath." Then she went on to the second question. "You asked what he was like. Well, I'll tell you this, he was the sweetheart of my life and a very loving father to you. He was a hard worker and was honest in all dealings." Ellen reminded Ira that he had been to his grave in Smith Cemetery. She asked if he remembered seeing his grave marker and what was written on it. Ira said he remembered seeing it but didn't remember the words. Ellen said that they would go back to the grave site this Sunday afternoon and they would read the inscription together.

Ira had more questions. He asked, "How did you get to know Papa? Was he a good hunter?" Ellen answered his first question by telling how she went with a cousin and friend back in Tinnin to a barbecue, dance, and singing in the town of Brandon. One of the young men there was so nice; we talked and danced. There was something about your Papa that got my attention. We saw each other many more times and were soon in love. We shared interests and felt good about being together. We courted a few months and were married.

Ira, you asked if your Papa was a good hunter? Yes, he was good but he didn't hunt a lot. He would sometimes take a rabbit or squirrel and maybe quail or a deer. He wasn't as good as your Uncle Nelson," Ellen explained. She continued, "Your Papa was a little like Pa. He wanted guns carefully used and only when necessary. Your Papa was never one to show off his use of guns."

Then Ira asked, "Mama, do you miss Papa?" Ellen responded, "Do I miss your Papa? Absolutely. Very much. Everyday. I don't think I will ever get over his death." At that moment, Nelson called out that a pig had escaped from its pen. Everyone rushed to capture the pig and return it to its rightful place. Nelson fixed the fence so the pig couldn't get out again. Ellen told Ira that their talking was good and that they would talk some more on another day.

Communication between Ellen and her family back home had not occurred for eight years beginning in 1864. Now that Ellen and her family had reconnected, communication was helping repair relationships. About the only form of communication was handwritten letters. Most letters were written on small sheets of paper 5 X 8 inches or 10 X 8 inches folded down the middle. Letters typically had two sheets of paper. The writing, ink or pencil, usually extended to the edge of the paper. Sometimes two letters by different sisters would be mailed in one envelope, which was usually 5.5 X 3 inches. The cost of postage for a letter was 2 cents from Clinton to Athens, and vice versa. Only a few days were required for delivery of mail from either location to the other. Railroads hauled mail, and except for crossing the Mississippi River, the route was fairly direct from Clinton to Athens.

A trove of old letters, receipts, and other documents was kept tucked away in a dilapidated trunk in the attic of the Shepard-Lee house. These documents became accessible when the last Lee to live in the house died in 1962. The documents begin in the 1840s. Some were letters that Ellen had received or sent in the 1870s. Letters to and from other family members were included. Statements about medical care, drugs prescribed, and receipts for purchases such as food products, cloth, shoes, and farm tools were in the trunk. Regardless, careful study has allowed reconstruction of family history rich in high moral standards and integrity. The writers took care to precisely share information so that family members were kept informed about some things.

The writing style was consistent regardless of who wrote a particular letter. The interior had a return address and date. Addresses were simple: person's name, county, and post office (typically the name of a town and state--no one had heard of ZIP Codes!). Ellen was nearly always addressed as Mrs. Ellen Lee, even by her sisters. The letters typically began much as the one from Mag dated November 3, 1873:

My Dear Sister Ellen,

I again seat myself to answer your kind letter which came to hand a few days ago. I no I ought to have written sooner but I have been very busy picking cotton in the week and on Sunday I go to the singing. My sweetheart came with me the past 2 Sundays.

The letters demonstrated good penmanship, some spelling issues, and no paragraphs. When the subject was changed, the writer would repeat the name of the person that letter was addressed to, such as "My Sister Ellen."

Letters often ended with an expression of affection. For example, the last few lines of the letter of November 3, 1873, had this:

I will close for this time as I have a chance to send it to the office. Kiss little Ira for me. I remain as ever your true and affectionate Sister until death. Write soon and often. So, good by for this time. From Naomi R. Shepard to Mrs. Ellen S. Lee.

Some words were spelled by sound, and others were misspelled, but largely the writing was quite good, considering that the Shepard sisters had very little schooling outside the home. Words that were used less frequently were more likely to be spelled incorrectly. For example, when one of the newly married sisters thought she had recently had a miscarriage, she spelled that word as "mistcarage."

Ellen's sisters often sent letters that shared their experiences in finding a man. They asked for Ellen's advice and help. Ellen identified a few in Texas that they could take a look at if they came there to visit her. She had met several possibilities for her sisters during the probate of Jasper's estate. Some worked in county and town government and others worked in business and agriculture.

The subjects in the letters touched on various aspects of life, particularly farm life. Most were written by girls and women, so the topics were naturally reflective of female interests. As a farm family trying to make it after losses during the Civil War, every member had to work in the fields at least a certain amount to compensate for the loss of laborers.

Sometimes a girl would include something about the progress being made in trying to care for an orphaned calf or other animal. The letters might also tell about weather, crops, harvests, or situations such as animal health and sickness. Unexplained deaths of residents in the community would occasionally be included. Letters might report on romance (or the lack thereof). No letters ever reported troubles with law authorities, as the Shepard family was always law-abiding and of high moral character.

Since Ellen and Ira lived in the Nelson home, mail to Ellen was addressed "In care of W. N. Bell." Such an arrangement might have created some suspicion or at least curiosity among her parents and other family members back home. Maybe Ellen explained it shortly after Jasper's death when she and Ira had to move from their farm home. However, in letters, the subject never came up.

Mag's letter of November 3, 1873, to Ellen in Henderson County talked about her and her sisters picking cotton, going to singings on Sunday, and sometimes being with their beaus/sweethearts. The letter stated:

I had a very pleasant evening yesterday. Me and my beau took a ride. Rachel and another young man took a ride; she doesn't claim him as a sweetheart as he is only 19 or 20 years old. My sweetheart's name is Sibley. I expect to marry him this winter about the first of January. I don't reckon the old folks will be willing but I can't help that Mr. Sibley and I are engaged. (Clarification: Plans changed; no wedding with Sibley ever took place.) Pa won't hardly speak to him though Sibley is very friendly. He is very stout and uses an artificial leg. He has a splendid education and can teach school or farm or get into most any kind of business. He was raised not *far from here near Raymond. Most of the young men around here drink too much whisky. Sister, I would be the gladest in the world to see you and Ira but if I marry I don't expect to. If I could see you I could tell you a heap. Sister, I don't believe Pa and Ma ever will be willing for any of us to marry. I think we ought to marry. They are getting old. Just suppose they were to die and leave us with just Ira. What would become of us?*

[Note: This Ira W. was the youngest Shepard child, the brother of Ellen and her sisters; he is not to be confused with Ira Jasper Lee, the son of Ellen and deceased Jasper H. Lee.]

The sisters commonly distinguished between the men in their lives with two terms, "beau" and "sweetheart." A beau was a man new to a sister or one whom she really didn't think would work out in the long run. For lack of another man, a beau was someone to go to a singing or barbecue with. A sweetheart was a man a sister liked and with whom she probably wished for a longer relationship--he might have been considered "marrying material." A sweetheart might have been someone the sister would go riding with. Riding would give a couple some time alone together for talking, embracing, and the like (nothing more, as the Shepard sisters were not into premarital sex).

Letters occasionally addressed whether a sister would go to Texas to see Ellen and Ira. Often a beau/sweetheart would be a reason not to leave for a while. Goodness, the beau/sweetheart might find another female while the sister was gone!

Ellen had apparently been identifying some possible men in Texas and telling her sisters about them. She suggested that the sisters might come to Texas to take a look at them.

But, to do so, they would come there to visit with Ellen and Ira. In one letter, her sister Mag wrote back:

Sister Ellen, you can tell the young man you spoke of wait-ing for me that he is a little too late. You can tell him that there are some other girls out here that I expect would marry if they had a good chance. Sister Rachel says she would like the best in the world to go to Texas but cotton has gone down so low she don't know for certain whether she will have the money to go or not.

Of course, all the sisters back home knew some of what was being written; anyone in the family receiving a letter shared it with everyone else. Those who wrote told about what they said. Sometimes the one writing a letter would ask others what should be said.

How much notice Ellen gave to Texas men is unknown. Maybe she did give a little notice--maybe just a little eye contact or twinkle. Most of the time she was too busy with life to think of another man. After all, who could replace Jasper? She remained single through the decade of the 1870s, even though some suitors came around. The young men that Ellen identified as potential "marrying material" for her sisters were probably also "marrying material" for Ellen herself. After all, good-looking Ellen was only in her mid- to late twenties during most of the decade of the 1870s.

Here is a letter (with minor editing) she received in 1872:

Mrs. Lee,
The undersigned after compliments and looks takes this method of approaching you on the subject of matrimony. Of all the female sex under my knowledge you are my first

choice. *If this meets your approval, will you please answer me as soon as practicable.*

I am truly yours,

S. B. Lusk

PS:

You are forever and constantly
Impressed upon my mind
It seems predestinated that together we
Should be combined
If your mind should be so impressed
That I should be thine
Let me know by writing me a line
That you are also desirous to become mine
And we will be joined together in
Holy wedlock by some devine
You may fix the time
Excuse me for writing with lead pencil
For I had run out of ink on hand
It looks so pail
But my love for you will not fail.
Sammie

Did Ellen know this man? Did she date him? Was he an honorable person with good intentions? Was he wealthy? It seems that he had at least some education to write such a letter and add a postscript poem. It is unknown if Ellen ever responded. Records do show that S. B. Lusk married a different woman in 1876.

In 1876 two of Ellen's sisters back home, Naomi and Sallie (Sarah), had men named Pink or Pinkney (Pinkney was usually shortened to Pink). One had the last name Bunyard; the other, Gary. In a letter dated December 1, 1876, Naomi told about her man. She said:

I have a Pink much more handsomer than hers (referring to sister Sallie), and I think more suited for me. He will be 21 in January. He has 3 more brothers and they are all nice looking boys. Sister Ellen, do you think it best for a girl to marry or live single?

Naomi did not reveal that Sallie had already married on October 19 to her Pink.

Rachel described the wedding of Sallie and Pinkney Gary in her letter.

She and Pink Gary looked very well the day they married though Sallie had been in bed all the week before that day with the neuralgia. She didn't eat a single meal at the table until the wedding supper. We had a very nice time. Every body enjoyed their selves so much. We had five large cakes and lemonade. We had a beautiful bride's cake to cut. Sister, the same person got the ring that got it when Mag was married. The old folks had to be willing for she said she would marry him regardless. Sister Ellen, I tell Mag that she is fattening slowly; she says it ain't so.

Now, for one sister to be talking of fat on another sister isn't much of a way to promote good family relations! Maybe the "fat" news wasn't shared. Being "fat" was not a genetic inclination of the Shepard family. If anything, some of them and their descendants were trim and muscled. They were active people.

In the 1870s, a wedding was typically a big social event in a family and the local community. The wedding ceremony was usually held in a small church or chapel or in a large room in a home. A minister or judge would conduct the ceremony. The location might have a few flower decorations set up by family members or friends. Members of the family would work together to prepare a meal or reception. They organized the event, cooked the food, set up tables and chairs or logs for sitting (if outside), cleaned the premises, and greeted guests. A family member good in sewing or the bride herself would make the wedding dress. In some cases, a ready-made, store-bought dress might be worn. A family member or friendly neighbor might do the bride's hair. Celebrations before and after drew the largest crowds and were in various community facilities, such as a dance hall, picnic barbecue area, or schoolhouse. People were typically hesitant about the use of alcoholic beverages but that didn't mean there was some slipping around to get a taste or two.

Brides wanted to look beautiful! After all, a wedding was the time when a young woman got a man for a lifetime commitment. The bride expected the groom to provide for her, keep her safe, and father their children. She also expected him to show her respect and be forever faithful. The groom expected the bride to honor him, follow his instructions, have and care for babies, run the home, and be attractive and submissive. Sometimes a groom expected the bride to do some fieldwork and work related to the vegetable garden and taking care of a run-about flock of chickens.

Bathing and personal hygiene often needed attention by the bride and the groom and wedding guests. Most homes had no bathroom. In the winter, bathing was often little more than sponging to wipe the body with a wet cloth. In the summer, bathing might be in a creek or spring pool, where the water was often cold. A few places had waterfalls that could be used. Deodorant and similar products were quite limited. No bride or groom wanted a wedding with the strong presence of body odor! So, both bride and groom did the best they could under the circumstances. Some folks said that a bride might like body odor on her groom, as it was a sign of manliness. Really? Maybe times change, as does tolerance for body odor on another person regardless of romantic association.

Brides and grooms might buy or make clothing for their weddings. Some would wear clothing that they had; guests often wore existing clothing. Trying to have clothing reasonably clean was a challenge. A cast-iron wash pot filled with water might have a wood fire started around it to heat water for washing clothing. Other times, clothing might be washed near the water in a creek--preferably a creek with clean water. To dry, clothing would be placed spread out on bushes or tree limbs. Not many folks had wire fences or clotheslines. Getting odors and stains out of dirty clothing was nearly impossible.

The wedding night would often be at the home of the bride or, less frequently, at the home of a relative or friend. Sometimes it was at the home where the bride and groom were going to live. Spending the night in a hotel or guesthouse was somewhat pricey for most couples. Not many such places were even available in the South following the Civil War. The honeymoon was only a weekend or couple of days, if there was one. Newlyweds often had to get quickly back to work tending crops or livestock on their farms. Regardless, no one spent very much on a wedding, as there was daily living that had to take place afterward.

By the late 1870s, all of Ellen's sisters had found men and were married, had been married, or were deceased. One of her brothers, James Alexander Shepard, was deceased (died at six years of age), and the other, Ira W., was a good-looking young man approaching 20 years of age. In his young life, he had a few favorite young women, and by 1880 he had a serious sweetheart. He understood the importance of a man's wife to his success.

Ira W. Was a capable young man and good catch for a compatible young woman. Most of all he wanted a good life and family. He wanted to operate farms and businesses that prospered. He would work hard to achieve his goals that, he felt, would lead to success. He held an interesting view of success: the progressive achievement of worthy goals.

Most of the marriages went as well as could be expected. One, however, experienced a major issue. The man one of Ellen's sisters married was, at the same time, involved with another woman. The sister had one child he fathered, and she experienced another pregnancy and miscarriage before her husband's affair was discovered. When she found out, the sister and her child went running back to the safety of the Shepard home in Tinnin. The man then drifted off to Louisiana with another woman. Counting the number of women he had is not easy--maybe four or more. The number of children he fathered is also unknown because the extent of his communal relationships is a mystery. The sister never married again. The situation with the man who was her one-time husband is unknown. (These were the kinds of things Pa wanted to protect his daughters from by trying to screen out the bad men they brought around.)

The sisters typically settled within 50 miles of their home place. Some lived on farms; others lived in towns or cities as the wives of store owners or clerks. The lives of two were ended in the 1870s, though prematurely, in yellow fever epidemics that swept a portion of the South. Even the best medical care of the time could not cope with some of the diseases and health maladies that appeared on the scene.

Clinton and Bolton usually had one or two doctors; much larger Jackson had several doctors. And, since slavery was over, the outbreak of a communicable disease could not be blamed on slave behavior.

Ellen began to feel that life was slipping by. Except for Georgia Ann's, she had never met the husbands or children of her sisters. This was just about always on her mind. She went about the routine of running the home she shared with Nelson, his daughter, Sarah Ellen, and her son, Ira. This wasn't easy and had become more difficult from the standpoint of a long-term situation. She had been away from Tinnin since 1864!

Ellen would also wonder what Pa and Ma thought of her living in the home with a man who was not her husband. Would they understand the relationship? Nelson and his parents had been so supportive and helpful in times of crisis. Certainly, he understood enough of Ellen to allow her and her son to continue living in the home until her situation in life was worked out. And, without Ellen, how would Nelson cope in raising his daughter? But not knowing what Pa and Ma thought, even when they lived hundreds of miles away, was probably easy to discern: they wouldn't think it was proper. A widowed woman should not live in a house with a single man. There were too many opportunities for unwanted relationships to develop. Regardless, Ellen didn't have a lot of choices. She was without a home, and the Bell family took her and her son in and gave them a place to live and provided food to eat. Ellen did a lot of work for Nelson and provided care for his daughter.

Some folks in the Tinnin community said that Pa and Ma should pray for Ellen and her son. Pa and Ma, particular- ly Pa, were not people who overtly prayed; it was a personal matter. Yes, they would say little prayers of thanks, but they felt that situations in human life that were created by humans should be solved by humans. Pa and Ma hoped that they had taught Ellen how to go about life in a positive, uplifting manner. Pa and Ma always thought that how a person lives and the kinds of relationships he or she has are indicative of the fundamental values of the person. (Of course, Ellen's marriage to Jasper didn't really reflect consideration for the input from Pa and Ma.)

Ellen tried to continue some of the traditions of the Shepard family, particularly as related to her sisters. These were things that she remembered during her childhood in Tinnin. Special days and holidays were recognized as best she could. She also wanted to fill in for her deceased sister, Georgia Ann, in raising Sarah Ellen with the traditions of her grandparents. Her son, Ira, also benefitted from continuance of the traditions. This suited Nelson just fine as long as he had no responsibility for them.

Birthdays, Christmas, and the beginning of the New Year were important traditions that Ellen tried to keep. Maybe she continued them around Nelson with the notion that a romantic relationship might develop. She had always resisted any hints or advances by Nelson with romantic inclinations. Of course, Nelson shared many of the same holiday traditions as Ellen and, no doubt, appreciated what Ellen did to help mark the special season and times in the lives of family members. These were appropriate in the lives of Ira as well as Sarah Ellen. Ellen's sisters continued Shepard family traditions with their men after marriage, though most were tempered by the traditions that their men had before marriage.

Ellen was always able to come up with small gifts for birthdays and Christmas. Sometimes, Christmas included one small, useful gift, such as clothing, and a large orange or apple; other times, a small amount of hard candy or some kind of nuts, such as pecans or English walnuts, might be included. A tradition was to have some sort of decorated tree. A native cedar 4 to 5 feet tall with a reasonably symmetrical shape would be cut about mid-December. It would be placed in a gallon bucket filled with soil. Decorations of various sorts would be placed on the tree. Sweetgum balls, pine cones, and small branches with red berries from holly trees would be used, depending on what was available. Candles were not used on the tree that Ellen prepared, as they were costly and, if lighted, she felt that they would pose a fire hazard. The few gifts would be placed around the tree's base on the floor. The gifts were opened on Christmas morning.

Birthdays involved homemade cupcakes, cookies, or a cake (Ellen was somewhat limited by the cooking stove she had). Often, a piece of clothing would be included as a gift. Ellen was a great believer in giving something that a person needed and would use in some way.

Celebration of the beginning of a New Year might have been the event that Ellen most liked to celebrate with traditional foods of the Shepard family for that time. Though a part of Pa's upbringing in Indiana, pumpkins were not included either in his Tinnin traditions or in Ellen's in Texas.

On January 1, 1880, Ellen prepared a special meal to commemorate the New Year. Her fixin's included dried peas, baked sweet potatoes, greens, corn pone, and a dish called Hoppin' John with molasses lightly poured over it. Her greens weren't exactly as Ma would have prepared in Tinnin. Ellen did not have collards, cabbage, or mustard greens: she had rutabaga greens. The rutabaga had been planted in the fall to grow roots, but this year the tops were very nice, and she used some of them before the roots developed. She left the plants so that root development would continue. The greens were cooked with a few slices of fresh hog jowl for seasoning and meat. Convincing Sarah Ellen, going on three years of age, to try some of these foods was a challenge to Nelson.

Pinda (peanuts) were not as widespread in Henderson County as on the farm in Tinnin. Not many were grown. Ellen was accustomed to a lot of pinda (she remembered that they raised them for the farm hands). Peanuts were versatile; they could be eaten raw, boiled, roasted, and, after shelling, prepared into other highly nutritious foods. Ellen tried to get Sarah Ellen to try pinda but had little success.

Ellen maintained some sort of family structure in her household. She wanted her son, Ira, and her sister's daughter, Sarah Ellen, to experience a family orientation though their families had been destroyed by deaths of parents. She often thought about family traditions with her sisters. She thought her son, Ira, could experience more valued traditions if he were in Tinnin with the Shepard family. Unfortunately a presence in Tinnin could not possibly be a part of life at this time. Maybe the future would be different.

A Big Decision

Years were passing by. Ellen felt lacking. Was she missing out on much of what life might hold for her? She spent hours thinking and dreaming. Her parents were getting older. Her sisters were into young adulthood and marriage. She had not seen her two brothers since they were little more than babies (one was dead, as he only lived into toddler years). Her son, Ira, would soon be a teenager.

An informative letter from Ellen's brother, Ira W. Shepard, was the first thing after the New Year in 1880 that got Ellen thinking about family. Ira W. was the youngest member of the family and was only about two years of age in 1864 when Ellen and Jasper married. After the marriage, she was forbidden by Pa ever to bring Jasper to the Shepard home. What her brother Ira knew about her was primarily what was shared with him by Ma, Pa, and sisters. He wrote a letter to Ellen on the last day of December 1879 that read, in part, as follows:

Mrs. Ellen S. Lee,

Dear and most affectionate sister, I once more in life seat myself to try and write you a few lines to inform you that we are all well at present.Sis we had right smart at Christmas and I believe most every body here did and I hope you had a heap of Christmas.Your sister Mag's husband is doing well with his store. We made a very good crop. I will be nineteen years old the twentieth of next March and weigh only 140 pounds. I have a fine bunch of hogs. I haven't told you anything about my sweetheart. She lives in Brandon in Rankin County and her name is Miss Lizzie Boggs. She is the Belle of Rankin County. Sister Ellen, do you ever expect to come back to Mississippi? If you want to and do not have the money to come home with, write to me and tell me and I will raise the money for you. I want to see you and Ira very badly. Tell Ira and little Ellen howdy and kiss them for me. Tell Mr. Bell I would like to have him come here to live. Well, I will bring my letter to a close by asking you to write soon and often. Excuse my bad writing and spelling. So, good by for this time.

Ira W. Shepard

As you read that letter, didn't you find it interesting that Ira W. talked about his "fine bunch of hogs" before his "Belle?" Maybe that was a reflection of the priority he placed women in his life but the writer of this doesn't think so. Giving the young woman the "Belle" title certainly elevates her status in his mind.

This letter from Ira W. tugged at Ellen's heart. It brought back a lot of memories of Tinnin and her family. Her memory of her brother was as a toddler just beginning to walk and run around a little. Now, he was an adult. She immediately wanted to see him and others in her family. She had heard that her brother was a smart, good-looking, and considerate young man. Maybe his relationship with his sweetheart will develop into marriage (but it didn't; the romance soured and Ira pursued another young woman as his "belle.") No doubt, Pa would like some grandchildren with the Shepard surname. Maybe Ira will take over the Shepard farm in Tinnin when Pa is no longer able to manage it.

Son Ira got to read the letter. It tugged at him somewhat the same way as it did his Mama. This led him to ask, "Mama, will I ever get to go to Mississippi?" Ellen collected her thoughts and said "maybe." TheN she asked if he would like to go. He replied, "yes." She then said, "why?" He talked about wanting to see Pa and Ma, his aunts and uncles, and cousins. He went on to say, "I don't have any kinfolk here in Texas but you, Mama. I would like to see some of my kinfolk. I think I would really like them. Maybe we could go hunting together."

Another event that really got Ellen thinking about the situation was the visit by the census enumerator for the 1880 U.S. Federal Census. Nelson Bell was the head of household and gave the information. Four people were in the household: Nelson Bell (age 31), Sarah Ellen Bell (age 2), Ellen Shepard Lee (age 33), and Ira Jasper Lee (age 12). Anyone who later looked at the Census information might wonder about what was going on in the household.

After the enumerator left, Ellen had a certain sadness come over her. She remembered that Jasper H. Lee, her husband, the love of her life and the father of her son, had given the information to the last enumerator in 1870. Interestingly, there were also four people in the 1870 Lee household! It had been almost a decade since Jasper died. She sat alone in a chair on the porch of the house and stared off into the distance. Her eyes moistened, and a tear rolled down each cheek. There, vividly in her mind, was the image of the love of her life. She missed him so much. She thought of opportunity in Henderson County. She thought of family and friends in Tinnin whom she had not seen in 16 years.

In a flash, she thought, "Return to Tinnin." She wondered if a return would be possible. She had the responsibility for running the household for Nelson. She also had the responsibility of caring for her 2-year-old niece and 12-year-old son. Life in Texas had not been comfortable since Jasper's death. Maybe sometimes Nelson wanted to have a romantic relationship, but that didn't suit Ellen.

Another concern was the future of the Mississippi farm property. Her sister Mag once sent a letter to Ellen that created concern about ever making a return to Tinnin. In the letter, Mag said:

Pa says if he can possibly sell the place he will and move to Louisiana next fall. I would rather move to Texas. If we should move to Louisiana and your side of that big Mississippi River we will certainly go to see you all then for it won't take so much money.

Maybe Pa had become weary after a decade of poor farm production and extra-hard labor. Getting farm workers and sharecroppers was a challenge that routinely came around each year. Pa might have also been observing what was happening in soil erosion on the hills. Plowing laid the land virtually bare. Hard downpours of rain would wash the topsoil and most other fertile soil away. Gullies were beginning to form in some hills. And, his children were growing up and leaving home, taking their work productivity with them. Son, Ira W. Shepard, had said he wanted to go farm in Sunflower County, Mississippi. This flat, fertile land of the Mississippi River Delta in the state of Mississippi was said to be the best cotton land around. So, if he did go to Sunflower County, he would not be taking over the Shepard farm in Tinnin. That would leave a need for someone else to do so. None of the daughters married men who appeared to have the interest or stamina. Maybe Ira J. Lee could do it as he became an adult. A lot of thoughts stormed through Ellen's mind. She thought that maybe her brother, Ira W., was dreaming and not being very realistic about the future.

To help in making a decision, Ellen quietly had a talk with Reverend McIntosh of the Presbyterian Church in Athens. She respected him a lot, as he always appeared level-headed and reasonable. He raised some good questions and offered support for Ellen in reuniting with her family. He did not personally see much future for Ellen and Ira in Henderson County. Society and Texas laws were harsh on single women. Reverend McIntosh did suggest that she share her situation with two or so trusted church members to get their opinions; she did, and they were supportive of a return (but did not want to lose her from their church community).

After a few days of quietly contemplating her future and going about work as usual, Ellen made up her mind to contact Pa and Ma. Beforehand, she quietly spoke with her son, Ira. She told him a little of what she was thinking about. He asked if Pa would let her come back and bring him with her. Ellen thought so, since Jasper was now dead (but she didn't say that to Ira). She went over in her mind what would be involved in a return. She knew she would need to talk with Nelson. It wasn't simple; things were more complex than merely picking up and leaving.

She began thinking about writing a letter to Pa and Ma. What would she say, and how would she say it? Of course, she wanted to ask if she and Ira could come back to live with them.

Before Ellen wrote the letter, she told Nelson early one morning that she wanted to talk with him when he came in from the field for lunch. All morning she thought about how to tell Nelson. After all, he and his parents had been so good to her. They took her in when she had no place to go. And, there was Sara Ellen, who would need to be cared for as a toddler and raised to be a moral, responsible young woman.

Noon came. Nelson ate, and Ellen said she had something to say. Ellen said, "Nelson, you and all of your Bell family have been very nice to me and my young son, Ira. I greatly appreciate all that you have done. However, the time has come for me to move on in life." Ellen continued, "I am planning to write my family in Tinnin to ask about returning. Though I am not sure, I feel that they would allow me and Ira to live in Tinnin. Nelson, what do you think?"

Nelson, though kind of shocked, said "okay" but immediately asked about Sarah Ellen's future. Ellen didn't have a good answer. She thought aloud that maybe one of Nelson's sisters would take Sarah Ellen into her family or that maybe Nelson could get a live-in housekeeper. Of course, there was always the notion that Nelson might marry again, but that didn't appear to be something that would be happening anytime soon.

Nelson was always a source of advice, comfort, and confidence for Ellen. She asked him for suggestions in writing the letter. Together they came up with a general approach. Ellen would be tactful, loving, and humble. She would not say "I am going to do so regardless of what you say," like her attitude when she chose to marry Jasper. She would first offer proper greeting and indicate that she loved and missed her family. She would tell Pa and Ma about their

12-year-old grandson, Ira. She would relate how the death of Jasper left her unsure of direction in her life. Settling the estate was long and left her with virtually nothing. (Fortunately, the Bell family took her in.) She would indicate that she feels that a return to Tinnin appears best for her. She would ask how they felt about her and Ira working and living with them. She would say that she hoped to hear from them very soon.

The letter was written and mailed. Ellen waited for a response. After a couple of weeks' wait (seemed like eternity), a response was received. Ellen hurriedly opened the letter.

Yes, you are welcome to return to Tinnin and live in our home. Come back soon. We miss you. We want to see grandson Ira.

She shared the letter from Ma and Pa with Ira and Nelson. Details for the return needed to be worked out. Ellen began planning. She knew it would take some time.

But, first, she would write Pa and Ma and thank them for offering to let her and Ira come there. She indicated that it would be about another year before she could return to Tinnin. She would keep them informed of her plans. She welcomed hearing from Pa and Ma about anything she needed to know.

Ellen shared a major concern in a letter to Pa and Ma: What would happen to Sarah Ellen Bell? Ellen was the primary caregiver of her sister, Georgia Ann's, daughter. She did not know how Nelson would cope if she left the child in his care. He was a good father, but he had a lot of farm work to do. Maybe he could get a live-in nanny or something. Pa and Ma did not think that Sarah Ellen should come to Tinnin with Ellen and Ira if and when they came. Pa and Ma felt that the needs of Sarah Ellen might keep Ellen in Texas. Of course, Sarah Ellen was a granddaughter of Pa and Ma that they had never seen. They would like to see her and bond with her.

Ellen's letters to Pa and Ma were shared among her siblings, particularly those living at or near their home. Some of them wrote Ellen with encouragement. Of course, the decision to allow Ellen to return to Tinnin was one for Pa and Ma.

Ellen thought about living arrangements in the Shepard home in Tinnin. There were four large rooms with very high ceilings downstairs on each corner of the house. A wide enclosed hallway went between pairs of rooms. The front of the hallway was used as a place for greeting and sitting with guests. The back was used as a bedroom though it lacked much privacy. The upstairs, though not all finished, contained considerable space that, with a little improvement, could be used. And, there was the large closet under the stairs that Jasper had used in courtship days when he stayed overnight at Ellen's home.

Next, Ellen thought about the people who would be living at the house if she and Ira returned. There would be Pa, Ma, and her youngest sibling, her brother Ira W. The house would have plenty of room--far more than needed and what she had become accustomed to while living in Texas. She also thought that her brother might marry and leave or that he might marry and bring his wife into the home so that he could take over the farming operation as Pa and Ma aged. There would be enough room either way.

Ellen spent almost the entire year of 1880 preparing for the return to Tinnin. Of course, she also continued to manage the household for Nelson and provide care for Nelson's three-year-old daughter as well as her own son, Ira. Ellen developed quite an attachment to Sarah Ellen; she was somewhat like a daughter that she didn't have and a sister to Ira.

She began getting ready for the return by assessing how to do it: What transportation would she use? How much would it cost? What could she take with her? How would she dispose of what she couldn't take? How would she tell friends and family goodbye? She realized that once she left she would likely never see them again.

Word got out in the local community about Ellen's possible plans to leave. The folks at Flowing Waters church were talking. Of course, she now went to the Presbyterian Church in Athens. When Brother Yonah heard about it, he came calling bringing a bouquet of gardenia flowers. He was so kind-talking and loving toward Ellen. He asked her about her plans. When he talked, it was so sweet that sugar must have been melting in his mouth. She told him what she was going to do. He asked if there was anyway to change her mind. He promised all sorts of things if she would stay and spend some time with him. She said her mind was made up. He persisted saying she might change if she spent time with him. Her answer was an emphatic "no." She said she had work to do and he should be on his way. He said if there is a change of mind, let him know. He got on his fine horse and rode off.

Ellen received letters from back home with suggestions on transportation. Some were from family members; others from friends who remembered her. They asked what she was going to try to bring with her, such as a bed and other furniture. Ellen soon realized she couldn't move the few items of furniture; she sold them for a few dollars. Some of the letters asked if Ellen had enough money and offered to send money if she would let them know what she needed. The estimate in one letter said that $60 would likely be enough for both her and Ira to ride the cars (train). The fare for Ellen would be $30, and for Ira it would be $15 to $20. Ellen immediately thought that she should have more than $60--there might be some things she needed to buy along the way.

A letter from her brother, Ira W. Shepard (now 19 years of age), dated September 22, 1880, offered his suggestion on the best way to return to Tinnin. The letter conveyed information on travel he had gotten from a friend:

Mr. Walter Baskins says it is the best for you to come by way of Palestine, Texas, through Arkansas in a stage coach and to St. Louis and take a barge down the Mississippi to Vicksburg. You can ride on a car (train) to Clinton.

Another suggestion in the letter was to take a boat from Shreveport, Louisiana, to New Orleans and then a barge or boat up the Mississippi River to Vicksburg. Some of these ideas seemed a little unwise and less than economical. Ellen wanted a route that was easy and manageable. With her meager money supply, she wanted a short route that was safe, affordable, and would get her and Ira to Tinnin as soon as possible. She was ready for a family reunion!

Ellen asked around Athens about transportation for herself, Ira, and their possessions. It made sense to her to ride the train from Athens to Tallulah, Louisiana. This is the same route that she and Jasper had used to come to

Athens 17 years ago; now she was reversing direction of travel. In Tallulah, Ellen and Ira would get a ride to the ferry to cross the Mississippi River into Vicksburg. In Vicksburg, they would hitch a ride to the depot for the train to Clinton. She carefully saved money, including small amounts from the sale of property she could not move, to buy train tickets and pay freight for one large box of personal belongings. She did not ask her family for money, though they offered to send money to her for making the trip.

She didn't have much in the way of physical possessions. Only a few things could be taken, such as clothing and the like. She began by disposing of other things. She asked Nelson if she had anything he might find useful. She identified items that might have some value; they could be sold. It was not easy to part with some things; sentimental attachment caused her to want to keep them, such as a cedar bucket that Jasper had bought in 1869. She had room for moving only a few things to Tinnin. And how was she going to transport what she kept?

The possessions she was taking with her had to go into either the old trunk that she bought secondhand after arriving in Henderson County or a big handmade wooden box. With Nelson's help, she and Ira got 12-inch board planks and constructed a box that was approximately a 4-foot cube. The box held a good deal of stuff and would offer some protection from damage. Once filled, it would be sealed by nailing planks over the top. The box would be shipped as freight on the passenger train. Between the weight of the wood and the contents of the box, it became too heavy for one person to lift. Train workers would load and unload freight.

Ellen had a trunk that she had acquired from a woman who was selling it secondhand after she and Jasper came to Texas. She would take it as baggage on the train. The trunk would have clothing, a few items for remembering Henderson County, and a trove of letters and papers (later found and used in family research). She also had the two old travel bags that she and Jasper had used 17 years ago, and these could be used as luggage. Ira would have one of them for his clothing and personal items.

Moving was also emotional for Ira Jasper Lee. He had always lived in Henderson County. He had a few friends from his involvement with the Presbyterian Church in Athens. One of these friends was a girl who could likely have become a sweetheart later as Ira became a young adult. And, she would have been a good one! She was likely one that would have met the approval of Pa and Ma Shepard. Her parents were prominent in the Athens area and actively participated in the Church. School really wasn't an issue; only a few were around, and Ira Jasper didn't attend. This part of Texas wasn't much into schools at this time. Some folks might say Ira was home-schooled, though that notion didn't exist at the time. His mother did teach him a lot but she had no standards or curriculum to follow.

One of the things that Ira and his mother would give up was the aging horse that had pulled the wagon for trips to town and was used for riding. Ira loved this horse so much. It would do about anything that Ira would ask. Ira and Ellen had named the horse Captain. It was a proud horse who could follow commands quite well. Maybe Ira could find and identify with a new horse after the return to Tinnin. Ira and Captain had bonded superbly. Nelson was going to keep Captain, and that helped Ellen and Ira feel better about leaving him, because they knew that Nelson would take good care of him.

The year 1880 was passing by quite rapidly. Ellen and Ira continued preparing for the return to Tinnin. Not all would be complete in the year. It would be 1881 before they would depart on a journey that would change the lives of a lot of people. Maybe Ira would grow to have a family and manage a farm. He had a lot to learn. He had a good teacher in his mother, Ellen, but more was needed. She felt that he needed a man from whom to learn, such as Pa. Her plans for Ira after they got to Tinnin involved getting Pa to teach him about life, farming, and, in general, how to be a gentleman on a cotton plantation.

Departure grew near. Ellen tried to wrap up all details at the Bell house. She told friends goodbye. She spoke with Reverend McIntosh, thanked him for his guidance and support, and told him goodbye. He announced in a church service that Ellen and Ira would be leaving, and members of the congregation wished her well. It was a sad but inspirational time with sincere people who really cared about one of their own.

Ellen wrote to her parents a few days before she was to leave, stating her plans and train schedule. When the letter was received in Tinnin, everyone paid attention to the details. She gave the details with the thought that a sister or two and Pa and Ma could make plans to meet her. She thought that if Pa and Ma would meet her and Ira in Vicksburg, healing of old wounds could begin and good relationships restored. Ira could begin getting acquainted right off with his grandparents. But, she didn't know what they would do.

The day of departure arrived. Ellen discussed final matters with Nelson. Leaving became emotional. Ellen and Nelson hugged and spoke, "Goodbye." Ellen expressed her thanks for all that he and his family had done for her and her son, Ira. She gave Sarah Ellen a big goodbye hug and several smacky-on-the-cheeks kisses that small children often enjoy. Ellen offered some words of inspiration for the three-year-old girl. Somehow, Sarah Ellen got a sense that she was losing something in all of this, because Ellen had been like a mother to her.

Nelson took Ellen and Ira to the depot in Athens in a wagon pulled by Captain. Ellen bought tickets to ride a passenger car. They all hugged goodbye again. Ellen and Ira boarded the car (train). Their luggage and baggage were placed aboard, and they were on their way. They waved to Nelson and Sarah Ellen as the trained pulled out of sight. Nelson and Sarah Ellen started the ride back to their home; Ellen and Ira saw the wagon disappear in the distance. Tears ran down both the faces of Ellen and Ira. They realized that they would likely never see Nelson, his daughter, or Captain again. Sad! But, there were exciting new adventures as the traveled to Tinnin.

The train was pulled by a coal-fired steam engine. It traveled at a speed of about 30 miles per hour across the countryside of Texas and Louisiana, over creeks and small rivers, and through the little towns. Ellen and Ira watched for fields, pastures, animals, houses, and features of the countryside. They wanted to have good memories of the lay of the land. The train made several stops in the towns. On the fourth stop near Shreveport, Ellen reached into her bag and pulled out two corn pones that she had cooked the previous day and brought with her as they traveled. She had two more that would be saved until later. They really didn't want to spend any of their limited money on whatever food might be available. It was getting dark. They would ride all night.

As daybreak occurred, the train traveled out of the hilly countryside into the low, flat land of the Delta. This was a sign that they were passing through Monroe and weren't too far from Tallulah, Louisiana, where they would leave the train. At Tallulah, with luggage and baggage, they caught a ride on a wagon going to the ferry landing on the Mississippi River. It had been 17 years since Ellen saw the Mississippi River; Ira had never seen it.

As the ferry was being tied up at the landing in Vicksburg, Ellen and Ira gathered their belongings. They got off the ferry, and two of the crew members unloaded their baggage and freight. Though the depot was not far away, Ellen and Ira arranged to be transported there in a wagon. Their baggage and freight were much too heavy to carry. Ellen had thought some of her siblings might meet her in Vicksburg, but none did.

Ellen bought tickets for herself and Ira to travel on the train from Vicksburg to Clinton. The train departed on schedule and made its way through steep hills and over creeks, crossing the Big Black River near Bovina. In a bit, they would pass through Bolton and arrive in Clinton.

What a glorious day! Just ahead down the tracks was the depot with a sign reading "Clinton." The train arrived on schedule. As it pulled to a stop, Ellen and Ira looked out the window. She looked toward the Women's Institute campus and the home of Reverend Autry where she and Jasper were married on March 2, 1864. She had so many memories. Ellen saw Pa and Ma standing on the platform wait-

ing; that made her feel wonderful. Ira had never seen them
and didn't know who to look for. Ellen pointed them out.
Ellen and Ira quickly got off. It was a clear, sunny day that
was just right for a reunion. Gee, the old folks looked good
to have aged more than 17 years since Ellen last saw them.
Hugs. Kisses. More hugs and kisses. Pa and Ma would get
to know their grandson Ira, who was barely a teenager but
would need to grow up fast on the Shepard farm. Ellen and
Ira checked to be sure that their luggage and baggage had
been unloaded before the train pulled out for its next stop
at the depot in Jackson.

Ellen had arrived in Clinton, but the return to Tinnin
wasn't complete. Pa and Ira loaded the luggage and large
freight box on the wagon and headed north to Tinnin. Pa
drove the wagon and talked about so many things along the
way, such as Monroe Street, which was developing into a
place where people built their homes in Clinton. The horse
pulled the wagon on out of town and toward Tinnin. They
passed Sumner Hill, Stafford Ridge, and Kickapoo and proceeded down a long trail through Shepard Hills.

Pa had questions: "What happened to your husband,
Jasper? Why did he die?" Ellen wasn't expecting those
questions on this day of reunion. She could tell Pa still
wasn't quite over the marriage. Ellen explained that he became quite ill on the fifteenth of November 1870 and died
the following day. She said the doctor came three times to
the house and treated him, but he died anyway. The doctor thought he had a heart attack or stroke. His body was
buried in Smith Cemetery.

After this, Pa asked, "Did you ever learn about his past?"

Ellen said, "Not much."

Pa said, "Well, I did. You might be surprised. I won't share the details today. I know you want to remember him as a good and honorable man dedicated to you and his marriage. I will talk to you sometime in private." Ellen really didn't want to know. It was sad that Pa had brought up this subject. By doing so, maybe it was to ward off any future matrimony ideas that Ellen might have after returning to Tinnin.

After a bit of riding, the horse turned onto the drive toward the Shepard home, which was on a ridge above the bottom of a small valley between the hills. They passed by a dug well that provided some of the water for the home. Pa knew how to evaluate water wells. He had been a well digger in Indiana before moving to Mississippi and had dug some wells after he moved. Pa spoke and said it was the best well around and kept water all year. Another well just behind the house provided water on a daily basis. It was also a good well but did not produce quite as much water.

The wagon pulled up to the big porch on the front of the Shepard home. Glorious! Ellen was so happy. She shouted and jumped for joy. Ira was very pleased to see his grandparents' home. But, Ellen quickly thought about her siblings. She found it interesting to see the home place without them around as children. She would quickly see that all were gone. She would hear that on occasion a sister would return with a child or so for a short while after a marriage developed problems. That was the reason Pa tried so hard to get them to make good marriage choices. Her youngest brother, Ira W., came running in from his work in a cotton field to greet and hug her. Ira got special treatment as the only grandson and young Lee around.

To Ellen, some things were different. Her parents had aged. There was no Bummer or Ritz, but there was a new dog named Howl. Ellen wanted to know how the dog got that name and was told it was because he howls at full moons. A new addition near the yard was six honey bee hives just south of the fence around the house. Pa warned not to go near the hives as the bees sometimes become agitated and could fly out and sting. Trees had grown and aged; some had fallen. Buildings had deteriorated; one in the animal lot had a collapsed roof. Former slave housing had fallen in or been torn down. A couple of new share-cropper cabins had been built. A new log corn crib was in the lot. Two new rat-cats named Sam and Samantha now kept guard over the corn in the crib. The allowed no rats! Some of the steeper hills were showing signs of gully erosion. Things looked so different. Ever so quickly, a flash came into Ellen's mind: "You can't go home. There is no such thing; home changes over time regardless of what you have in your mind. When you go away and return, it is not the same as when you left. Many things are different. But, it is always home."

Ellen was so happy to see her parents and brother and to be at home that everything that caused them to be apart for 17 years was forgotten. Ellen was glowing with happiness. The return to Tinnin was now partially achieved. Next, adjustment and the final adaptations would fully give her a return.

ADJUSTMENT TO RETURN

The year was 1881. Ellen had returned to Tinnin. She went about filling the emptiness she had beforehand and seeking happiness in Tinnin. What would it take for a complete return to Tinnin? Maybe it would involve her son, Ira.

After being away about 17 years, she would need time to adjust. Would she be able to have a satisfied life in Tinnin? Considering their relationship in 1864, would she be able to get along with Pa? Could she accept the maturity and aging of her family? After all, her parents were older; she was older. Pa was now 67 years of age, Ma was 51, and Ellen was 34. Her siblings had reached adulthood, married, and moved away. So many changes influenced Ellen's ability to readily adjust to Tinnin.

It was Ellen's nature to pitch in and strive to make the best of situations. She knew that she and her son, Ira, would be expected to do their share of work around the farm and home. A surprise she first learned about the farm was that the amount of land was now much less. Hard times after the Civil War resulted in her father selling and losing acreage.

Without sufficient income to cover some debts in which land had been used as collateral, he lost acreage by foreclosure of the lien holder. Altogether, the farm acreage was now close to 400, a decline of some 800 acres while Ellen was living in Texas. She wondered if she had been there, if she could have done something so that the property wouldn't have been lost. Maybe she could have helped Pa make smart decisions and not have to sell or lose land for failure to make timely loan repayments. Oh well, that was water under the bridge; no turning back. Plus, 400 acres should be sufficient to support the now smaller family.

After arrival, Ellen and Ira got somewhat settled into a large room that would be theirs. A couple of small beds and not much else was in it, though there was enough for them to get by on for a while. Ellen then went outside and showed Ira around. This was a good time for her to see things that had changed. She showed Ira the water well and went over how to draw water to keep it clean and safe to use. She showed him the privy, animal lot and outbuildings, smokehouse, chicken yard, and bee hives, along with the garden that had a few things growing in it. The same site for a garden was used for many years; it was good for early-season, mid-season, and late-season vegetable crops, depending on the kinds planted. Then they walked down to the spring branch that brought good water within a hundred yards of the house. After they looked around a bit, it was late afternoon and time to go back to the house. Ma would soon have dinner. Ellen pitched in to help finish getting it ready.

Dinner was simple. Traditional food was prepared for an evening meal of the Shepard family. Boiled dried peas seasoned with ham hock, corn pone, fried salt pork meat, raw onion, and pickled zucchini relish. Five people were at the table: Pa and Ma, Ellen's brother Ira W., and Ellen and Ira Lee. There was no longer need for a separate children's table. This "table emptiness" made it seem somewhat lonely. Pa said a quick blessing that included thanks for bringing Ellen home safely. Conversation was nice. A lot of reminiscing took place. Ellen got brought up to date on her sisters. Ira W. talked a little about his sweetheart in Rankin County, but somehow the feeling was that maybe the relationship wasn't going to be a long-term one. Talk about neighboring families revealed a lot of change over the years Ellen was gone. The school had a few months of class each year. Mason Chapel continued much as before with an itinerant preacher named Pastor Summer. Pa talked some about the farm and challenges with finding labor and managing sharecroppers. He said the hill land was just not as productive as it was when he first got it in the mid-1840s. No doubt, erosion of topsoil was taking its toll.

Ellen and Ira were tired and sleepy from the long trip. So, it was time for bed. The window shutters would be folded shut. The outside doors of the house would be latched securely by the last person to come inside, Pa usually.

Pa thought Ira needed a little instruction about his approaching manhood. He didn't check with his mother before doing so. He thought men know men better, and after all Ira was now 13 years of age. He took him out on the front porch. He talked about the budding whiskers on his face and the hair beginning to grow other places on his body. Pa indicated that he might want to shave his face a little, but some whiskers, if trimmed and neat, would be okay on the farm. He talked about bathing and washing areas where body odor may readily develop. Frequent sponge bathing may work, Pa said. This would be done with a cloth, soap, and a wash bucket of water. Pa said never to use the drinking water bucket for bathing. Ira needed some of this "man to man" talk. Neither his mother, Ellen, nor his uncle, Nelson, had talked about such.

The discussion continued. Pa asked him if he liked girls. Hesitantly, Ira said he did like them but that he was kind of shy around them. No one had ever talked to Ira about that subject, either. He said that there was a girl he left in Athens that appeared to have potential but that he might never see her again. Pa asked if he knew about animals and their lives; Ira said yes (all young folks on a farm with animals "know" about them). Pa said the humans were sort the same as farm animals but are mostly very private and cautious about what they do. Pa told him that he would talk some more about being a man and how to relate to girls sometime soon. Always be kind and respectful, and never take advantage of females, he said. Pa further said some things are only for married folks. Now, Ira had a lot of questions in his mind. Boys are usually always ahead of parents and grandparents when these subjects are brought up.

Pa ended by talking about taking his before-going-to-bed pee each night off the porch (just as he had done most nights since 1857). This was probably something Ira didn't need to be told a lot about, but since he was a new man in the Shepard home, Pa felt an obligation to inform him. Anyway, Pa believed relieving oneself "off the porch" (either the front or the back porch) was better than wondering around the yard in the dark (might step on a snake or a pile of fresh dog crap) or using the slop jar in the bedroom, which he said was mostly for the women. He told Ira that he had learned that women didn't like to use a slop jar that had earlier been used by a man--something about the odor. Of course, it could be emptied and rinsed out, but that was a morning task for the next day. Pa told him to go to different places around the porch (not the same place each time) and never on the porch floor. And, that was the end of Pa's instructions for the night. Then, it was off to bed.

The first thing Ellen wanted to do the next morning was take a ride around the farm and the Tinnin community. She got permission from Pa to use a horse and the one-horse wagon to do so. Ira helped her with hitching (he knew how to do it, but he needed to learn the way things were done on the Shepard farm). She had Ira drive, and with instructions from her, they rode to the fields on trails used to get around on the farm property. They talked a little about the fields, the creeks that ran through them, and the way overflowing creeks could ruin young crop plants. Some fields were now planted to different crops than before Ellen was gone, and she told Ira that Pa would give him the details. As the passenger, Ellen jumped out of the wagon and opened and closed gates along the way. She told Ira always to close any gate that he opened: "Leave gates the way you find them." In their ride, they passed five fairly new sharecropper houses and a couple of falling-in former slave cabins. The other slave cabins that Ellen remembered had been torn down.

Ellen showed Ira where the Union troops came onto the farm and camped. She told about how the family prepared for arrival of the troops and the threat to burn the house. Ira wanted to know why it wasn't burned. Ellen explained that Pa was raised in Indiana and had different views on slavery, the Civil War, and how to honestly and fairly relate to all people. He told the troops that he had voted the Union ticket and that no Confederate soldier lived in the house. That, without doubt, saved the house.

After looking around the farm a little while, it was time to explore the Tinnin community. They rode back to the house and up the driveway to the main dirt road and turned right. To Ellen, it seemed that fewer houses were being lived in and more were getting into a bad state of repair. They rode by the Zachariah Ratliff Family Cemetery. Ellen told Ira about some of the people buried in it and that Pa and Ma wanted to be buried there when their time came. One of the things that Ira noticed was that some graves appeared to be outside the bounds of the cemetery. He wondered who they were; he wondered if maybe some had been slaves. His curiosity led to asking, "Mama, who is buried in the graves outside the bounds marked by large rocks?" His Mama said she didn't know all the details. He was surprised to learn that a couple of them were his distant Ratliff relatives who died as small children. She also said that some graves might be those of slaves and the children of slaves who died quite small. She told him, to the best of her knowledge, no slaves had been buried there since about 1860.

Next, they rode by the schoolhouse and Mason Chapel. Ellen told Ira that she went to the Tinnin School a few months each year for eight years. The school usually had one teacher, and all grades met together. She said that he was likely beyond the age to go to school. A teacher=s home was next to the schoolhouse so that the teacher, who was paid very little, would have a place to stay.

Mason Chapel was somewhat run down but still served a few families in the community. It needed repairs, including a new roof. Ellen and Ira stopped at it and went inside. Surprisingly, the preacher, Brother Summer, was there. Ellen introduced herself and explained how she used to go to church there but had been away in Texas. Brother Murrow welcomed her back to Tinnin and indicated that she and Ira would be welcome to come to Mason Chapel. Brother Summer said that George and Sarah Shepard and some of their family attended. Services were on Sundays with even calendar numbers. Preaching began at 11:00 a.m. Sometimes there were special events, such as singings and barbecues--sounded like old times to Ellen. Brother Summer said he would visit the Shepard family on Saturday afternoon and looked forward to seeing Ellen and Ira as well.

Ellen and Ira next headed for the Ratliff Store, which was about like it had been when Ellen went away in 1864. She told Ira that his maternal great-grandparents, Zachariah and Susan Tinnin Ratliff, had started the store and operated it for several years. They stopped the wagon out front, hitched to a porch post, and went inside. There wasn't much to see. It was typical for a small country store. The amount of goods for sale was in stark contrast to the larger mercantile stores found in Vicksburg and a few other cities.

The store had a few food items, such as sugar, salt, coffee, and tea, which were on shelves in pottery jars. Several bolts of cloth and sewing supplies were kept on a large table with a cabinet at one end. Limited ready-made clothing and shoes were near the back. Tobacco products, moonshine liquor (on a shelf out of sight), and a few things used as medicines, such as paregoric (an opium product), were near the cash box. Behind the counter with the cash box were bullets and gunpowder. Small pieces of hard candy were in a pottery jar next to the cash box. Several small wooden containers had the seed of common small-seeded vegetables, such as turnips, radishes, and carrots. Larger boxes held pea, butterbean, okra, and squash seeds. There were bins of cornmeal that had been ground at a water-powered stone mill on the Bogue Chitto Creek.

Ellen introduced herself to the person running the store. Ellen told her that she grew up in Tinnin but had been away 17 years and had just gotten back. She asked if she had been in the area long. The store clerk said about 15 years. She said that she had moved from Brandon, where for a while she was a housekeeper at Sister Annie's Boarding House. Further, she said that place had some very interesting people, with some scary, and others nice. Wonder what the store clerk really knew about the men at Sister Annie's? Ellen didn't ask her about the men.

Ellen then asked the store clerk if she knew a few folks in the Tinnin community, including Samuel Echols, Rufus Tilman, and Margie Mason; these were youngsters from her childhood that she had gone to school with for a while. The clerk said she knew two of the individuals Ellen named: Samuel Echols and Margie Mason. Both still lived in the community and occasionally came into the store. Mason's Chapel was named after one of Margie's grandfathers. After a few minutes of talking, they discovered a distant kinfolk relationship with the parents of Ellen's mother. Now, that kin relationship was special to Ellen. The discussion and relationship might prove quite meaningful to her in the years to come. Ellen tried to explain the kinfolk relationship to Ira, but it didn't make much sense to him. He would learn more in the next few years.

Now it was time to head back to the Shepard house. They passed a couple of homes, and Ellen told Ira who lived there when she was growing up in Tinnin. So many changes made it difficult to explain the community. How life in Tinnin had changed since 1864!

Ira had a question for his mother, and it kind of caught her by surprise: "Do you have any old sweethearts around here?"

Ellen thought; she said, "A couple of beaus but no sweet-hearts. I am sure they are all married, have moved away, or are dead. Your daddy was the only sweetheart I ever had."

Then Ira wanted to know if she was interested in finding another man; Ellen hedged her response and never said a flat-out no.

The next Saturday afternoon, a one-seat, horse-pulled buggy came into sight up the hill from the Shepard home. Brother Summer was coming for the visit he had men-tioned to Ellen and Ira. Everyone gathered on the porch to welcome Brother Summer. He said a prayer and read a short Bible passage. He and the family talked about differ-ent things, with emphasis on the return of Ellen with her son. Brother Summer wanted to know if Ellen's son, Ira, had been baptized.

Ira quickly spoke, "No, but I might want to be."

Then Ellen related church experiences in Texas. After a few words about Flowing Waters Church, she talked about the Presbyterian Church she and Ira had attended. She told that it was about peace, love, hope, and joy. She said that the Presbyterian minister didn't preach about the hot fires of hell and scare everybody. Interestingly, Brother Sum-mer said that his sermons didn't get into hot-fire subjects very often, though he was somewhat oriented in that direc-tion. He wanted people to know that sin had consequences. The visit ended with a prayer, and the family said that they would be at the next preaching service.

Pace of activity would soon pick up on the farm. Crop time was at hand. Some field work had already been done. Ira needed to learn the details from his Grandfather George and his Uncle Ira W. They were more than willing to have

198 RETURN TO TINNIN

another person to help in the fields and to manage the sharecroppers. Ira was ready to get started. He viewed the return to Tinnin as a great opportunity that he should seize and develop. He wanted a good life on a farm. He knew of the hurt his mother experienced when the farm she and his father had was repossessed.

Ira had some farm experience from living with Nelson Bell in Texas. Ira's father, Jasper, died when Ira was too young to be taught farming. Ira knew a little about cotton, corn, and other common crops. He was ready to learn more and become more important on the Shepard farm. His mother, Ellen, assured him that she would be around most of the time to help keep him on the right track. She so strongly wanted him to be successful; she did not view failure as an option. Maybe she was an over-protective mother!

The Shepards mostly used mules as draft animals. Ira learned a lot about mules the first summer. Between the teachings of Pa and those of his mother, he learned that a mule was a cross of a male donkey and a female horse and was smarter than either parent. Good care of mules was a must. They needed feed, including corn or oat grain and grass or good-quality hay, along with water. The also needed rest. They were never to be abused. Mules were valuable animals that could work long hours at a steady pace.

Pa stressed the importance of having good relationships with animals that were expected to do work. He would say, "Treat 'em right, and they will treat you right."

Ellen would reiterate with "Be kind to animals, and they will be kind to you."

Pa told Ira that the mule named Isaiah would be his to use and develop a bond with. Isaiah was a whitish-gray, medium-sized mule approaching eight years of age. He said Isaiah had always proven to be good in following commands and pulling a consistent load.

Maybe Ellen and Pa shared some of the same sense of how to go about life and get things done. Anyway, Ellen wanted Ira to learn the right ways of doing things--likely for his future benefit.

Ira learned how to hitch horses, oxen, and mules to wagons from his mother and Uncle Nelson in Texas. These wheeled vehicles had tongues that extended forward alongside or between (in case of two) the animals. Now, he would learn how to hitch to various equipment, including plows and cultivators. Ellen explained that it was all more complicated than he probably thought. He first learned about hitching one mule to a singletree to pull a turning plow, cultivator, or log. He learned about putting collars, hames, trace chains, bridles, blinders, bits, lines, and belly bands on mules. He learned how to hitch a pair of mules using a doubletree to a middle buster plow or disk harrow. The process was similar to that of one mule but was complicated by having two animals that had to be hitched to work together. The Shepards did not use more than two-mule teams on implements.

With all of these, Ira learned how to manage mules by giving commands. Ellen reviewed the most important commands in field work, such as "Get up" for "Go," "Whoa" for "Stop," "Gee" for "Turn right," and "Haw" for "Turn left." Ira learned how to use the plow lines to help direct a mule and motivate it to pull. Holding plow handles so that the plow point would go into the soil just right--not too deep--took some time and strength and helped develop his arm muscles. Holding the handles of cultivators so that the soil was tilled and weeds were destroyed without damaging or destroying crop plants took greater care.

Pa cautioned Ira about the dangers of mules kicking, biting, pawing, and mashing (as against a barn post or a tree). Pa jokingly told him that some of the best working mules are just waiting for a chance to kick or bite the person who all day tells them what to do. When behind a mule, stand to the side and never directly to the rear. This makes it harder for the mule to land a solid lick. Kicks to the head, shin, or in the belly are most serious. A few mornings later, as Ira was hitching his mule, Isaiah, to a plow for a few hours of work, he stood directly behind him about two feet from the rear legs. Isaiah sensed it and quickly lifted a foot and landed a blow onto Ira's right thigh. It hurt! Ira called Isiah an unrepeatable new name. Of course, the new name didn't matter to Isaiah. Luckily, the result was just a big bruise and no broken skin or bone. From then on, Isaiah never had a chance to land a solid kick on Ira but that doesn't mean that Isaiah wasn't tempted to try.

Ira learned so many things that first year. Planting seed required soil preparation early in the growing season. There were differences in how cotton and corn were planted. He learned to identify crop plants and distinguish them from weeds. He learned to use a hoe to go about work known as "chopping cotton" without damaging the plants and how to cut weeds from growing corn. He learned that chopping was to thin cotton plant populations to promote growth and development, remove weeds, and loosen the soil. Harvest required even different skills.

Some learning occurred vicariously, as it did one time in early August when Ira went to gather chicken eggs from nests in the chicken house. A typical part of his noon hour routine was to get the eggs that had been laid in the morning. The house had a row of ten nests constructed of lumber to form foot-square places where hens could lay. Pine straw lined the bottom of each nest to protect eggs from breaking. Ira had become accustomed to reaching inside, grabbing eggs, and placing them in a basket. On this day, he stuck his hand inside where eggs usually were and felt something cold and scaly, and this reminded him of a large lizard. He jerked his hand back and peered inside. There was a coiled chicken snake. It looked huge (but might not have been). He had never seen one that close-up before. Ira ran to the nearby shed, got a garden hoe, and lifted the snake out. The snake's body had three egg-shaped bulges caused by the whole eggs it had eaten. He carried it on the hoe some 75 yards away and left it in the woods. Ira told his Mama about the chicken snake; she asked why he didn't kill it and said it would return and eat more eggs. For some reason, it was never seen in the chicken house again. Ira kept mum; maybe he did kill it and didn't confess to doing so.

In late August, the teacher at Tinnin School came by. She introduced herself as Miss Spell and said she had recently graduated from a college in Jackson and was newly hired as the teacher at Tinnin School. She said she had been told that a boy had recently moved here from Texas. She wanted to talk about enrolling him in school. She said that school would begin the first of October after much of the cotton crop had been harvested. She said she would be teaching reading, arithmetic, writing, and beginning science (something new at Tinnin). Ellen and Miss Spell talked about ages, costs, and school days. Ira didn't think he wanted to go; he thought he was too old and knew enough, anyway. Miss

Spell said that most students quit school by age 14, which she thought was a little early. Miss Spell said goodbye and told them to let her know. She got on her horse and left. Ellen talked with Ira and thought it over; Ira would not be going to school.

Ira had a little experience picking cotton in Texas with Nelson Bell, so that wasn't a totally new experience when the time to pick cotton arrived. Ellen usually picked side-by-side rows when Ira picked. Getting cotton harvested was viewed as getting cash in one's pocket. Pulling a pick sack, ever so rapidly removing white seed cotton from the bolls, and quickly putting the cotton into the pick sack required repeated motion all day long. The faster one went, the more one could pick. Care was needed, however, to keep the sharp spines on the bolls from making sores on the hands. Once full, a pick sack was weighed (usually at 60 to 70 pounds) and emptied into a cotton house--a small building on the edge of a field for putting cotton after picking and weighing until there was a bale (about 1,100 pounds). And it took a far greater mass of picked cotton than one would think to make a bale!

Once there was a bale, it would be hauled in a wagon to the gin in Pocahontas. Gin workers would use a big flexible suction pipe to lift the cotton up from the wagon. About ten minutes would be needed to unload a bale from a wagon. Suction would move the cotton with seed, known as seed cotton, to the gin stands where the seeds were removed and separated from the lint. The seed would be sent to a seed bin for weighing and the lint would go into a compress. Ira liked driving a loaded cotton wagon to a gin so he could wait around an hour or more for ginning and go to a store to get a special candy snack or a handful of pork cracklin.

Pa wanted to be sure Ira knew about tagging and weighing the ginned bale, which was the important part of cotton ginning. Both happened as the bale was taken out of the compress wrapped in bagging and ties (bagging and ties held the compacted lint together and gave the bale a rectangular shape). Tagging involved placing a durable paper tag with a wire tie on the ginned bale for future identification of the owner. The number on the tag would also be used to associate the lint with the grade of the cotton. Weighing involved using a big beam scale for getting the weight of the bale in bagging and ties. Most bales were within the range of 500 pounds. After tagging and weighing, a sample of lint would be taken for grading the cotton and setting the price per pound. Cotton grade was based on two major factors: length of individual fibers (often one and one-eighth inches) and color (very white was desired; open white cotton in the field exposed to rain might turn dark and be less desirable when ginned). Keeping up with tag number, weight, and grade was essential. There were a couple of cotton merchants in Pocahontas who would use that information to buy the bale without physically seeing it. The seed were usually traded for the cost of ginning. A boxcar parked on the rail siding near the loading platform would be filled with bales of cotton and pulled by a locomotive as part of a train to a textile mill or to a port for export to Europe.

Almost all appeared to go routinely the first cropping season. Pa and his son, Ira W., ran things. Grandson Ira carefully observed the goings-on. He would sometimes talk to his mother about the events of a day. Ellen was proud of the way her son went about work and learning. She often offered encouragement for him to learn new things and bragged on him when he did. In the back of her mind, she thought that one day her son might be the boss of the Shepard farm.

Cropping season ended. The sharecroppers had worked out well. Cotton harvest was good: 32 bales of high quality cotton were ginned. Corn harvest was good, as well as that of other crops, such as sweet potatoes and pinda. It was at that point that Shepard son, Ira W., began to reflect on his future. He was now 20 years old with a promising adult life ahead. Hill land required a lot of work. Productivity of the soil appeared to be going down. Where would he have the best future?

A change was on the way for the Shepard farm. Ira W. Shepard decided he would strike out on his own. He had found a young woman he wanted to marry. And it was not the "Belle of Rankin County" he had earlier described to his sister and that he was so deeply in love with just about a year ago. The "Belle" didn't last until marriage; situations and compatibility resulted in loss of sweetheart status. His new sweetheart was Mary Ella Collier. Together, they talked about their future. They decided to leave the hill land in favor of the nearly level and highly fertile land of the Mississippi Delta in Sunflower County, Mississippi. Ira W. had heard that it was the best cotton land on Earth. He was told that only about 10 percent of the Delta bottomland had been developed. Ira W. viewed this as an opportunity for him to be successful and gain wealth. The undeveloped land would take a huge amount of clearing to bring it into cotton production. He just hoped to get several hundred or thousand acres.

Ira W. talked to Pa about his tentative plans. Pa was a bit surprised, for he had thought that his son would be taking over from him in a few years. But, that appeared not to be the case. Ira W. told Pa that his grandson, Ira, was young, smart, and energetic and that with a few more years on the farm under Pa's direction, he could take over, and the farm would continue.

On December 1, 1881, Ira W. Shepard (age 20) married Mary Ella Collier, and moved to the Sunflower County community of Caile, near Inverness, Mississippi. It was a big move for a young man who had no wealth but had a lot of smarts about farming and success in business ventures. As of this event, the Shepard family no longer had a child who had not married, though two had married, gone away, and moved back home for different reasons. In any case, the two who were no longer married and had again married and moved away.

Operation of the Shepard farm was now solely in the hands of Pa, and he was reaching the age of losing some of his stamina and interest. Maybe some of what Ellen had in mind for a "complete" return was now unfolding. And, it related to the advance of her son, Ira, in taking over the farm. But he had a lot to learn. Ellen encouraged him, taught him, and worked beside him. She wanted him to be able to do a good job.

After Christmas was over and with the year 1882 beginning, Pa asked Ira to come talk with him. Ira was approaching age 14. Though Ira was not yet an adult, Pa felt he could be a lot more involved on the farm. Ellen wanted in on the conversation as well, because she had a vested interest in her son being successful. After all, she would work side-by-side with Ira, as needed, to help him learn the ropes. So the three of them sat on the front porch in late afternoon sunlight with coats and hats on to protect themselves from the chilly January breeze in central Mississippi.

Conversation dealt with how to make the farm more productive and have more money at the end of the year from
the major cash crop: cotton. Several things were discussed.
The first was labor to do the required work. There were
very few people to hire who would work hard, and money
would be needed to pay their wages. The three talked about
the use of sharecroppers. Ellen mentioned how sharecropping helped her and Jasper get their start in Texas. Pa indicated that two sharecropper families had been used over
the past few years. Maybe it was now time to expand a little
in that direction.

Over the next few days, they decided to continue with
the two existing sharecropper families from last year and
add another for the 1882 crop year. Each would have about
20 acres of good crop land. Some 10 to 15 acres would be
planted to cotton, and a couple of acres to corn. Any remaining land could be used as the sharecropper wished for
gardening and other crops. They made arrangements with
the sharecroppers from last year and told them to put out
the word that they were looking for another sharecropper.

Ellen felt that there should be a written agreement between Pa and each sharecropper. She checked around with
other farmers that had sharecroppers and asked if she
could have examples of agreements. She was able to get a
couple agreements to use in creating what would be used
on the Shepard farm. Both were handwritten, were not
very legalistic, and had little detail, but they were helpful.
Ellen drafted what her family might use; Pa agreed with it.
Contact was made with the two sharecroppers of the past
year. The use of a written agreement seemed okay to them;
they thought a written agreement better than an oral one,
though Pa Shepard was a man of his word. A new share-

cropper was found and agreed with the use of a written agreement. He thought a written agreement would be good because he believed his previous landlord had cheated him.

A major issue with written agreements and sharecroppers was that most sharecroppers could not read or write. One of the Shepards' sharecroppers had a wife who could read a little. Ellen read the agreements aloud. Each sharecropper signed with an "X", because he could not write his name. The signing (X-ing) was typically witnessed by a Shepard family member. Nevertheless, the sharecroppers were very trusting of Pa and his family. Pa had earned the trust through years of honesty and fairness. Pa tried extra hard to be a person of high integrity.

Each agreement typically contained the sharecropper's name, the date, the cropping year, the kind of crop, the field location on the farm, the number of acres, and the work responsibilities of the sharecropper. The agreement also included the division of crop yields. Most sharecroppers worked on thirds. This meant that they got two-thirds of the money from the sale of cotton and the landowner got one-third. It they worked for Pa on other things, such as building a fence, they were paid a daily amount in cash. Most of them had very little, and the daily work was important. The rate was typically $1 to $2 for a hard day of labor.

Part of each agreement dealt with Pa providing "furnishings" to the sharecropper. Furnishings included what the sharecropper's family needed to live--primarily food and occasionally money for clothing. Small cash amounts would be advanced to the sharecropper. Ellen kept a record of the advances in a small paper tablet. The amounts would be totaled and deducted from the sharecropper's portion of the proceeds from cotton sales. The Shepards didn't have much extra money for making advances. If they needed to, they would themselves borrow money. Ellen was very careful to keep all records honestly and accurately. What the sharecroppers received was meager enough and important to them. Since most could not read or write, it would be fairly easy for a dishonest person to manipulate records to the detriment of the sharecroppers. Ellen never wanted this sort of thing to happen. Sometimes problems developed, however.

Shooting craps and sipping moonshine can get you put in jail! Yes, one of the men sharecroppers learned it the hard way. On a Saturday night, several men were enjoying a little evening entertainment behind Ratliff's store. For some reason, the deputy sheriff showed up and saw what was going on; once they saw him, the men fled. Only one was caught and he was from the Shepard farm. The deputy sheriff took him to the Hinds County jail in Jackson and locked him up.

Word of the man's predicament was sent to his family on the farm and the woman of the sharecropper family came to Ellen. She sobbed telling what had happened and wondered how she should would get him home. Ellen said she would go and do what she could. She asked the woman (probably his common-law wife) and Ira to go with her. They left in a wagon early the next morning and got there before noon. Ellen explained to the jailer that they needed this man to work on the farm. He took them down a hallway between rows of cells with lonely and frightened prisoners. Prisoners (nearly all were black) reached out through the bars with extended arms and open hands; they just wanted to touch somebody from the outside. Near the end of the hall, they saw the man they wanted and he was happy to see them. Ellen found out that if she paid his fine of $13, the man would be released and could go back to Tinnin with them. The fine would be placed on the furnishings account that Ellen maintained and settled in the fall. Now, that was one happy man who would forever hold Ellen in high regard.

The farm operation continued much the same through the 1880s. Ira Lee matured in farming and management skills; Pa was slowed by aging, but his mind was still sharp. Of course, Ellen was always around to advise and assure that things went well.

Though the cash crops were doing okay, Ira felt that the farm needed to produce more of what the family needed, aka, to be more self-sufficient; Ellen agreed. The goal was to produce more of what they needed to live and, maybe, help the sharecroppers as well. The first action was to add new, young fruit trees to the orchard. The orchard was still much as it had been during the Civil War; the trees were getting old, and some had died. Ira and Ellen ordered 20 two-year-old fruit trees (5 apple, 10 peach, and 5 pear) from an out-of-state nursery. In addition, they got twelve improved pecan trees shipped from a nursery in southern Mississippi. The fruit trees were brought to Bolton by train by a man named Arthur Stone, who worked for the Green Tree Nursery Company in the mountains near Asheville, North Carolina. The train transported the trees as freight. A time was set, and Ira and Ellen went in a two-horse wagon to pick them up at the depot in Bolton. When they arrived at the depot, three other people were there to get trees, but they were soon gone. The only trees that remained outside on the platform were those that belonged to Ira and Ellen. They had brought the cash to pay for them and the freight.

Ellen noticed that the man who brought the trees was a nice person who apparently had some education. They chatted briefly about how to set out and care for the trees. For some reason, Ellen and Arthur clicked. He was a single man and interested in romance. Ellen wanted to know more about Arthur. She asked a couple of questions, such as where he lived and where he had gone to school. He asked her a few questions as well, such as if she was married and where she lived.

Arthur had to go on to Vicksburg and deliver another batch of trees. He would come back through Bolton on his way to North Carolina. He told Ellen that if someone would meet him in Bolton when the train came back, he would go to the farm and help set out the trees. He indicated that a shovel and some "old" horse manure from the barn would be needed to set them out. He said he would help shovel the manure into a wagon and help mix it with the soil to assure that nutrients were available for the trees to grow. He also said that the trees would need to be watered so that the roots were moist.

A check of the schedule revealed that the train was due back the next day at 9:36 a.m. Just when Arthur was boarding the train for Vicksburg, he touched Ellen's hand as a sign of interest in her; this made her feel good as well.

Back at the farm, Ellen and Ira unloaded the trees and put a little water on the wrapped roots to keep them in good condition until the next day when the trees were to be set out in the orchard. The next morning they were off to meet the 9:36 train. They didn't know if Arthur would show up but felt that his help would be good to have. He said he would do the work without pay as appreciation for their buying the trees.

The train arrived on schedule. Arthur got off with a small overnight bag. They rode to the farm. Arthur got right to work; he was fast and organized. Ellen and Ira helped. He knew how to move with a shovel in hauling horse manure and digging holes. He tried to follow good practices in setting out each tree. He dug the holes twice the size of the root mass; mixed manure with the soil; filled the hole around the roots, and created a small dike around each tree to hold water. Ira brought buckets of water from the spring branch. Pa came to the orchard and met Arthur just about the time the work was finished.

Arthur commented that this orchard site was an excellent location for fruit trees. He suggested that the orchard be expanded and produce fruit crops for the local market. He particularly liked peaches and apples for this area. He said he would be happy to work with the family on developing an orchard plan and getting this underway, if they had interest. Pa said he would talk with Ellen, Ira, and others about it.

It was now getting near noon. Arthur had to be back in Bolton for the 4:15 train that afternoon. Ellen asked him to have lunch and said that they would drive him back. Ma didn't have anything special prepared, but Arthur ate. He and Ellen sat together at the lunch table. There might have been a little twinkle in their eyes.

Over lunch, they talked about various things. The Shepards wanted to know about life in the mountains and about his family. He indicated that his wife was dead and his three children were adults and now gone from home. He said he was 45 years of age. Pa was inquisitive, as he had been in the past. He wanted to know details on a few things, such as work history, church going, and relationship with the law. Arthur said he had been in the fruit tree business about 20 years. All in all, he sounded pretty good to Pa and, of course, to Ellen. Then it was time to take him back to the depot in Bolton. They made it on time, and he caught the 4:15 train that would take him east where he would transfer to another train to go north to Asheville. Ellen told him to write her; likewise, he asked her to write him. They waved at each other as the train pulled out of sight.

Six days after Arthur boarded the train, she received a letter from him. Arthur was proposing that he come to Tinnin in a few weeks to talk about how to expand the orchard and add nut trees, specifically, pecans. She quickly wrote him back and said to come on--just let her know so that she could meet him in Clinton (closer than Bolton). Ellen quickly told her family that Arthur was coming to talk about fruits and nuts. As soon as those words were out of her mouth, Arthur was labeled as the fruit-and-nut man. Ellen didn't think it was too bad of a name if he actually showed up and provided good advice. Maybe there was also a romantic part.

Arthur came. He and the family talked about expanding the fruit-and-nut orchard. He gave specific suggestions about the kinds of trees to set out. He included how far to set them apart, how much manure to use in the holes that were dug, and how to water the small trees to assure that they lived. He said he would send another letter once home with the kinds of trees and offer a quote on cost. Ellen did have a few minutes of alone time with him in the orchard area near the dug well. Mostly, they talked about getting Ellen to travel to Asheville and visit the area where the fruit tree business was located.

Exciting! Maybe romance would blossom in her life once more. In about a week, she got another letter. But, as she opened and began to read the letter, she saw it was different. Arthur said he would be happy to help get the orchard expanded with quality fruit trees. However, he went on to say that he was now renewing a long-term relationship he had for several years with a woman who lived west of Asheville in a little place called Waynesboro. That sort of deflated Ellen and left her with an empty feeling the rest of the day.

Regardless, when Pa talked to Ellen and Ira about expanding the orchard to make it more productive, they decided not to do so. Ellen had a range of reasons, including lack of workers who knew about fruit production. No contact was made back with Arthur. The orchard was never expanded and maybe a good opportunity was missed, but times didn't seem to be right.

Ellen was seeking more in her personal life. Farm life was going well. She was so proud of the progress of her son.

After going to Mason Chapel for a few years, Ellen decided to venture into Clinton to the larger Baptist Church operated in association with Mississippi College and the two-year Institute for Women. The college had been disbanded and buildings deteriorated during the U.S. Civil War. Some buildings were used in the war effort, including use of the chapel as a hospital. After a few decades, recovery of the college was now underway. The Baptist Church expanded as the college regained status. It would take 15 to 20 minutes in a horse-drawn wagon. Wow! So different from the Presbyterian Church in Athens and from Mason Chapel. The Clinton community did not have a Presbyterian Church, which she would have preferred.

The Baptist Church had a larger congregation. Ellen observed that it appeared to superbly meet the faith and social needs of most of its long-term members; of others, not so well. She observed that how well the needs of people were met varied with commitment of the individuals to Baptist doctrine. She observed only one color of skin among its members: white. She thought a lot about skin color. She often pondered the questions: "Why couldn't all people worship together? Weren't those people who had other than white skin entitled to a good place to worship that met their needs?" She observed that people with other than white skin had a few places of their own "color" for worship. Occasionally, Ellen would talk to sharecropper families about faith and what it meant. No doubt, some of her feelings on skin color were shaped by the teachings of midwest-raised Pa.

Ellen also observed that only men were involved in leadership roles with the church; she always felt that women could do as well as men (and better than some). Certainly, she felt, God would not place men in positions of superiority over women and keep women from using their abilities. Right or wrong, she came to the realization of her own that long, long ago in Christianity, men themselves had structured things so that they could assume superior positions, i.e., be the bosses. She figured that they never relinquished that conviction and enjoyed keeping women subservient. She thought that as men promoted the idea that this was the way it was supposed to be, beliefs about this spilled over into secular laws and family living.

Some of the Clinton church members were farmers, but most had non-farm jobs with the institutes (colleges), schools, local stores, government, railroad, and cotton gin facilities. Overall, their level of education was a little higher than the average of the white people in the community. They had organized Sunday school classes, Sunday school papers, and other resources for learning. This experience helped Ellen further realize that the church was made up of people with different personalities, values, and beliefs, though all mainly followed Baptist doctrine.

A church service involved music, announcements about upcoming events (such as marriages) or happenings (such as recent deaths), Bible reading, testimonies, and a prepared message by the preacher. During the sometimes fiery sermons, one or more men might shout "Amen!" or "Tell "em!" Of course, there would be a time to take up collection; the preacher would even talk a minute or so about giving to the "Lord's work." He said he liked to see folks digging in purses and pockets for contributions. No service was complete without an altar call, also known as "come to Jesus time," to be "saved." Every week or so, one or two local people and a couple of students at the colleges would go down front and make a profession of faith. There would be a prayer, and the people who had just been "saved" would be told about a future baptism. The individuals would be introduced to the congregation and asked to stand near the exit door after the service to be greeted by church members. Ellen didn't always agree with the conservative tone of the sermons. Nevertheless, they were usually well prepared and provided useful information for her life.

Several groups were active at the church. Of course, she got into a Sunday school class. She was asked to assist the ordinance committee. Ellen could only assist; she could not be a committee member because she was not a member of the church. This didn't dampen her participation. She never had in mind joining this church. The ordinance committee prepared for communion, baptism, and similar special services in the church. Communion involved using tiny pieces of bread along with a small amount of wine. Ellen was a good worker. She would sometimes bake the unleavened bread used in communion. The wine was really only grape juice, though sometimes it might be on the borderline of fermentation. And people who took communion would often joke about the alcohol content of the wine having an influence on their thinking and walking.

Being involved with the ordinance committee gave her the opportunity to meet and work with a number of people. And, there was an unmarried male member of the ordinance committee who dressed well, was neatly groomed, and spoke language signaling education beyond normal in the local community. He apparently worked a job with a local college and earned a fairly good income. Ellen was intrigued by him and wanted to get to know him better.

His name: Rufus Barker. Maybe!

Another Life

Since returning to Tinnin, Ellen had experienced a renewed life. It was energetic and held potential for the future. But, she was always seeking new opportunities for herself, her son, and her parental family. Getting involved with church activities at the Baptist Church in Clinton resulted in meeting new people and having more social contacts outside her family and the Tinnin community.

This led to her becoming involved with groups or clubs; some were religious, and some were not. The adoption of new methods in the home and on the farm was often initiated in these groups or clubs. Some focused on education for a better life on the farm and in the home. Ellen kept thinking about what she could do to help Ira and Pa have more income and produce more food.

Nothing gained greater enthusiasm from Ellen than changes taking place in home food production and, secondly, farming. Some of the new implements and methods took years to be adopted in the rural areas of the South. These new developments made farm life a little easier and more productive. They also improved the use of foods produced on the farm and made vegetable gardening more beneficial.

Just prior to the U.S. Civil War, factory-made agricultural equipment had begun to rapidly come onto the farm scene in the North. The war, however, delayed its use in the South. Before the war, labor was plentiful on most farms in the South; thus, there was little need to reduce the hand labor required. The North had a big advantage in the use of new technology with many factories opening there. Some would say that the first American agricultural revolution occurred between 1862 and 1875. No doubt, new equipment promoted recovery from the war in the 1870s and 1880s once it reached the South. As more equipment was used, labor needs decreased. The loss of slave labor was an incentive to adopt labor-saving implements and methods. Animal power had largely replaced human power in preparing land and tilling crops. It would still be quite a while before engine (mechanical) power would replace animal power.

With a draft animal and an implement, such as a turning plow, one person on the Shepard farm could be much more productive than before. So, by 1890, many things based on animal power were available and being used. The Shepards already had iron plows and side-row cultivators. Ellen encouraged Ira and Pa to get a two-horse straddle-row cultivator, spring-tooth harrow, and seed drills/planters. Using these developments allowed them to get more production with less human effort. Agricultural leaders of the time were well aware of labor reductions. In 1850, it took 75 to 90 hours to produce 100 bushels of corn from 2.5 acres of land. By 1890, only 35 to 40 hours were required to produce 100 bushels of corn from the same amount of land. Labor hours per bale of cotton went down about the same, though cotton required much more labor than corn. That kind of information really impressed Ellen. She wanted to adopt all new technology that would help the farm and

family life. She was innovative in the use of much new technology based on animal power.

A limited supply of new implements was available for
the farms in the cotton-growing areas of the South. Ellen
and Ira would acquire what they could afford that they felt
had potential to improve productivity and reduce the need
for hard labor. The production of the sharecroppers had
become a major part of cash income on the farm. There
were four sharecropper families on the farm in the early
1890s. It was Ellen's notion that the sharecroppers needed
to be treated with respect and helped in their work. Buying
newly-developed farming tools would certainly be good.

Ellen's role in operating the farm was expanding. She
and Ira regularly supervised the sharecroppers in the fields.
Ellen was more involved with families in the barely-more-
than-shack houses. Most of the families had three or so
children. Ellen often had contact with the women, who
maintained their shack-like homes and worked a good deal
in the fields. She would sometimes talk about health, food,
and other family issues. She might help sick children get
the care of a doctor. She was very saddened when one family's few-months-old baby got sick and died without medical care. Lacking resources, the family quietly buried the
baby just off the front porch of their house under a tree.
Ellen found out only by asking the mother about the baby. No marker was placed, though people familiar with the
family knew what was under the little mound of earth in the
yard.

Ellen was helping Ira develop abilities with sharecroppers. She wanted him to care just as much about the well-
being of them and their families as he did about the farm
productivity of cotton, corn, and a few other crops. Share-

croppers were good people who had spiritual needs just like other people. With this in mind, Ellen helped share-croppers organize and establish a small Wells Church very near the Shepard farm. It affiliated itself with the African Methodist Episcopal Church. She donated a little money to help get it going. At first, it had a minister who led a service once a month. Other sharecropper families in Tinnin were also served by the church. When services were held, excited and loud singing and preaching could be heard for a mile or so around in the community.

Ellen also got into home food production. Preserving what was produced was important to her. She studied home canning using glass Mason jars, which were invented in 1858. It took many years for glass jars and canning techniques to become widespread in the South. Families had to have money to buy the jars, and they needed to know how to use them safely in food preservation. Glass jars were certainly handy when compared with the pottery containers used with some kinds of food preservation, such as fermenting, salting, and sugaring.

In the early 1890s and as an outgrowth of being involved with church, Ellen got into a canning group. They learned the differences in foods and how these differences affected canning (for example, tomatoes were said to be acidic, and snap beans were said not to be). They studied how to prepare foods for canning, how to use heat to destroy harmful bacteria, how to seal jars properly, and how to store canned food to prevent spoilage resulting in sickness of a person who might eat a spoiled food.

Jellies and preserves were popular items from wild berries, such as blackberries, and from farm-raised fruits, such as peaches and apples. They were prepared with heat and a great deal of sugar. The sugar acted as a preservative to prevent spoilage. Covered with a wax seal (layer on top), the sugar-based foods would keep several months, and maybe up to a year. People liked the sweetness of jellies and preserves, especially when spread on bread.

To some extent, Ellen became a local authority on canning among people in the Tinnin community. She taught some of her relatives and friends. People would ask her about canning and how to do it. She was sometimes asked to demonstrate in the homes of other people or to bring a sample of something she had canned.

A tragedy struck one day with an aunt who had learned about canning from Ellen. She had prepared snap beans and put them into jars. The jars and lids had been heating for a while in the small oven of a wood stove. It was amazing how hot a wood fire could be! She opened the oven door to check on things. A cool burst of air blew inside the hot oven, instantly causing one of the jars to explode. The force sent glass all around the oven and out the door. Some of the hot, jagged, sharp glass hit the woman's face. The hot fragments made deep cuts and burns. She was placed on a pallet in the back of a wagon and quickly transported to a doctor. He examined the burns and cuts and cleaned away the broken, jagged glass. There wasn't much more he could do. He sent her home and said she should take it easy for a few days. He suggested applying a bit of butter every now and then to soothe the wounds. Gradually the cuts and burns began to heal. It was obvious that her face would forever have deep scars which served as reminders of this canning tragedy. Word spread rapidly through the community. No one ever heated jars in an oven again. A hot-water bath in a large container was typically used until newer devices, such as pressure cookers, became available.

The canning accident really got Ellen's attention. She went to see her injured aunt several times (the woman lived only a couple of miles away and attended Mason Chapel). From then on, she was always very careful when telling people about heating jars. This accident frightened Ellen, and, she took a less active role in canning. She continued canning for her own home use but with great care for safety. As leader of the family, she was responsible for having food available at all times.

Ellen refocused on farm operation in the early 1890s. She always kept the records carefully and accurately. She learned how analysis could be used to identify crops and fields that produced the greatest cash returns. She had heard that there were specialists in such at the new Mississippi A&M College that could offer guidance in keeping and using records, but she did not make contact.

Ellen began analyzing possible farm alternatives. She occasionally mentioned her thoughts to Pa and Ira. She believed that the Shepard farm should begin producing more vegetables for the "city" market in nearby Jackson. The city had somewhat recovered from the destruction by Civil War armies and was making steady growth. Many people lived in town and, except for small yard beds, had little garden space. Their jobs also used most of the time that was needed to grow gardens of much size. She counted at least a dozen grocery stores that might be interested in selling fresh vegetables; it didn't seem that any other farm was regularly trying to meet potential demands. These stores were in the white part of town on Capital and State Streets and Robinson Road or side streets that crossed them. Many of the residents there worked in state government offices, banks, and related regular-paying jobs. Ellen's count did not include those stores in the Farish Street area mostly frequented at that time by black residents with lesser discretionary income.

Ellen developed an informal plan in her head and shared it with Pa and Ira for their input. Ma wasn't involved; her health was deteriorating fairly rapidly and much more so that Pa's. Ellen proposed beginning fresh vegetable production for the Jackson market. She named the stores she had identified and described how no farm was regularly providing fresh vegetables. She also stated that residents in the central part of Jackson had no opportunity for gardening of much size. Next, Ellen listed potential vegetable crops to grow by season of the year: spring: greens, potatoes, carrots, snap beans, English peas, and squash; summer: peas, butterbeans, okra, tomatoes, and squash; and fall: greens, root crops, and late English peas. She then went into the advantages of the land they had. Iit was fertile and the soil was loose and relatively easy to till. She thought that sharecropper families could be hired some of the time on a day basis to help produce and harvest the vegetables. This would not take them away from their major cash crop of cotton. Now, what did Pa and Ira think?

Pa was concerned that the vegetable production would cut into the cotton and corn production. Ellen explained that most of those crops were produced by sharecroppers who had a few extra days every now and then. She didn't see how the vegetable production would cut into their cotton work if they were occasionally hired on a daily basis. Further, cool season vegetable crop work would be at times of the year when cotton was not in the field. A benefit to the sharecroppers was that they needed a little extra money from day work. Ira was interested in how any vegetables might be delivered once produced. "By horse and wagon,"

Ellen said. That meant that he might get to take the wagon into town and go to various stores; he kind of liked the idea. Pa also wanted to know if the stores would actually buy vegetables from them for selling to customers. Ellen didn't know but agreed to check with a few next week when she went to the Hinds County courthouse to pay property taxes for the year. Discussion ended with agreement to try a few vegetable crops the first year and expand if they worked out okay.

The family would need to get the fields determined and decide on which vegetables. Pa suggested yellow crookneck squash, pole snap beans, okra, and, maybe, tomatoes. He also suggested that they plant a few acres of sweet potatoes for fall harvest and delivery to the grocery stores.

Ellen talked about another idea for expanding farm productivity. This one was mostly for consumption on the farm by themselves and sharecropper families. In addition to the chickens they already had, she mentioned keeping a few ducks, geese, guinea fowl, and turkeys for eggs and meat. Turkeys and guineas were most favorably viewed in early discussion. Guineas were hardy and had requirements about like chickens. Turkeys were very desirable for meat but were not quite so hardy, as they were subject to health problems. It was agreed to begin with guineas and delay turkeys for another year. The six guinea hens and one guinea rooster they got worked out well. Two of the hens sat on a nest of eggs and between them raised 11 young guineas. A few eggs were also available for use in cooking. Three of the young guineas were slaughtered when they were large enough. The guinea flock was increasing! After a year, turkeys were brought in and they didn't fare so well. Between predatory fox and disease, none survived the year.

Ellen had an even more compelling case for geese, especially weeder geese. She explained how they could be used to control weeds in cotton and other crops. She had investigated this and told how they would "work" from daylight to dark, 7 days a week, nipping troublesome grass and certain broadleaf weeds as they sprouted from the soil. Geese would occasionally eat insects that might be pests of cotton. The geese would not damage cotton plants. She said geese seldom get disease and that it was best to start with young goslings (about 6 weeks of age). Waterers and shade should be placed in a large field. Feeding them a little corn so that they will be eager to work in weeding was appropriate. She thought this could help conserve labor in chopping cotton. She also indicated that the young geese would grow and themselves be suitable for Christmas and other special meals.

Getting Pa and Ira to agree was not easy. They wanted to know what kept the geese from leaving a cotton field. They asked to visit a farm where weeder geese were used. No farms in the local area did so, but Ellen had heard of one a couple of miles north of Vicksburg. They agreed to ride the train to Vicksburg and see for themselves. Contacting the farm to arrange a visit was not easy; the farmer with the geese did not respond immediately to Ellen's letter. She would keep trying to reach him.

The yard around the Shepard house was stark and not very welcoming. Ellen had that on her mind since returning a few years before. The yard near the house had been made by scrapping the ground with a hoe so that no grass, weeds, or other vegetation grew. The ground was hard from years of scrapping and compaction. Some of the yard was shaded by the large, old cedar trees. She took it on herself to establish a few flowering plants around the yard. She liked woody shrub-type flowering plants such as crepe myrtle, camellia, and, most of all, gardenia. She liked bulbs including daffodils and tulips. Flowering annuals for the summer included zinnia and the poppy. She got a few cuttings of gardenias and camellias from neighbors and set about rooting them. She bought daffodil and tulip bulbs in the fall and zinnia and poppy seed in early spring at a mercantile store in Clinton.

Ellen understood that plants needed good place for their roots to grow. She used a shovel to hand dig three beds: one for zinnias, one for poppy, and another for daffodils and tulips. Holes were dug for planting the woody shrubs. She brought chicken manure from under the roost in the henhouse to add to the soil so there would be extra fertility for good plant growth. She was careful to add only enough manure--not too much, as it could burn the roots and reduce growth. She set out all that she had in the yard. Most things grew the first year. It would take a few years for the woody shrubs to flower. The bulbs and annuals flowered the first year. Of the annuals, she particularly liked the red poppies. They brought color and brightened the whole yard area. She planted more poppies the next year. It seems that everyone enjoyed the flowers that she had. She expanded the beds for poppies in subsequent years. (Note that the painting on the cover of this book depicts red poppies growing in the yard.)

A few years go by...

Not long into the decade of the 1890s, Pa seemed to be slowing down even more. Ma had already done so. Their health was gradually deteriorating. They were less able to move about. Their knees were not as strong and did not bend as well as in the past. Their feet were sometimes sore in ways not accustomed to. They seemed forgetful and put things in the wrong places. Occasionally they would attempt to do things they shouldn't, such as the time Pa was going to empty the slop jar into the water well, thinking it was one side of the two-holer; Ellen saw what was about to happen and rushed outside to stop it. He said he was just trying to be helpful. Though not contaminated, water was not used from that well for a while. Sometimes Pa and Ma both suffered shortness of breath and weakness. Occasionally, Ma had fainting spells. Ellen had to keep a close eye on them. More of the farm responsibilities were now on Ira's shoulders. He could handle them; he was now the farm manager.

Pa's health seemed to fail rapidly in late winter and early spring of 1895. By May, he could no longer walk on his own, nor could he control body functions. Dr. W. S. West, of Clinton, was called to the house. He said Pa appeared to have something he was just learning about called senile dementia. He explained that his brain no longer did what it was supposed to do in human life. Dr. West said to keep him comfortable, provide food and water, hand feed as needed, and try to remind him to frequently use the slop jar so that his clothing and bed would not regularly get soiled. That was about a full-time job for Ellen, but she, as with past situations, put forth extra effort.

On May 10, 1895, Dr. West was sent for, and he came to the house. He examined Pa and pronounced him dead. He had lived 81 years, which was a long life for a man born before 1850. Ma was beside herself; she just could not understand how her life could go on without Pa. She had sat by his bed continually for the last few days and offered food, water, and comfort. She slept very little. She loved George so much. She had worked side by side with him for years in running the home and farm. But, Ma, herself, was already showing more signs of failing health.

A mortician from Baldwin Funeral Home in Jackson assisted with arrangements, including bathing and dressing the body and moving it to Mason Chapel and then to the cemetery. The family parted from the tradition of bathing the body and dressing it themselves. Pa's body would be kept at home for visitation. A simple casket was used. It was placed in the front room with a fireplace. No one was currently sleeping in that room, and it had become sort of a parlor. A couple of neighbors took turns sitting up with the casket and body all night--a tradition in the community. Neighbors dug a grave in the Zachariah Ratliff Family Cemetery in Tinnin. The grave was in proximity to Ma's parents but with space for Ma to someday be buried between Pa and her mother and father.

The Shepard children were notified, and most arrived in time for the funeral. Ma, with help, was able to attend the service and go to the cemetery. Some family traveled a hundred miles or so to be present. All wanted to pay special tribute to Pa. A few people brought flowers from their yards to place on the burial site.

It was May 15 by the time the service was held. Ira went early to check on the crops that morning. Quite a coincidence that day: The first cotton bloom of the year had opened. It was a beautiful white in the early morning, and he knew it would turn pink by the time of the funeral. Never before had there been such a beautiful bloom this early in the cotton-growing season. Wonder why it occurred on the day of Pa's funeral? It was the funeral of the man who had farmed the land a little more than 50 years. Ira picked the bloom and took it to Mason Chapel for all to see. He placed it on the lapel of the jacket that Pa wore--so touching! It was closed in the casket and buried with the body. This was a very fitting thing to do because life all these years in Tinnin had depended on cotton to produce a crop that could be sold for cash. Pa would always say, "You have to have blooms in order to have cotton, and the more the better."

Pastor Summer held a funeral service at Mason Chapel, followed by a short grave-side service at the Zachariah Ratliff Family Cemetery in Tinnin. He talked about how George W. Shepard was a man of high moral character; promoted equality among all people, even though it wasn't the popular thing to do; and was a good farmer and steward of the land. One of the things he mentioned was Pa's love of farming, especially cotton. He said an interest in cotton farming was amazing for a man from Indiana. Then he told about Ira picking the first cotton bloom of the year from the field earlier that day. Was it a sign of some sort? Did it signal a loss? Not a dry eye remained in the crowd. Pastor Summer conducted a dignified service that included the congregation singing a couple of hymns, one of them Pa's favorite, "Amazing Grace."

Ellen increasingly became the leader of the family. Without Pa, Ira at age 27 would become head of the household. This was quite important in those times, when men enjoyed greater authority than women. Regardless, Ira just about always deferred to his Mama. She was wise and experienced, and she knew how to assess possibilities, determine risks, and make good decisions. Her life with husband Jasper and as a single woman for more than a decade after his death in Texas taught her a lot about the world. Ira and his mother never had differences of opinion that resulted in heated situations.

Almost immediately after Pa's funeral, Ma had a spell, and Dr. West was summoned. Ma was under his care for much of the summer, with the need increasing in July and August of 1895. In those two months, Dr. West made 14 house calls to the Shepard home to administer to her needs and see if something could be found to reverse her failing health. Ellen stayed close to her bedside except when one of her sisters could be present. But, Ma was in serious condition. The physician had a hard time being specific about her health issues. He thought maybe it was blood sugar problems, kidney failure, or circulatory problems.

Dr. West visited four days in a row the last of August and pronounced Ma dead on August 31, 1895. No death certificate was filed because it was not required by law; therefore, the cause of death is unknown. Ma, in general, had deteriorating health and failed to thrive. Dr. West charged $2.50 for each house visit but only $1.50 on the day he pronounced her dead. No records of any medicines were kept. Dr. West administered some medicines as part of the care he provided during some of his visits. The last days of Ma's life likely included the administration of paregoric (a sedative) to lessen pain. No one wanted Ma to suffer in pain as her life was ending.

Plans were made for Ma's funeral. She would be buried alongside her husband and near her mother and father in the Zachariah Ratliff Family Cemetery. A walnut wood casket lined with velvet was bought at Baldwin Funeral Home in Jackson and delivered to the Shepard home. A mortician would handle details, such as bathing and dressing the body. Plans were that the body would lie in state in the home for a couple of days before burial. As with Pa, a couple of neighbors sat up all night with the body. All of Ma's daughters and her son were notified, and they made every effort to attend the funeral, along with their spouses and children. Ellen greeted mourners at the home. Ira assisted as he could.

The morning before the service, Ira went to one of Ma's favorite places on the spring branch near a cotton patch. Ma would sometimes work in the patch when she could get some time away from the house. A couple of shade trees not far away made it kind of a cool, restful place. Ira picked an open cotton boll with glistening white locks of seed cotton. He placed the open boll in the casket on her right shoulder, similar to what he had' done with Pa and the cotton bloom.

As with Pa, Pastor Summer conducted a memorial service at Mason Chapel. Held on September 3, 1895, the service was composed of an opening prayer; Ma's favorite Bible scripture, the Twenty-Third Psalm; a couple of her favorite hymns; a message; and a closing prayer. The message included facts about Ma, such as her place of birth, the name of her husband, the number and names of children and grandchildren, and her strong role as a mother. The preacher mentioned that an open cotton boll had been brought from a patch near her favorite spot on the spring branch. A short grave side service followed. Ma was buried in the space that was left between Pa's grave and her father's in the Zachariah Ratliff Family Cemetery in Tinnin, Mississippi.

Engraved granite markers were ordered and installed at both Pa's and Ma's graves. The engraving on each included full name, date of birth, and date of death. The two markers were placed on solid ground. After about four years, the settling of the graves resulted in the markers leaning and tipping over. Ellen saw the condition, and the next day dispatched Ira and one of the sharecroppers to upright and stabilize the markers. They did the best they could with this job, but settling continued. Maybe it was also due to the shifting nature of the earth (loess soil over limestone rock) in the area.

The Shepard house at one time was home to a large family, and sometimes an extended family. Now, for the first time, no Shepard lived there. Ellen and Ira were the only occupants. Their last name was Lee, though Ellen could profess she was a Shepard. Things around the house became kind of sad. There wasn't much activity. Ellen's and Ira's minds began to turn to thoughts of what might be in store with the turn of the century. The year 1900 was only a few years away.

Ellen was quite busy with closing the estates of Ma and Pa, as well as keeping the house up. Ira was busy with the crops and overseeing the sharecroppers. Neither Pa nor Ma had a will. Ellen had learned that his was not a good idea. Ellen knew that both should, but she was not able to persuade either of them to have one drawn up by a qualified lawyer. They would say it would cost too much money. Or, maybe Pa and Ma found it difficult to make decisions about the distribution of their possessions among their children. One might feel shorted.

A couple of months after Ma's death, the group of siblings gathered at the home to discuss final estate details. Personal effects were fairly easy to handle; each child or child's heir got something. Furniture and the like stayed with the house. Animals on the farm and unharvested crops had value and needed to be settled. Ira and Ellen were to move forward with harvest and with the sharecroppers. Since Ira and Ellen already owned some of the animals, there was no urgency to deal with them, but those they didn't own were to be purchased or sold. Money derived over the fall from the farm was to be divided among the heirs. Ellen and Ira were to keep records of all harvests and sales.

Ellen knew the importance of properly handling the estate. She had experienced a bad situation in Texas when her Jasper died. She talked with a lawyer in Clinton about the legal aspects of settling the estate. He explained that, under Mississippi law, each of the Shepard children was entitled to an equal share of the estate. Three daughters were dead and their heirs were entitled to a share of the estate. One son, James Alexander Shepard, died quite young without any heirs, so his share would be divided among the other siblings or their heirs. Ellen and Ira agreed that the lawyer would prepare the needed paperwork and guide them as they went along. This was not going to be nearly so long and drawn out as the experience in Texas settling Jasper's estate.

The major estate item was the farm and the home and outbuildings on it. Ellen and Ira needed the home for living. No decision was made immediately. The heirs agreed to discuss it at another time. Until then, Ellen and Ira would continue just as they had been. A year passed, and the siblings had a reunion. They again talked about what to do with the farm.

A range of opinions were offered, but it was agreed that Ira, with support from his mother, would go about buying out each heir's share of the property. Each would have an acreage of equal value based on the going rate of farm land. Georgia Ann Shepard Bell was dead, so her spouse at the time of her death (Nelson Bell) in 1878 would be the heir. Margaret "Mag" Shepard Shields died in childbirth in

1885 (she had three sons who were abandoned by their father, Dick Shields, to B. F. Mulholland of Brandon for raising. These sons were her heirs). Sarah Sallie Shepard Gary
and her husband Pinkney Gary died in 1878 in the yellow
fever epidemic; she had no heirs. Naomi R. Shepard Bunyard married James Pinky Bunyard in 1877 and died in the
same 1878 yellow fever epidemic as her sister Sarah; she
had no heirs at the time the estate was settled. Ellen would
help Ira get things figured out. He would use the services of
a bank to borrow the needed money. Discussion went back
and forth on some things. In the end, everyone seemed to
agree. Ira began to make arrangements to get the money he
needed.

Ira was able to make land payments so that all was covered by the end of 1899 or shortly thereafter. His mother
did not ask for a payment. The approximately 400 acres of
farm property would be all his; this sounded good to him.
Making the payments might require extra attention to saving money all year. A receipt in the family records from B. F.
Mulholland, of Brandon, dated January 14, 1899, shows the
following: "Received of Ira J. Lee the sum of seventeen dollars and fifty cents, this being the amount due as interest
on the Shields boys portion of the Shepard estate at 10% interest for the year 1898." (Mag was the boys' mother.) Documents also included banking receipts and statements from
the Bank of Brandon and the Bank of Pocahontas.

The Shepard surname would continue in the Mississippi
Delta, though the big house in Tinnin had no one with that
name living there. Ira W. Shepard, who lived in Sunflower
County, wrote Ellen on July 11, 1898, that he had a new
son born June 30. The birth was difficult.He state that a
Dr. Donald from Indianola had to be summoned to deliver
the baby. The letter indicated that the doctor put Ella un-

der the influence of chloroform and used instruments to make the delivery. The baby weighed 8 pounds. Dr. Donald charged $20, which Ira W. stated was good money spent; otherwise, Ella would have died.

In the same July 11, 1898, letter, Ira W. Shepard wrote about the war between Spain and the United States. Apparently an acquaintance from Sunflower County was in the army involved in the fighting. But, how would this war be so much on his mind? Maybe it was a memory from his experiences when soldiers came through the Shepard farm in Tinnin during the U.S. Civil War. His letter stated:

Sis, the war is getting very hot. I am afraid the whole world will be in before it ends. The Spaniards are making it pretty hot for the Americans. They had a very bloody fight last week. A great many Americans were killed. Surely, England will go with us.

Ira W. was referring to the Spanish-American War over independence for Cuba. The war was prompted by the sinking of the battleship Maine in the harbor of Havana and lasted 10 weeks in the summer of 1898. Hostilities spread around the globe. The Spanish empire collapsed afterward. It is amazing how Ira W. could have been so well informed about the war when he lived far away in rural Sunflower County! Maybe telegraphy or a letter from a friend in the army gave him the information.

Ira J. Lee appeared to be developing a health issue. He was increasingly having difficulties breathing. He was only 30 years of age when Doctor W. W. Farr, of Bolton, Mississippi, wrote a medical statement on November 12, 1898, as follows: "I hereby certify that Mr. Ira Lee is within my charge as a patient and is unfit for road service." Though not cited in this statement, it appears that his health issue was related to asthma and not tuberculosis. Statements by family members (now deceased) who knew him spoke of his bouts with asthma. Road service had to do with citizens keeping up the roads (trails) that were in rural areas. County governments did not have road departments that maintained rural roads. Medication and life style allowed Ira to live more than 40 additional years.

In the years immediately after the death of Pa and Ma, some changes were made on the farm. The number of sharecroppers was reduced to three families. Some of the change resulted from a tragedy. Midmorning on a Wednesday as the adults of the Davis Trimm family were away from home in the field, a small child decided to add wood to the coals in the fireplace. In doing so, the piece of wood knocked a red hot coal out across the hearth onto the wooden board floor. In a few minutes, the coal had ignited the wood and a blaze ensued. The child knew there was a problem and got the other two children outside as the flames began to engulf the structure. Ellen happened to peer out a window in the Shepard-Lee home and saw the flames. She dashed up the hill to the house that was now almost totally consumed. The children were safe; she took them with her to the field to tell the adults. Now this family really had very little; even that was lost. Ellen arranged for clothing, a few home furnishings, some food, and a place to live in an older house on the farm. She even gave them a little money to help with this disaster.

At the end of the crop year, the Davis Trimm family decided to no longer sharecrop on the Shepard farm. It had found another farm and moved. This saddened Ellen and Ira, but they thought it might turn out to be a good idea because of the need for supervision, as only Ellen and Ira were available. Ellen also provided family support and the furnishing that was made available throughout the year for living.

The production of vegetables was about ended. Some for use by the family and sharecropper families were continued. Labor to produce vegetables was simply not available. Ira didn't have time to make deliveries to the grocery stores in Jackson. In addition to the garden vegetables, sweet potatoes and pinda were grown. These were popular with the sharecroppers. Ellen and Ira also liked them. Other farm-produced food crops included honey, chicken and guinea eggs, cow's milk, and pork. Pork was produced only in cool months, however, because no refrigeration was available to keep the meat from spoiling. In cool months, pork could be smoked and salted as ways to keep it safe to eat.

A possible new crop that Ellen and Ira had thought about was sugar cane. They had some land that they thought would be productive in sugar cane. Sharecroppers could be hired as day labor to grow, harvest, and process the cane into syrup. Some new equipment would be needed, such as a roller juice extractor and a large pan over the wood-fired oven for cooking the juice. Ellen and Ira agreed that he would investigate the possibilities, including costs. Income could be gained from selling the molasses syrup and a limited number of whole stalks of cane for chewing through the grocery stores in Jackson that had taken some of their vegetables.

Something was happening in Ira's life that caused him some distraction from farming. He had met a young woman who stirred a romantic flame in him. A serious courtship developed in 1899 between Ira and Carrie Cheers Hendrick, who lived on a farm in a nearby German community in Madison County. Ellen thought this relationship was probably a good idea. She had met Carrie and considered her to be a good fit for the family. After all, Ira was now 31 years of age. He should be sufficiently mature to wisely choose a life partner.

Ellen encouraged Ira and Carrie to include life on the new Lee farm in any plans they might make. Yes, the name had changed when Ira paid off the Shepard heirs and changed legal records in the Hinds County courthouse. Ellen was proud that this had been done. This helped assure the future for the old Shepard place, which had now been in existence more than 60 years. And, of course, Ellen planned to continue living on the farm in the big house her father had built in 1857.

Was Ellen about to give up on romance in her life? A man she met at the Baptist Church in Clinton some time ago briefly got her attention. His name was Rufus Barker, and there was a hint of potential romance.

What about the seemingly nice man? She talked with him a little; he was a gentleman with education and a good job, and he appeared to be considerate of others. Things never clicked between them, however. He was too "churchy," Ellen thought. She knew to watch out for individuals of this type. They were likely hiding some sort of mean spirit, such as she had seen in Texas. Ellen was busy with things in Tinnin and did not give the time for in-depth assessment of "Mr. Churchy." Of course, she had Mason Chapel there close to her home and was now back much more involved with it.

A New Household

Ira and his sweetheart became engaged in May 1900. Carrie Cheers Hendrick was an attractive 18-year-old farm woman. She was born in Coahoma County in the Delta area of Mississippi and grew up in the hills of a German community known as Gluckstadt in Madison County. Though she had some wonderful traits, she could certainly have used some polish in how to get along with people.

Courtship lasted about a year. Ira and Carrie were busy with plans for a future together. Their planning involved moving forward with the new Lee farm and living in the old Shepard house. During the course of the year, Ellen's sister Rachel and her 12-year-old daughter, Addie, had moved back because of a failed marriage (word was that her husband had taken up with another woman). These two additional individuals took a little more space in the house, but it was still plenty large for a newly married couple.

In June 1900 the U.S. Federal Census enumerator came by the Lee place in the Tinnin community. He gathered information from Ira, the head of the household. The Census report indicated that four people lived in the house: Ira, Ellen, Rachel, and Addie. A blended-generation family had mostly lived in the house for the past quarter century. In another year, there would be an additional person. And, beyond that, maybe a new, younger generation.

Ira and Carrie were married on August 7, 1901. Her mother Louvenia Stone Hendrick, attended the wedding but her father, William Hendrick did not because he was in the State Insane Asylum in Jackson, Mississippi (why and how long he was there is unknown). Ira's mother, her sister Rachel, and Rachel's daughter, Addie Conrad attended. Ellen likely had some reservations about the marriage but, she thought Ira was old enough to make his own decisions. There is no evidence that Ira had a previous sweetheart. The newly weds had no honeymoon travel or anything; trains and ships were big in some places but not in Tinnin. They would be at their home.

There wasn't much time in the summer to take a break from work on the farm, but early August provided a couple of weeks of slower pace. The crops were mostly laid by, and harvest would get underway in early September. The slower pace allowed the couple to get everything all set in their part of the home for their "comfortable" living. It also allowed Ellen, Rachel, and Addie to adjust to a newly married couple being present in the house. Of course, Ira had lived there for about 20 years and had grown to adulthood there. With the new bride, somewhat of a division of responsibilities was thought to be needed, but making it work was not so easy.

A challenge for Ellen was how to get along with Carrie, who could be very sweet and nice. One moment she could really turn on the charm. But, at another time, her unpleasant personality would be evident. This was true from near the beginning of the marriage. It appeared that she would not be easy to deal with. Rachel and Addie also saw the two sides of Carrie. Ira appeared to always get along with her reasonably well; she deferred to him as the male head of the household. Wasn't that what all women were supposed to do in 1901?

Adjusting to Carrie took some effort from everyone, including the sharecroppers (she made a couple of negative statements to them). Besides not being able to get along with people, Carrie also preferred not to do much housework and cooking. A few housekeeping issues related to her and Ira's part of the house included not sweeping the floor, letting the fireplace and wood-burning stove accumulate too many ashes, and allowing the guard dog, barn cat, and a few hens to come inside the house. She would do enough cleaning to get by in her and Ira's quarters and not much elsewhere in a house that five people shared. Most cleaning was left to Ellen and Rachel. Of course, Carrie found ways to avoid work on the farm and around the barns. She was sometimes grumpy with the sharecroppers and their families, and this did not build good will. Making friends in the community was a challenge to her. Ellen began to wonder if this marriage was going to work out; she didn't want Ira to have a failed marriage. There was never any notion that Ira did not have a strong commitment to Carrie even though the two of them did not see eye-to-eye on many things.

Why was Carrie so difficult? Ellen thought that maybe it was just her personality; but then she thought it might be something else. Of course, personality is shaped by the environment of an individual in their young, formative years. Her father had problems; maybe he was an alcoholic, as were many men in the South following the U.S. Civil War. Another thought some people had was that Carrie was abused as a child. We know that one of Carrie's daughters as a mature adult spend time at Whitfield--the new state mental institution. We also know that another of Carrie's children was diagnosed by a medical professional as having been sexually abused as a child. In terms of Carrie, we can only propose these few possible explanations.

Fall was moving toward winter. Life on the farm revolved around crop seasons. By now, most crops were harvested. Some of the cotton, though picked, still needed to be ginned. Sweet potatoes and pecans needed to be harvested. A couple of good-quality, extra-fat pigs were being fed to reach more than 150 pounds by November in preparation for slaughter once the weather was cold. That was usually about late November or early December. Cold weather was needed to maintain the meat until it was seasoned or smoked to prevent spoilage. Christmastime would soon be at hand.

Just about the time folks were somewhat adjusting to Carrie in the house, she announced, after a little more than three months of marriage, that she thought she was pregnant. That kind of changed some of the attitude toward her. Ellen was excited to know that she would soon be a grandmother. Ira was happy (he was looking forward to a son). Ellen was hoping that if the baby was a girl, her name would include Ellen, and that if it was a boy, his name would include Jasper. Carrie's pregnancy progressed normally, but there were times when she took advantage of her "condition."

Ira knew that a new baby would require a little money. Figuring out how he could get it might become a bit of a problem. He went about operating the farm much as usual in the 1902 cropping season. Sometimes Carrie would seek attention as a pregnant woman and disrupt things a bit. In early summer, they took some advance income on cotton that would be harvested in the fall to buy a few things needed for the baby. One thing, in particular, was a wooden crib with rockers and a thin pad on the bottom. The rocker crib would serve this baby and any future babies and generations. It was a nice, sturdy crib. The only problem with it was that it might turn over if rocked too vigorously. The baby in it would fall out and, possibly, injure itself.

Though Ira wanted his mother to assist with the birth when the time came, she said no. There was a midwife in the community. When Carrie appeared to be going into labor, the midwife was summoned. She observed the situation and announced that a doctor was needed. Dr. E. B. Poole came from Clinton to deliver the baby on August 20, 1902; he charged $20 for the home delivery. The baby was a healthy girl. Carrie and Ira had decided ahead of time that it would be named Ellen Louvenia Lee if it were a girl; they had also chosen a name for a boy if needed. Everyone was happy about a daughter/granddaughter, though Ira had spoken of wanting a son. No doubt Ira was hoping for a boy who would grow up and become a major part of the farm work. Grandmother Ellen was delighted with the name.

Carrie was 20 years of age when she became a first-time mother. The baby's father, Ira, was 34 years of age when baby Ellen was born. New grandmother Ellen was 54. Both Ira and Ellen were somewhat older than they thought they would be with a firstborn child and grandchild. Generations change; ages of marriage and parenting sometimes change. For example, men tended to be several years older than women in marriages; younger women supposedly liked older men because they brought them security. Ellen was 16 and Jasper was 37 when they married. Ellen was approaching 19 years of age when her son, Ira, was born and close to the same age as Carrie. Jasper was nearly 40. With a newborn, some age differentials did not dampen spirits or interest in caring for a baby.

Carrie cared for new baby Ellen Louvenia Lee. She nursed her; changed her diaper for the first few days, held her in a comforting manner, and otherwise cared for her. Then she grew impatient and tired with some of the routines required in mothering. She got other people to care for and rock the baby. Maybe she was suffering from something that many years later would be called postpartum depression. At first, grandmother Ellen was happy to be involved. Later, she tried to teach and motivate Carrie as a mother to do what was needed; success was slow. After all, the baby was the responsibility of Carrie and Ira.

Somehow it seemed that Carrie did not want to do any more than was essential for the health of baby Ellen Louvenia. Of course, she breast-fed the baby; no wet nursing was involved (there was a sharecropper woman on the farm who could have served as a wet nurse). One biological factor that was likely fortunate for Carrie and Ira was that lactating tends to reduce fertility and delay the next pregnancy a bit.

As baby Ellen developed, began walking and started speaking a few words, her grandmother Ellen would take her to church or to stores in Tinnin, Clinton, or Pocahontas. They developed quite a bond. Grandmother was trying to help baby Ellen grow and develop a personality of kindness and caring. Sometimes baby Ellen would get a new dress, compliments of her grandmother. She was a beautiful two-year-old little girl!

Ellen was observing that attendance at Mason Chapel had dwindled to a very few individuals. All appearance was that it would soon close; some members had already started going into Clinton, and others into Pocahontas. Ellen and Rachel decided that they would become involved with the Pocahontas Methodist Episcopal Church. Pocahontas was a tiny community where they took cotton for ginning, bought supplies at a mercantile store, and had gotten to know some of the people. The Methodist Church had begun several years before in a vacant house on the Lane plantation. In 1902, a new church building was built in Pocahontas. It really looked like a church of the time, with a steeple, double front door, and large, ornate windows. Men's and women's privies were to one side behind the building. A new cemetery was being started several yards behind the church. The church in Pocahontas was a longer wagon ride to get to it from home than Mason Chapel, but it had some appealing features. This was a church that Ellen enjoyed and one in which she became more secure as a Christian believer.

Soon after going and aligning herself with the Pocahontas ME Church, Ellen invited the minister to have Sunday dinner with her, Ira and Carrie, and Rachel and Addie Conrad. The new minister, Reverend Presley, accepted the invitation. Ellen worked hard on the previous Saturday getting ready for the preacher. To some extent, Ellen's mind drifted back to Easter Sunday in 1863 when her parents had the minister over for dinner just before the Union troops came storming through. Ellen just about had everything ready. Food preparation was well underway--every preacher was served fried yard-bird chicken and vegetables to go with it. She knew some last-minute things would need to be fixed on Sunday, such as boiled rice. The floors were clean, cobwebs were swept from the ceilings on the porches, and a fresh Sears catalog was in the privy.

For some reason, Carrie did not like what was happening and the notion that the preacher was coming to the house she lived in (but not to her living quarters). Ellen had invited everyone who was at the house to be there for dinner and had talked with Carrie about how she was preparing. In somewhat of a fit of rage, Carrie took a pan of dirty dishwater and poured it over the floor around the dining table. Ellen became furious at this, but she didn't confront Carrie about it. Ellen got a mop and started cleaning up the floor. It took a while to get the floor reasonably clean again. Fortunately, there were no more incidents at this time.

Everyone, including baby Ellen, went to the Pocahontas ME Church that Sunday morning. They participated in the worship service and departed quickly afterward for home. Of course, Ellen checked with Reverend Presley to remind him of the dinner. When home, Ellen worked feverishly to get everything ready, while Carrie sat on the front porch with baby Ellen. Rachel and Addie also helped; Ira was out checking on crops.

About 1:30 that afternoon, Reverend Presley came down the hill in a nice one-horse carriage. (Why was it that preachers around Tinnin always had nice horses and carriages?) He pulled up to the front gate and hitched the horse. He walked to the front porch and was first greeted by Carrie. Oh, how she hugged him and poured out her personality! She told him how wonderful his sermon was and that she was so happy to have him at her home for dinner. Every other person greeted him afterward. He was invited inside to the dinner table, where everyone took a seat. Carrie began as if she were the hostess entitled to welcoming the preacher, asking him to say a blessing and offering food to him, beginning with the fried yard-bird chicken. Ellen let her get away with this behavior; she thought it was far better than a confrontation while the preacher was there. As the meal ended, the preacher thanked Carrie for the wonderful meal and thanked all others there for inviting him. Ellen and Rachel washed all the dishes after the preacher left. Carrie had gone back to sit on the front porch.

In early 1905, Carrie was again pregnant. Ira just knew that this baby was going to be a boy. All went well during pregnancy. With the help of a midwife, Carrie gave birth to a baby girl on May 20 of that year. The baby was named Sudie Willie Lee. No one knew where Carrie and Ira got the name; it was not used in the family. Ira was upset that Carrie had a girl--probably something she had eaten, he said. He vowed to change what Carrie ate before another baby. Anyway, Sudie Willie thrived with limited care from her mother, but of course her grandmother was always there. Baby Ellen was now reaching three years of age.

It was Ira's contention that girl babies just resulted in more field work for the men. Maybe not so much at a young age, but as they got older, they required more clothing, food, and the like. A girl was not expected to work in the fields as much as a boy. Some women worked part-time in the fields; however, they could not usually work full-time because they had responsibilities around their homes.

Grandmother Ellen enjoyed watching her granddaughters grow and develop. She continued to take the older Ellen to special little places. But, there was work to do to maintain the home, prepare meals, gather eggs, and help look after the garden. Just as in past years, Ellen continued to support the sharecropper families and help them have better lives. For some reason, though, Ellen did not feel as energetic as in the past. However, she still felt good and went about her daily chores. Ira suggested that she see a doctor, but she chose not to.

Another one on the way! About the time Sudie was 14 months of age, Carrie was again pregnant. When the date of giving birth was a couple of months away, Ira began trying to make certain that the new baby was a boy. He thought he had all the girl babies he wanted.

On one of Ira's trips delivering a wagonload of sweet potatoes to a couple of grocery stores in Jackson, Mississippi, he rode along Farrish Street. He saw a "New Orleans" store and two voodoo and hoodoo shops. Though the distance from New Orleans and Atlanta, where voodoo queens were well known, wasn't that great, these probably weren't much more than cheap fortune-teller places. One shop had a lot of signs: "Get Rich," "Stay Healthy," "Have Good Crops," and "Catch the Big Fish." A sign that really got his attention was "Get the Baby You Want." Ira stopped the wagon, hitched the horses, and went inside. He had never seen anything like it. The shop had unusual pottery and paraphernalia on its shelves around the walls that, together with silk cloths and burning incense, created a unique atmosphere.

The voodoo queen, in an apparent or imitated trance, was selling and administering magical powders and charms. She had a big glass ball and was dressed in a way he had never before seen. The queen spoke in language he had never before heard but could understand (combination of Cajun and Gullah). The queen asked if he had matters to be discussed or things he wanted advice on. She said that she could do almost everything that a well-known New Orleans voodoo queen could do based on African spiritual folkways. For a dollar, she would give the answer to one of his questions. So, Ira wanted a boy, and no one would miss the dollar. After payment, the conversation began.

The voodoo queen wanted to know the matter. Ira said, "I want a baby boy. I have only girls." The voodoo queen asked if he had a wife. He answered, "Yes." She asked if his wife was "with child." He said, "Yes, she told me she was 'with child.'" The queen proceeded by saying that since she was already "with child," the baby was "set." He could, however, do some things. She never said that what he would do would make a bit of difference. Ira was gullible about this.

The voodoo queen, with very strong confidence about getting a boy baby, said for his wife to be very choosey about the kinds and sources of the foods she ate. The voodoo queen said for her to eat cooked pig's liver from a male hog. This was the most important thing. She should eat the liver regularly or at least several times a week. She should eat other meats only from male animals, such as roosters and bulls. She gave Ira a small package of some sort of granular powder for his wife to sprinkle on her food. The queen mumbled something about the powder containing ground ram horns and salt.

The voodoo queen told him that she would tell him some more for another 50 cents. This had been sounding so good to Ira that he dug the coins out of his pocket. She continued with instructions: In addition to the expectant mother's eating only meat of male animals, she should dig a few sassafras roots in early February and boil them in water to make tea. She should season the tea with a small amount of tallow from a male animal. The queen also gave Ira a very small amount of a shredded leaf-like material to sprinkle on his wife's tea. It was said to be from the leaves of a male gingko tree.

In the end, the voodoo queen poured a bit of fragrant incense into a small bowl and blew on the surface of the liquid so that fragrance increased. As the incense was rising, she majestically waved her hands and magic wand above it. She said a goodby and told Ira to keep a positive attitude about the baby. Ira felt happy all the way home. The queen also said that he might come back to consult with her the next time he was on Farrish Street. The special treatment that she could provide next time would cost only a dollar. She further said that the treatment had guaranteed results, but she never said what the results would be.

Had Ira done what he needed to do to have a boy baby? The horses and wagon made the trip back to Tinnin in a little less than three hours. Ira told Carrie what to eat and went so far as to slaughter a small male pig to get the liver and other flesh. He made her some sassafras tea and sprinkled some of the ground leafy substance on it. He also put some of the potion of ground ram horns on the only small piece of male pork liver he was ever able to get her to eat.

Time for the delivery of another baby was at hand. Would Ira's magical efforts to get a boy work? He was concerned that his wife didn't follow the instructions very well. If he tried to talk to her about, she became sullen and "bullheaded." On March 1, 1907, Ivie Carrie Lee was born. Just as with the previous two babies, she was born right there in their home and was healthy. Ira could not believe that the baby was a girl; he felt that he had done all he could but admitted that he didn't understand all that was involved. He felt the voodoo queen had let him down (but he never told anyone about this silly encounter on Farrish Street).

Three babies created additional demands on the household. Also, changes were taking place with other people. Addie, Rachel's daughter, got married and moved to live with her husband in the Mississippi Delta. Rachel decided to go live with them when their first baby was due. Rachel thought maybe she could help with the baby or on the farm that her daughter's husband was starting. Maybe, she wanted to escape some of the noise, activity, and rudeness she had been living amongst.

If all-girl babies wasn't enough for Ira (and he learned to really love girls), he now had the additional issue of the arrival of the cotton boll weevil. The boll weevil entered the U.S. from Mexico in 1892 and traveled 40-160 miles a year across cotton-growing areas. Ira first noticed punctured cotton squares and bolls in 1908. This activity by the weevils destroyed squares and bolls reducing cotton yield--not so much the first year but a little more in years after. Various home-prepared approaches were tried to prevent loss, such as sprinkling ashes from the fireplaces on cotton plants. Soon various commercial insecticides became available. These were used to some extent but the cost cut into profit. The boll weevil was a huge issue throughout all cotton growing areas and resulted in the price received for cotton increasing. Fortunately, damage most years to Ira's crop was minimal.

More than three years went by before Carrie again thought she was pregnant. Ira asked her how she knew; she mumbled a few things. He reminded her that while she was "with child," she should regularly eat liver from a male pig and eat only meat from male animals (no hens, sows or cows). He wanted a boy but resigned himself to taking whichever. He had talked to some farm folks in the community about a possible curse on him that had resulted in having only girl babies. They had several thoughts about what to do, but none that he believed would work. He figured that if high-priced voodoo didn't work, nothing would. Anyway, he had grown to love the three daughters he had. If he could just get them old enough and motivated to go to the fields!

On August 20, 1910, a baby boy was born--same day of the month as Ellen Louvenia was born. Ira was so proud to have a boy; he took a peek at it between its legs just to be sure. Ira harnessed a horse to the one-horse wagon and dashed around the Tinnin community telling everyone he saw: "I have a boy! I have a boy! I have a boy!" The boy was named Jasper Henry Lee. Ellen went on and on about how wonderful that name was. She talked about her husband, Jasper, and that the name was the same as Ira's father's name. Further, Jasper was a longtime given name used with the Lee surname all the way back to England.

Now, there were four little ones in the home. Managing them could be a challenge. They had a mother who wasn't always energetic, patient, or considerate. One of the things Carrie did after the babies were several months of age was to put long dresses on them; both the girls and the boy wore dresses. As an aid in baby management, a bedpost or other heavy piece of furniture would be set on the tail of a dress. The baby could tug, scratch, cry, and exert itself to roam about but was kept confined within a range of a few inches of the bedpost. At the same time, it would get some exercise but could not wander off and get into something, such as a fireplace or hot stove.

Ira and Carrie had an increasing family. Ira had to figure how to produce more food for the family and crops for cash so that he could buy what little else the family needed.

Three sharecropper families remained. Maybe he should go back to producing more vegetables; maybe he needed to start producing sugar cane, as he and his mother had considered nearly 10 years earlier. After discussion, Ira agreed to do both: grow a few more fresh vegetables for the grocery stores in Jackson and raise a few acres of sugar cane from which to produce molasses for sale and home use.

The sugar cane, in particular, would require a source of seed or planting joints with buds. Planting was in early spring in plowed land. Maturity would be reached in October. Harvest would require cutting the cane and hauling it for evaporating. A roller juicer that could be connected to a long pole and turned by a walking mule was bought to mash juice from the harvested stalks. The juice would be collected in a barrel. A cooking pan over a fire pit or oven would be needed to evaporate excess water from the juice. Gallon syrup cans were ordered through the DeWeese Store in Pocahontas. Everything was on hand and ready by the time of harvest in late October. Unfortunately, this time coincided with cotton and corn harvest, but Ira was able to work it out by using sharecroppers as day laborers to do the work. The syrup produced the first year was very good. Folks around the community bragged about how good it was. Ira was able to sell about 125 gallons.

The years 1910 through 1913 passed rather quickly. Farming continued much as it had. The children were growing and coming along well. In mid-1912, Carrie was pregnant. More or less, having babies was becoming routine for Carrie. Ethel Naomi Lee was born on April 28, 1913. And, as Ira said in announcing the new family member to people in the community, "I have been blessed with another girl." Ira's thoughts about girl babies had changed. The oldest girl,

Ellen Louvenia, was now approaching her teenage years and could help care for the new baby.

Another year went by on the farm. And there was no need for guessing Carrie was pregnant again. On April 4, 1915, she gave birth to a boy who was named Ira Nelson Lee. This name reflected the man and family that rescued Ira and his mother, Ellen, in Texas in the 1870s, named Walter Nelson Bell. This was the sixth baby born into the family. Ellen sent a letter to Nelson Bell's daughter, Sarah Ellen, in Texas telling her about the naming. The baby was sickly, and a doctor was summoned from Clinton. Dr. W. D. Potter examined Ira Nelson at about two years of age and gave some kind of medicine that had little positive influence (the charge was $10 to travel the five miles from Clinton, including the medicine he left). Ira Nelson died a few days later, having lived two years and two months. The cause of death was unknown. So many childhood ailments went around the countryside, and medical care was quite limited. Maybe his death had something to do with his mother not keeping her family's rooms in the house clean. Ira Nelson was buried in the Zachariah Ratliff Family Cemetery in an unmarked grave (though initial intention was to permanently mark it).

Ira and Carrie were heartbroken over the death of their baby. They had been fortunate with their previous five babies and were thankful for the health of those children. Ira Nelson had lived long enough for the family to love and appreciate his two-year-old abilities. Fortunately, the first-born son, Jasper Henry (fourth-born child), was living and healthy.

The death of Ira Nelson stirred feelings among the sharecroppers. One or two from each family turned out for the short burial service held for him at the Zachariah Ratliff Family Cemetery. Grandmother Ellen was so appreciative; she hugged them. Now, not often did a person such as Ellen hug a sharecropper, but Ellen was unique. She appreciated and respected all people regardless of color and other differences. She had always shown courtesy to sharecroppers, including when one of their children would die. The model of respect Ellen had shown was returned to her on this sad occasion.

Income had been doing better on the farm. In fact, most all farms were doing better (partly because of demand by Europe during World War I). On a trip to Pocahontas to gin cotton in the fall of 1916, Ira saw a display by a salesman for Flora Motor Company: a new 1917 Ford Model T Touring Sedan automobile. What Ira saw intrigued him. He talked to the salesman and asked if he would come to the farm and demonstrate it to members of his family. The salesman drove up at the Shepard (now Lee) house on the next Saturday afternoon. Most of the family had no idea what an engine was nor how a car operated. He went over a few details about the engine, drive train, steering, brakes, and the like. He reiterated that no horse was needed and explained that the engine and wheels caused the vehicle to move forward or backward. In addition, no hay or grain was needed but the engine used gasoline! He told about how the steering wheel was connected so that the direction of its turn would also turn the wheels and cause the Model T to go another way. The salesman bragged about the steering located on the left side for the first time and that the vehicle weighed only 1,200 pounds. Further, it had an electric horn that could be sounded to alert other people that you were driving through. "Sounds like fun," he said. Ira, Carrie, Ellen, and the older Lee children were so excited about it. They wanted one. The $360 price was a deterrent; they agreed they would need to wait another year or so to save the needed money. Just thinking about getting a new Model T was a motivation to work harder.

Until this time in the marriage of Ira and Carrie, she had been pregnant or lactating at least 13 of their 15 years of marriage! And, the number would likely increase. There would probably be more children. Ira no longer insisted on boy babies. He had learned that girl babies were nice.

Ellen's health was continuing to show signs that had caused her to slow down. She had put up with so much stress, tragedy, and poverty in her life that the effects were becoming evident. Yet, she maintained a happy, pleasant disposition and was always cheering other people. She was known as an innovator and leader. One of her sayings became, "if you are not out front leading, you are getting behind."

Ellen was also saddened by the death of her sister Rachel in the same year as Ira Nelson's death. Rachel was her last surviving sister. Only her brother Ira W. Shepard (the youngest Shepard sibling) survived longer than the sisters.

Another source of stress was the Selective Service Act of 1917. World War I was raging in Europe. President Woodrow Wilson only had about 100,000 soldiers he could commit to the European allies who desperately needed fresh soldiers. He asked congress to enact legislation to require all men to register for a military service draft. In a few months, some ten million men in the United States signed up. News that a draft was underway reached Tinnin but not the details. Ira and his family were worried that he might be drafted and shipped to Europe. Fulfilling his duty, Ira nervously went to the Selective Service office in Jackson to register and found that the registration applied to men born after 1872 (he was born in 1868). He was safe! He hurried back to Tinnin with the news and that brought great relief to his wife and mother, in particular. Their worry was about who would run the farm and be head of household if he was away in war. They were also concerned about his mother's health.

Ellen's wisdom helped so many people. In about the last few months of her life, when she was still a fairly sharp thinker, her granddaughter Ellen Louvenia Lee sought her advice. Ellen was in her upper teen years and somewhat ready to strike out into the world for herself. She told her grandmother that she couldn't get along with her mother, Carrie. She wanted to know what to do. She was thinking of completing what schooling she was taking and heading out on her own. She said she had a beau and that he might become a sweetheart. His name was Glenn. During the conversation, Ellen thought back to her own years at home and how Pa had rejected her sweetheart. He forbid him to come to the house after they were married.

Ellen encouraged her granddaughter to assess her possibilities very carefully and always go about doing good things for other people. She told her she was smart to get an education but that she would need a job when she left home. Ellen Louvenia was thinking that maybe she and her sweetheart would strike out but that didn't happen immediately, as they were later married in Clinton and lived there a short while. Both went on to have successful careers.

Just as their conversation was ending, Ellen Louvenia said there is one more thing: Mother may need help. Since the birth of the last baby (Ethel), she has been taking paregoric a couple of times a day. Ellen Louvenia continued, "You know this drug is addictive. I believe she is into it so that she depends on it to get through the day. I hope she doesn't become a mother again until she is no longer dependent on paregoric." Ellen was amazed that she lived in the same house as Carrie and did not know about this. She told Ellen Louvenia, "I will talk with Ira about it. There would be no need for me to infuriate Carrie by bringing it up with her." Ellen did remember to mention this to Ira and apparently the situation was, at least temporarily, handled. Maybe Carrie had a natural inclination for using such and it might be an issue later in her life.

The ravages of age were catching up with Ellen. She lived life without engaging in things that were known to damage health, such as drinking alcohol and using tobacco. Preventive health care had not been a part of her life. It was not done much in the South at that time. She had lost some of her teeth, which made chewing food difficult. Carrie would tease her about being a slow eater.

Another sign of aging was that Ellen was becoming forgetful. She could put something down and not remember where it was. Sometimes things were put in the wrong places. She or other members of the family would search for them. One day she put kitchen scraps in the pie safe. Another day she went to the garden to get eggs from the hen nests and returned with six squash. Everyone except Carrie tried to be helpful and patient. Carrie would avoid Ellen, and if she saw something about to happen that was not right, Carrie wouldn't stop it but would go ahead and let Ellen suffer the consequences. This was sad to Ellen. Sometimes she would sit and hold her head in her hands and cry.

Age was depriving Ellen of the ability to move about and be active. Some of her joints were stiff. Balance was occasionally a problem, particularly after first standing up or getting up out of the bed. She would hold onto a chair or bedpost, or she would lean against the wall. And with time, these problems were getting worse. Only a couple of times did she fall; fortunately, she did not suffer any major injuries or bone breaks. Each time, it was hard for her to get up and stand.

Ellen Loretta Shepard Lee died March 21, 1918 (born September 7, 1847); she was 70 years of age. She lived more than 47 years after husband Jasper's death. She had done so much for so many people. She tried to always do the right thing and be nice. Little did she know before her death that she would not live to see additional grandchildren produced by Ira and Carrie. There was another boy (who died at birth) and two more girls. She would have been proud that almost all grew up to have lives marked by goodness in most regards.

Even with decline, Ellen had maintained the lovable, friendly smile and personality and the kind disposition that endeared her to so many people. But, death is nearly always sad. Regardless of how religious clerics try to explain death, death means that life has gone. Materials in the body decompose to become minerals of Earth. No one had ever proven to Ellen that life in the ever-after existed. She thought that was based on faith and that took a lot of faith.

Ellen's wake and visitation were at the Shepard (now Lee) home. Baldwin Funeral Home was in charge of delivering a casket, bathing, and dressing the body. Usually, a family member dressed the body, but there was no one in the home to do it. Certainly, proud and disagreeable Carrie would not have anything to do with the body!

Ellen's body lay in state for a couple of days in the front parlor of the house. Neighbors Elzy Ratliff and Herbert Echols (both formerly Mason's Chapel attendees) sat up all night both nights with the body, which was a tradition with some families. A number of people stopped by to greet the family and pay tribute to Ellen. She was thought of as a wonderful person who had touched many lives. Of course, there were a few in the community who did not appreciate her friendship with the sharecroppers and others of lesser means. Many of those who stopped by the house brought a dish of food of some type to leave for the family.

A couple of sharecroppers dug the grave in the Zachariah Ratliff Family Cemetery. They said that this was the least they could do for an honest, considerate woman. Ira W. Shepard, her brother, came for the funeral from his home in Caile, located in the fertile farmland of the Mississippi Delta. A few nieces and nephews also came. The absence of sisters left sort of a hollow feeling in the family (all sisters were deceased). Of course, the children of Carrie and Ira were there, along with a few citizens of the community.

A short service was led on the front porch of the house by Preacher Presley of the Pocahontas ME Church. A few people sat (Carrie was one). The casket with the body was on the porch. The service included statements about the life of Ellen, a reading of the Twenty-Third Psalm, and a group singing of the hymn "The Old Rugged Cross." When the preacher gave people a chance to say something, two people spoke: Ellen's brother, Ira W. Shepard, and one of the sharecroppers. Both said very touching things about the love and kindness Ellen had for the people around her, even when the people had different skin color, lived in shabby houses, and went to different churches. Tears rolled down the cheeks of almost every adult on the porch, including Carrie. The preacher closed the porch service with a short prayer.

Sharecroppers served as pallbearers and transported the casket and body on a wagon from the house to the cemetery. That was unheard of in this part of the South. Society typically had the practice that such people did not mingle outside of field work. Ellen would have been so happy about what the sharecroppers did.

After a short statement and prayer at the cemetery by Preacher Presley, the group sang "Amazing Grace," the same hymn sung at the services for Jasper and Pa. The sharecroppers then lowered the casket and body. They began to slowly fill the grave with shovels of earth, remembering all the while that Ellen was one of the few people who had ever been nice to sharecroppers. No doubt, her kindness and respect were learned from her mid-western father, George W. Shepard. A half dozen people had brought flowers from their yards. These were placed on the earth mound of the filled grave. Of the flowers, Ellen would have most appreciated the bouquet of five beautiful red camellia blossoms. What wonderful memories she had of red camellias!

Ira, Ellen's son, was heard to say: "My mother is home. Ellen is back. She has truly made a "Return to Tinnin. Praise the Lord."

Yes, a "Return to Tinnin!"

AFTERLIFE PRESENCE

Ellen was dead. Her physical body had been fittingly buried in the Zachariah Ratliff Family Cemetery. (A local preacher might say that a separation of soul and body had occurred.) Family members were still in mourning. She continued to have a major influence on her descendant family. With almost everything they would do and the decisions they would make, they would ask themselves, "What would Ellen do?"

Though she had died, her values and teachings were still much alive. Some of her descendants were having a hard time getting over her death. They wondered why she had to leave Earth. After the funeral, Brother Murrow told Ira to contact him if he could be of use. Ira sensed a need. So, to help with grieving and adjusting to life without Ellen, he asked Brother Murrow to meet with family members and talk about adjusting to the death of a loved one. Ira and Carrie arranged for him to come to their home on a Saturday afternoon. He did; the family was ready to listen attentively.

Ira welcomed Brother Murrow. He had the adults and older children seat themselves in somewhat of a circle. Brother Murrow sat in one chair in the circle. He began with a short, comforting prayer. He mentioned the wonderful life of Ellen that had ended on Earth on March

21–just a few days ago and the first day of spring. He talked about how she was related as mother, grandmother, and mother-in-law to members of the group. He said that she loved each and every one of them. He further mentioned the most appropriate celebration of her life that the family had held with her funeral.

Calling on his Methodist religious teachings, Brother Murrow went on to say, "We will all be with her again in heaven." Some of the older children were thinking that rejoining her would be wonderful but that it was frightening because it would require that they also die an earthly death. They were not yet ready to die, and some doubted that they would ever be ready. They thought of death as scary; it was the end of earthly enjoyment and of being with people they loved.

Brother Murrow, using his church background, explained that "when she died an earthly death, her soul was raised into heaven to be with God. This is because she was a born-again Christian and faithful member of the Pocahontas Methodist Church. This was her immortal being or, as some would say, spirit. We will all have the opportunity for our souls to join her one day in heaven when our physical lives end." What he was saying was raising more questions with the children than providing answers. They began to think about the need to be baptized into the church and living lives that merited being in heaven with Ellen.

Brother Murrow talked about death and how it is hard to explain. He said he was not a medical doctor and could not explain death in those terms. "But," he said, "based on my studies, death occurs when the body is permanently unable to do what is needed to carry out life processes." He further said, "Death can be explained in several ways, such as biology and brain activity. If the heart stops or breathing ceases, death will likely occur quite soon." He went on to talk about how the decline of Ellen's health over the past months was preparation for her family and friends that the death process was gradually occurring. She was losing her ability to go about life as she had in earlier years.

As the discussion continued, Brother Murrow asked each individual to remember and speak one special thing about their dearly departed family member. Ellen Louvenia, the oldest grandchild, began by stating that she really liked how her grandmother would take time to listen and help in making choices. Sudie mentioned how she would take time to teach about cooking and other things a young woman needed to learn in running a home. The other older grandchildren also made statements, ending with Jasper Henry (now called Henry), who indicated that she had a good sense of how to identify and use new ways of farming. Then Ira, her son, talked about several of his mother's wonderful qualities, including her ability to be strong in bad situations. Carrie, her daughter-in-law, did not make any statements.

After family comments, Brother Murrow indicated that the family had offered wonderful ways of remembering Ellen. Then he wanted to offer a comment. He said, "I remember Mrs. Ellen Lee as a friendly, moral, and supportive member of the church who sought to do God's will. Though she did not agree with everything I preached about, she was always carefully listening and thinking about what I said as the word of God." Then, Brother Murrow stated that a lot of wonderful things had been spoken that day. He said, "The family is healing from her death and, given a little time, will be fine. It is good to have memories, but we can't let memories overcome our emotions. We must have a reasoned approach. Don't let your sorrow take over your lives; go about routines, and that will help you through. Occasionally visit her gravesite for a quiet time and reflection. I ask each of you to pray about your feelings in the loss of Ellen. God will help you through if you seek his guidance." He then said a short ending prayer and told everyone goodbye. He got into his buggy and left. The family waved to him as he rode up the hill and toward the main road.

Ira told the family that he now felt a lot better. He indicated that Brother Murrow had done a good job of helping the family understand how to adjust to the death. He asked each child to think about what the preacher had to say and use it to guide his or her thoughts and actions. Ivie, one of Ellen's granddaughters spoke up: "Yes, he said a lot, but I don't understand all of it. I am going to continue to think and pray about it."

The next morning was Sunday, and off to church they went. When Monday came, it was back to routine in the home and on the farm. Spring was here and time to get fields ready for crops. Sharecroppers were at work, as well as a couple of hired hands and older children. Fortunately, the weather was good, and over the next several weeks all land was readied and planted. Good showers and warm temperatures helped the seeds germinate and give a good stand of cotton, corn, and vegetable crops.

After Ellen's death, Ira and Carrie would have two more children: Edna was born on August 1, 1919, and Lyda on April 19, 1923. These two did not have the opportunity to get to know their grandmother Ellen. They would certainly have benefited from her presence in the home. A couple of the older daughters gave much time to the care of Edna and Lyda...maybe they were surrogates for their grandmother in this regard. Anyway, seven of the nine children born to Carrie and Ira lived into adulthood and assumed productive lives as citizens in the communities where they lived.

Ellen had always felt that men had a big advantage over women. She had firsthand experience in that regard while settling the estate of her deceased husband, Jasper. Maybe Ellen was an early feminist or women's rights and suffrage advocate. She knew that the women's suffrage movement had been underway for many years. Anyway, 1919 would have been a good year for her, and 1920 an even better year. In 1919, the U.S. Congress passed legislation to allow citizens in the states to vote on the 19th Amendment to the Constitution, which granted women the right to vote. On August 18, 1920, Tennessee became the 36th state to ratify the amendment. (There were 48 states in the Union; a three-fourths' majority of the states was needed for ratification.) Ellen's home state of Mississippi was not one of the states that voted to ratify the amendment. In fact, Mississippians voted in opposition to ratification on March 29, 1920. That action by voters in her home state would have been hurtful to Ellen, as she was typically an early adopter and progressive when it came to women's rights and new technology. Unfortunately, the nature of voters in the state was to oppose progressive people and ideas. Some say that this same notion has held back advancements in important areas for another century.

In June 1920, the U.S. Federal Census enumerator came to the Lee home and farm in Tinnin. Ira Jasper Lee was head of the household—same as in the two previous Census reports. One person was missing this time: Ellen Loretta Shepard Lee; three new children were present since the last Census in 1910. Individuals listed by the enumerator were Ira Jasper Lee (age 52), Carrie Cheers Hendrick Lee (age 38), Ellen Louvenia (age 17), Sudie (age 15), Ivie (age 13), Henry (age 9), Ethel (age 7), and Edna (8 months). The family had certainly changed since the previous Census!

A little more than four years after the death of Ellen and about one year before the birth of Lyda, Ellen Louvenia Lee announced she was getting married. In June 1922, she married Glenn Edwards. Immediately, there was a tremendous amount of wailing and crying by her mother, Carrie. Was this due to her sadness about her daughter moving away, or was it due to the loss of her daughter as a source of household work? Maybe the sadness was due to both, but most likely the latter. Some family members have thought it might have been associated with occasional bouts of mental illness that Carrie suffered.

The new Mr. and Mrs. Edwards lived a short while in Clinton and wound up living for many years in Montgomery, Alabama, where they were highly successful in business. To some extent, Ellen Louvenia Lee Edwards was viewed by other family members much as Ellen Loretta Shepard Lee; she was looked up to as a person who could make good choices and be successful. One indication of success is that during the Great Depression of the 1930s, Ellen and Glenn took a cruise on a Holland-America ship from New York to Cuba and back to New York. That was virtually unheard of in the Tinnin community, where the only travel to great distances was as soldiers going to war. Ira, Carrie, and their children were always excited by a visit from Ellen Louvenia and husband, Glenn. Ellen Louvenia and Glenn had no children.

Most years were relatively routine with Ira and Carrie. One year that stands out, however, is 1923. On September 3, they bought a new Ford touring car (#8228213) from Flora Motor Company in the nearby town of Flora. Ira paid $469 cash at the dealership. He and Carrie had saved the money since the good farming years of World War I. This was the first vehicle of any kind that the family had owned with an engine. Three of the older children went the day it was bought (Carrie stayed home, as she had baby Lyda to care for). The family rode in a horse-pulled buggy to Flora. Sudie and Ivie had to drive the Ford car home, as Ira did not understand all the mechanical devices. Henry also wanted to drive it and did so for some of the distance (he was 13 years of age at the time). Henry's main duty was to get the horse and buggy back home following the car.

Ira tried to learn to drive. When he did get in the driver's seat to drive, the car would jerk about and kick up dust; Ira didn't understand gears and clutches. He often killed the engine. The car would sometimes go off the pig-trail roadways and wind up in a ditch or bumping into a tree. No family members would ride with him. Even animals were frightened. In fact, Ira never learned to confidently drive a vehicle. His reasoning was that the front fenders covered the wheels and he could not see the direction they were going when he turned the steering wheel. This was okay with the older children in the family, as they were anxious to drive if given the opportunity.

Ira and family had first looked at a Model T when Ellen was alive. She wanted them to get the car in 1917. Flora Motor Company had a salesperson demonstrate the car at the farm. The Lees did not buy at that time, as they felt the price was too high. But Ellen always wanted to try new things; she was an early adopter or innovator. Even with the Ford touring car, horses and wagons were still much in use. The car was never used to transport products; in fact, it wasn't designed to do so. Ira had great pride in the family's first automobile.

Expansion of U.S. agriculture during World War I to meet demands in Europe resulted in overproduction and low prices for farm products in the 1920s. Agriculture was in a depression. The U.S. Congress attempted legislation that would bring relief but without very good results. About 600,000 farms, or one in four in the nation, were sold to meet financial obligations; fortunately, Ira was able to manage his farm so that it survived. Times got really tough late in the 1920s, but Ira held on. He often thought about his mother, Ellen, and how she endured the hard times she faced. Hunker down and be self-sufficient...buy very little.

Tough times on farms in the 1920s resulted in the Lee daughters (who were approaching marrying age) looking for ways out of farm life. They had heard that some towns and cities had thriving manufacturing industries with good jobs. Ellen Louvenia had married before the depression was so severe. Now, Sudie and Ivie were each looking for a man who would take them away from the harsh reality facing Ira and Carrie. Each found her man about the change of the decade. But, another and more extensive great depression was on the way. With Sudie's and Ivie's marriages, Carrie wept and wailed considerably; some folks said that she had "weeping fits." To Carrie, the marriage of a daughter was like the death of a person she loved. As before, she got over the marriages after a couple of weeks of weeping episodes. Carrie and Ira realized that the size of their family was shrinking; Carrie was now beyond the age of producing more babies.

A major event in 1930 was the opening of a bridge over the Mississippi River in Vicksburg. Prior to the bridge, ferries and boats were used to cross the river. The new bridge connected a roadway in Mississippi to a roadway in Louisiana. Crossing the river had been a major issue for family members (and everyone else) for many years, including newlyweds Jasper and Ellen as they traveled to Texas in March 1864. The opening of the bridge was billed as an historic occasion in central Mississippi. Ira wanted to go; Henry would drive. They agreed to go in an automobile for which they had traded their 1923 Ford touring car. On May 1, 1930, they skipped out on farm work and made the trip to Vicksburg to be one of the first cars to drive across the bridge. The roadway to Vicksburg wasn't a very good highway, but it was adequate. To great fanfare, the bridge was opened to automobile, pedestrian, and railroad traffic. With cantilever engineering, it was a major construction fete. The bridge was 8,546 feet long (a mile and a half), with 116 feet of clearance above the typical water level in the Mississippi River. Wow! Ira and Henry had a lot to talk about when they returned home late that day.

Crossing on the bridge gave Ira and Henry the notion that they could later drive to Ira's birthplace in Henderson County, Texas. They could see the burial site of Ira's father and of Henry's grandfather (Jasper H. Lee) and look around the area. Possibly they could see relatives who were still living in the area, including children of Sarah Ellen Bell.

Interestingly, no married daughter ever returned to live with Carrie and Ira, either as a newlywed seeking a first home or as a single woman who had experienced marital issues. The home lacked the loving vibrancy of their grandmother, Ellen. It had the unpleasantness of their mother, Carrie. Ira was there as the head of household, but he was very involved with farming. Ira had many of the gentlemanly qualities that his mother, Ellen, and her father,

George Shepard, tried to teach him. Carrie, however, set the tone for the home, and it was not always pleasant. Times were tight, money was short, and few modern conveniences were present in the home.

Money got so short that son Henry took a job with the railroad in the mid-1930s. He, by and large, gave up farming for a while to work as a laborer in track maintenance for the railroad. It was good to have a small paycheck for the Lee family. One interesting thing Henry gained was Social Security through the U.S. Railroad Retirement Board (RRB). In the early 1930s, President Franklin Roosevelt took office during very difficult economic times in the United States. He pushed the 1934 legislation that would aid railroad employees and serve as a model for Social Security legislation. In 1935, President Roosevelt signed legislation creating the controversial (but very beneficial) Social Security Administration, which applied far beyond railroad jobs. Henry was covered with enhanced benefits, though, until his death many years later. His Social Security number had an "R" at the end, designating "railroad."

Ira and Henry made their long-planned trip to Henderson County, Texas, in 1937 after Henry had gotten one of his paychecks for his railroad work. The bridge over the Mississippi River made it possible for them to drive. They were in the Athens, Texas, area only a couple of days, but that was enough time for them to see what they wanted. Ira got to see his father's grave marker in Smith Cemetery. The epitaph for Jasper Henry Lee mentioned that he was the father of Ira; no mention was made that he was the husband of Ellen, but such was the status of women at the time.

It was interesting for Ira to visit the area and try to figure out where things were when he was a boy. Ira even thought about what his life would have been like if his mother, Ellen, had not made the return to Mississippi. Anyway, there was no going back. They had been able to cope with the challenges of life in Mississippi.

Henry worked for the railroad for only a few years. The health of his father, Ira, began to deteriorate, and Henry was needed to operate the farm. Ira had long experienced asthma and breathing problems. Now other health issues were apparently occurring. At that time in the Great Depression, few people sought the assistance of a doctor unless they were very ill—maybe too far gone to ever get better.

Henry always had a special fondness for his grandmother, Ellen. Maybe she showed him special attention when he was quite small. After all, he was her only grandson to survive beyond early childhood. Henry had some of her traits about work and honesty. He also had some traits of his mother, Carrie. But, most of all, it was his father, Ira, with whom he shared so many things in common.

Henry was at home on the farm in the Tinnin community. He did not plan to leave or go anywhere. He would carry on the family farming tradition. He had a small place in the back of the main hallway for his bed and belongings. Henry really wasn't very comfortable in the house with his limited privacy. The marriages of a couple more sisters freed up space. So, he was able to occupy a larger front room. He lived in the house with his parental family and one younger sister who had not left home.

On a fall day in 1939, on the one-mile drive from home to the Ratliff Store for some Prince Albert tobacco (yes, Henry unfortunately smoked roll-your-own cigarettes at that time in his life), he passed an attractive young woman who was out walking between the schoolhouse and the teachers' home. He didn't stop that day; he waved and tipped his hat. A couple of days later, he was on the same short trip at the same time of day, and there she was making the school-to-home walk accompanied by another young woman. Henry couldn't resist; he stopped and introduced himself. They said that they were new teachers at the Tinnin School and stayed in the teachers' home along with a couple of other teachers. Henry asked if they would like to go to the Ratliff Store (only a quarter of a mile) and get a cold cola. He thought for sure that they would say no, but to his surprise, they said yes. They probably assessed Henry as an honorable young farmer who meant only good. Plus, he had a car to ride in. They got in, and Henry drove off—most likely with a big grin on his face.

They each got a cola and sat on the porch steps at the store. They talked a bit. One said she had a boyfriend; the other didn't mention anything about a boyfriend. Henry observed that the one without a boyfriend appeared to be highly intelligent and was a beautiful young woman. She said her name was Doris Sloan. He drove them back to the teachers' home and asked Doris if he could come to visit her the next day after school. She said yes, and that led to what became the romance of a good-looking young woman with another Jasper Henry Lee (sounds like somewhat of a repeat of 1863–64, doesn't it?).

Henry and Doris continued a relationship that grew into a certain closeness that led to a marriage proposal. The celebration of the rites of marriage was held on August 3, 1940, with Brother Murrow officiating. The ceremony was conducted at the home of Edna and Brunner Huddleston (one of Henry's sisters and her husband) in Jackson. Edna and Brunner were married about five years before. The big room that Henry had gotten a couple of years ago in his childhood home would now belong to the newlywed Mr. and Mrs. Lee. They would get another room to use as a kitchen. Of course, the toilet was a two-holer privy out back.

Doris was no longer a school teacher. Two factors were at work: State law prohibited married women from teaching, and the Tinnin School was consolidated with the Clinton School. Doris was a full-time homemaker, and Henry a farmer. By the first of October, Doris suspected she was pregnant. Pregnancy was confirmed in another month. So, Henry and Doris went about preparing for the birth of their first child; and, likely, there would be several more. They took an unusual step at that time for rural people by getting some prenatal care and planning for delivery of the baby in the Jackson Infirmary. Doris had a college degree and knew about health and maternity care.

Ira carried on work as long as he could. He lost weight and became lethargic. He would sit and rock for long hours on the front porch of his home. Sometimes he would fall asleep in the rocking chair. He would always dress neatly in a farmer sort of way that included high-top shoes, long-sleeved shirt, long pants, and a hat, even while sitting in the chair.

Shock and sadness struck on January 1, 1941, with the death of Ira. The family somewhat expected his death because of declining health. There was considerable grieving in the family about the death of Ellen Loretta Shepard Lee's son. Carrie whimpered and mourned with occasional bursts of wailing. All the Lee children and their spouses began to arrive at the house. Conditions were rainy, wet, and muddy. The decision was made to bury Ira in the cemetery at the Pocahontas Methodist Church rather than with his mother in the Zachariah Ratliff Family Cemetery. The mud was too bad to get to the family cemetery, which was beginning to suffer from neglect, anyway. Ira's viewing was at his home. Brother Murrow delivered the eulogy in the Pocahontas Methodist Church.

The family worked to overcome the loss of Ira. Lyda was the only unmarried child at home. She was going to college in Clinton. She had a big role in comforting her mother after the loss of Ira.

Late on May 28, 1941, Doris thought she was going into labor. Henry drove her to the Jackson Infirmary, where a boy was born the next day. Henry was so proud to have a boy, as he had grown up around all girls. Plus, Henry thought, when he was older, he could get the boy to work on the farm and plan transition of the farm to the next generation. Doris continued being a housewife and new mother to their son. Coping with the antics of her mother-in-law was a daily challenge and source of anxiety.

Farming routine went as well as could be expected for the next year. World War II had broken out. Pearl Harbor in Hawaii had been attacked. All of Europe was at war and countries were fighting on one side or the other. Government rationing of food, clothing, and other products was instituted to assure plenty of resources for the war effort. These actions meant that Henry and Doris's home would continue to provide a place to live meagerly without modern conveniences of electricity, running water, heat, and plumbing for kitchen and bathroom.

Things don't always go as planned, as was true on January 20, 1943. Before Henry left home that morning to go grind corn with a hammer mill at the Ratliff Store, he held his son, tossed him gently in the air, and kissed his Doris goodby. Henry and a helper positioned the steel-wheeled Farmall tractor in just the right place for the wide belt to transfer power from a rotating pulley on the side of the tractor to a pulley on the hammer mill. All was up and going well. The belt and pulleys were turning at a high speed (was it too fast?). Corn was being ground to the proper size for meal.

Suddenly the big rotating belt lunged off the pulley wheel and wrapped around Henry's right arm just above the elbow. The rotation of the heavy belt was powerful. In a twisting motion, it almost totally severed the arm a couple of inches below the shoulder. Henry was flung to the ground. He temporarily lost consciousness. His helper called out. People from the store rushed to Henry's aid. Blood was flowing. The twisting motion of the belt that pulled the arm off had closed some of the blood vessels, which reduced the rate of blood loss and helped him remain alive. The bones in the upper arm were broken, jagged and protruding from the flesh.

Henry regained consciousness and was able to stand up and walk, though he was somewhat wobbly. As he walked, his right hand drug along on the ground, as skin and tissue holding the arm to the body stretched several inches long. He made it to an automobile that was used to rush him to the Jackson Infirmary for care. Emergency room personnel went about amputating what remained of the arm and hand. The nub of bone that remained was covered with skin stretched from above where the arm was removed. Anesthesia was limited at that time and no doubt he experienced a lot of pain. He had a blood transfusion to replace some of what he lost. His body was in shock. Hospital care helped him survive. Doris stayed around the clock at his bedside.

After several days in the hospital, Henry returned home where Doris provided tender and loving care of her man. Henry could no longer hold his son. He was not able to do farm work of any sort for a while. Gradually he regained some abilities but was always handicapped by having one hand. He was a right-handed person and now had to learn to use his left hand to do more things. He had a farm to manage. Fortunately, spring and the start of crops were a few months away.

A horrible accident had occurred. Coping with the consequences would not be easy. As was often the case, the spirit of Ellen would be alive in the resilience of a young severely traumatized family. Yes, Ellen's teachings and modeling of how to deal with adversity continued in her Lee descendants. And, as you may surmise, there is a lot more to this story that is for another time. Henry's life lasted 47 years after the loss of his right arm. In spite of the handicap, he was able to accomplish a great deal.

Epilogue

Ellen Loretta Shepard met and fell in love with Jasper Henry Lee in late 1863 and married him in early 1864. He was more than twice her age and was not from her home area. His charisma had an amazing appeal to Ellen. She was immediately attracted to him, but, she knew very little about him.

Considerable modern-day investigation into Jasper's history was needed to uncover some of his past and determine a little of what Ellen did not know. Diligent search of government records from the mid-1800s, including U.S. Federal Census, license applications, and court records, provided a wealth of information. Review of old letters and documents kept by Ellen and other family members yielded interesting family life information and directed some of the genealogy research. Current-day DNA analysis of descendants helped locate and confirm genetic matches among descendants of the families involved. A complication in searching for the whereabouts and actions of Jasper is that he sometimes went by only his middle name of Henry; he would be shown in records as Henry Lee.

Full details are not available on Jasper and never will be; however, a great deal of reliable and compelling information has been located. Jasper was most likely born in Richland County, South Carolina, in 1827. The names of his parents or any family members living at that time are unknown. It has been suggested that his mother was unwed and he took her Lee surname (no proof of that). Apparently he never told Ellen about his family, or if he did, he revealed very little. She never talked or wrote about it.

Young women didn't have many potential husbands as the U.S. Civil War was winding down. Bloody battles killed thousands of young men, permanently maimed thousands more, and left many with mental illness and alcoholism. Ellen was caught in that situation as well as deteriorating conditions at home due to the loss of farm productivity and a way of life built on labor-intensive cotton production. Families also lost many possessions to plundering by Union and Confederate troops. In the mid-1860s, the future didn't hold a lot of promise for many young people in the war-ravaged deep South.

So, when Ellen had a chance to develop a romantic relationship with Jasper, she did so. In a matter of weeks, they were talking about marriage and future life together. She had introduced Jasper to her family. Instantly, Pa did not like him nor think he was up to the standard of marrying his oldest daughter. It seems that Jasper was never able to answer Pa's questions in a straightforward manner there were always unexplained gaps in his life. What was the nature of his life before he met Ellen? The couple moved ahead with plans to marry without Pa's approval. Sadly, this led to Pa rejecting both Ellen and Jasper by not allowing Jasper ever to come to the Shepard home again.

Maybe Pa had some sort of special insight into Jasper; maybe it was the unanswered questions that gave that insight. Where was Jasper born, and where did he grow up? Who were his parents? Had he been married before? What kind of work had he been doing in his young adult years? Had he been in Union or Confederate forces? Getting answers was not easy then and has not been easy to this day.

As a young adult (teenager), Jasper wandered from his home in South Carolina in the late 1840s. Some people have thought that in the 1860s he was running from conscription in either the Union or Confederate military during the U.S. Civil War. He traveled a bit and worked on farms and at manual labor kinds of jobs. He was sometimes thought to have hidden in the woods, barns, or other places. Mostly, he lived without resources. His travel was by hitching rides, walking, and riding trains. By the time Jasper reached Brandon, Mississippi, in 1863, he had been married or lived in communal relationships three times. A child resulted from at least one of these relationships but there might be others. None of the relationships lasted more than three years. Probate records from Attalla County, Mississippi, indicate that he shared an inheritance with one of the women whose father died. The relationships were in Alabama and Mississippi. All evidence is that Jasper provided no support for any children he fathered, except for about two years for his son, Ira, who was born after his marriage to Ellen.

Various other scenarios on Jasper have been given. One is that he was from Virginia and found his way south across the Carolina's and on to Mississippi. Another is that he was from Georgia and moved westward as the Civil War was ending. Another is that Jasper, his mother, and a sister traveled from North Carolina to settle in Madison County, Mississippi, where, according to slave records, they lived and owned slaves for several years before he met Ellen.

Regardless, Jasper and Ellen married in 1864 and had a son four years later. Ellen probably never got much accurate information about Jasper. It is hard to see where Ellen, based on her moral values, would have accepted some of the behavior of Jasper as the man to whom she would dedicate her life. There is no evidence that Jasper was anything less than a gentleman with Ellen always kind and considerate of her.

They lived together as Mr. and Mrs. Lee for six years and eight months after marriage. Such a short married life left Ellen a widow while still in her early 20's. Ellen was known as a wonderful, smart, kind, and considerate woman who appreciated all people regardless of skin color and other differences. Tinnin was her home, and to Tinnin she returned. She died there in 1918. Seven of her nine grandchildren had been born to her son, Ira, and his wife, Carrie, by then.

The Zachariah Ratliff Family Cemetery in Tinnin where Ellen, her parents, and other family members were buried has not been used in a century. Ellen was the last person buried in it. Today, the gravestones have weathered, fallen over, and broken; it is not accessible by vehicle and requires walking through heavy growth on posted land. Trees have filled the location. It is hardly recognizable as a place where people are buried.

No doubt, as *Return to Tinnin* demonstrates, the moral values of Ellen's family (the Shepards) compensated for what might have been lacking in Jasper.

Ira Jasper Lee Pedigree Tree

```
                                          b:
                                          m:
                                          d:
                        Jasper H Lee
                        b: Mar 27, 1827 in South Carolina
                        m: Mar 02, 1864 in Hinds County, Mississippi
                        d: Nov 16, 1870 in Athens, Henderson Co.,
                        Texas (Smith Cemetery, Athens, Texas)

                                          b:
                                          d:

Ira Jasper Lee
b: Feb 03, 1868 in Athens, Texas
m: Aug 07, 1901 in Hinds County, Mississippi
d: Jan 01, 1941 in Tinnin, Mississippi
(Pocahontas Cemetery, Pocahontas,
Mississippi)
                                          George Washington Shepard
                                          b: Jul 16, 1814 in Kentucky
                                          m: Jan 20, 1845 in Mississippi
                                          d: May 10, 1895 in Tinnin, Mississippi
                        Ellen Loretta Shepard
                        b: Sep 15, 1847 in Tinnin, Mississippi
                        d: Mar 21, 1918 in Tinnin, Mississippi
                        (Zachariah Ratliff Family Cemetery, Tinnin,
                        Mississippi)

                                          Sarah Elisabeth Ratliff
                                          b: Jun 24, 1830 in Tinnin, Mississippi
                                          d: Aug 31, 1895 in Tinnin, Mississippi
```

Relationship of Ellen Loretta Shepard to her
parents, husband, and son.

CPSIA information can be obtained
at www.ICGtesting.com
Printed in the USA
FFOW01n2033210617
37006FF